CONSTRUCTIVE READING

D1710556

LB
1050.45
. C 75
1993

8-95

CONSTRUCTIVE READING
Teaching Beyond Communication

Edited by
Stanley B. Straw
University of Manitoba
and
Deanne Bogdan
Ontario Institute for Studies in Education

Boynton/Cook Publishers
HEINEMANN
Portsmouth, NH

71980

CONCORDIA COLLEGE LIBRARY
BRONXVILLE, N.Y. 10708

Boynton/Cook Publishers, Inc.
A Subsidiary of Reed Publishing (USA) Inc.
361 Hanover Street   Portsmouth, NH 03801–3912
Offices and agents throughout the world

Copyright © 1993 by Boynton/Cook Publishers, Inc.
All rights reserved. No part of this book may be reproduced in any form or by
electronic or mechanical means, including information storage and retrieval systems,
without permission in writing from the publisher, except by a reviewer, who may
quote brief passages in a review.

Every effort has been made to contact the copyright holders and students for
permission to reprint borrowed material. We regret any oversights that may have
occurred and would be happy to rectify them in future printing of this work.

Editor: Robert W. Boynton
Production: Renée M. Pinard
Cover design: Tom Allen/Pear Graphic Design

Library of Congress Cataloging-in-Publication Data

Constructive reading : teaching beyond communication / edited by
   Stanley B. Straw and Deanne Bogdan.
        p.   cm.
   Includes bibliographical references (p.) and index.
   ISBN 0-86709-329-3
   1. Reading comprehension.   2. Books and reading.   3. Self
-realization in literature.   I. Straw, Stanley B.   II. Bodgan,
Deanne.
LB1050.45.C75   1993   93–2295
372.41—dc20   CIP

Printed in the United States of America on acid-free paper
97 96 95 94 93   BB   1   2   3   4   5

Contents

Acknowledgments

The overall project of which this is a part began nearly a decade ago at lunch at the hotel where the Executive of the Canadian Council of Teachers of English was meeting in Toronto. The idea to compile and edit a series of papers on theories of reader response and the pedagogical implications of those theories emerged as we began to see similarities between the individual work we were carrying out in response to literature. This similarity was a greater surprise to us at the time than now seems possible. One of us was working in the aesthetics of response, the other was working in reading comprehension theory. In the mid 1980s, they were seen as very different fields. But the more we talked about the theoretical and pedagogical issues within aesthetics and comprehension, the more we discovered we were talking about the same issues, though we often used different language to describe those issues. We were also seeing similarities between our own work and the work of our colleagues. It was our goal back then to develop a dialogue between the people in theories of literary reading and the people in reading comprehension theory.

The project has resulted in two edited books, both published by Boynton/Cook Heinemann: the present volume and its predecessor, *Beyond Communication: Reading Comprehension and Criticism.* The first of these, *Beyond Communication,* attempts to explore what the fields of aesthetic reading and reading comprehension can say to one another and how each can broaden and sharpen its perspective by adoption and accommodating the perspective of the other. This volume has drifted away from that attempt at dialogue between the two fields in that we have focused primarily on the reading of literature. We see this book as a kind of *application* of the notions presented in *Beyond Communication*, and the subtitle, *Teaching Beyond Communication*, attempts to capture that notion of application.

The main title of this book, *Constructive Reading*, attempts to capture our beliefs about the nature of the reading process (that it is constructive) and what teaching beyond communication really means: that is, that reading must be taught as an act of constructing, aided perhaps by some textual blueprints and by some teacher scaffolds. But textual blueprints and teacher scaffolds cannot substitute for the act of constructing meaning on the part of the reader. Nor can construction be seen as a solitary act. Our research and investigations have convinced us that the most important blueprints and scaffolds that readers use in constructing meaning are those provided by the communities to which the readers belong.

This set of essays, hopefully, addresses those important issues of community which we think are so critical to the act of reading. We would, therefore, like to acknowledge, as much as possible, the members of the communities we ourselves belong to who have helped us in constructing *Constructive Reading*. First, and most important, we would like to thank the authors who contributed to this book. Though they belong to academic communities from New South Wales, Australia, to Vancouver, British Columbia, to Houston, Texas, they also belong to a community of researchers and teachers who subscribe to the basic constructive nature of reading. Without our contributors, and without the encouragement, hard work, and support of those contributors, this book would never have been conceived or completed.

Second, we would like to thank our institutions and administrators for supporting this project in a variety of ways. We would like to thank the Ontario Institute for Studies in Education for two small-scale grants directed towards this project, and the Faculty of Education, University of Manitoba, for a time-release grant from the Research and Scholarly Development Fund. We would like to thank our administrations, Malcolm Levin (Assistant Director, Academic, at the Ontario Institute for Studies in Education [OISE]), Dwight Boyd (Chair, Department of History and Philosophy of Education at OISE), John Stapleton (Dean, Faculty of Education, University of Manitoba), and John Seymour (Chair, Department of Curriculum: Humanities and Social Sciences, Faculty of Education, University of Manitoba) for offering financial and personal support for this project. We both feel lucky that we work in institutions with administrators who appreciate the kind of work we carry out academically.

Third, we would like to thank the people associated with our institutions that directly worked on the preparation of this manuscript: Margaret Brennan (Administrative Officer, Department of History and Philosophy of Education), Jill Given-King, Ruth Niebor at OISE, Louise Sabourin (Secretary of the Department of Curriculum: Humanities and Social Sciences), Edna Wooler (Secretary to the Associate Dean of Education in the Faculty of Education), and Sandy Baardman at the University of Manitoba. All of these people worked diligently on different aspects of the manuscript–typing, mailing, researching, eyeballing. When our energies lagged, these were the people who helped us believe the manuscript would finally become a reality.

Lastly, we would like to thank the important people in our lives who must constantly put up with our shifts from elation to depression and back again. Our thanks for the love, patience, and support we have received from Stasia Bogdan, Elisabeth Bogdan, Joseph Bogdan, and Roger Lagacé, our partners and families.

Stan Straw
Deanne Bogdan

Introduction

Deanne Bogdan
Stanley B. Straw

In *Beyond Communication: Reading Comprehension and Criticism* (Bogdan & Straw 1990), we make a number of interrelated hypotheses about the state of the art in reading—both reading comprehension and literary reading. The first hypothesis is that reading comprehension and literary reading are developing in parallel and converging ways; a number of the articles in the book attempt to trace how the two fields have been coming together (Hunt 1990a; Hynds 1990; Straw 1990a). The second hypothesis is that the history of reading in general can be traced through a number of phases or periods differentiated by a variety of factors, one of which is whether communication is seen as the primary purpose for reading. Finally, we suggest that a revolution of sorts in conceptualizations of reading is taking place in both reading comprehension and literary reading: what we call the "communication contract"—that is, the assumption that the main purpose of reading is for communicative purposes—is being replaced by an "actualization contract," a contract that readers have with themselves and with the discourse communities with which they identify rather than a contract readers have with either the author of a text or the text itself. Within the communication contract in reading, readers accepting the purposes of reading to be primarily communicative place themselves in particular roles with reference to both the author and the text. An actualization contract, on the other hand, is really an agreement that readers have with themselves and their communities about how they are going to use texts—a *social* contract about how texts are implicated in *social* contexts.

Some reviewers (e.g., Stotsky 1992) have suggested that our view of the convergence of reading comprehension theory and literary theory is wishful thinking; in some arenas it appears that, although the two fields may have a great deal in common, they are not coming together in any

1

meaningful way. We feel, however, that it is at the point of instruction—when teachers are attempting to help students become better and more sensitive readers—that the two fields do in fact become integrated. That is the point of this book. Since we believe that many of the perceptions drawn from reading comprehension theory and research are being absorbed by teachers of literature and that a significant number of perceptions drawn from the reading of literature are finding their ways into the teaching of reading, we think it is appropriate to collect together a group of essays on how teachers might deal with the significant move from a communication contract to an actualization contract.

As we point out in *Beyond Communication,* the actualization contract implies that readers search out or find meaningful texts that will help them understand the events in their lives. The most telling aspect is that this new conceptualization of reading—and therefore of the teaching of reading—is seen as a constructive and collaborative process. The recognition of the constructive and collaborative nature of reading can have powerful implications for how teachers deal with language in their classrooms. We have attempted to pull together some exemplary teachers, theorists, and researchers in reading and literature to discuss what a move to an actualization contract might really mean to what teachers do in their classes. Our chapters contain a rich variety of approaches: from how to use literary critical theory in teaching reading to how teachers might rethink their own roles in instruction.

Reading and response-to-literature teaching and pedagogy made a major leap when the work of Louise Rosenblatt (1938, 1978) became acknowledged in the middle-to-late seventies; this recognition is probably the best indicator of the revolution from communication to actualization. Rosenblatt suggests that the act of reading literature is a transactional process, a point of view often seen as an alternative to the more traditional, empirically based notions of reading as transmission and translation (Straw & Bogdan 1990). The recognition of the transactional nature of reading has signaled a significant shift in the ways in which we as teachers conceptualize and therefore teach reading and literature. On the one hand, transmission and translation theories of reading and response imply that meaning is present in text, that meaning is determinate (that a single meaning for a text can be arrived at), and that the reader's task is to "figure out" what that meaning is. Here reading is much like working out a crossword puzzle, in which there is a correct answer and the reader's task is to solve the puzzle (i.e., get the meaning). Reading is viewed as the application of learned skills to text such that mastery over the skills will lead to mature, competent reading. In contrast to this is a notion of reading as a transactional and constructive act. From this view of reading, meaning is not present in text (though the text may be one source of knowledge) but is built up by the reader during the act of reading: the reader draws on a number of knowledge sources in order to create this meaning. Among these knowledge sources are the text, the reader's knowledge of the features of language, the reader's background experiences and worldview, and the reader's social context. The important contribution of transactional/constructivist approaches to reading is that they view reading as a *meaning-constructing process* rather than a *meaning-getting process.*

Theories of reading and literature as transaction and construction can have a profound impact on the ways we as teachers envision our role in instruction—the ways in which we attempt to expand our students' discursive practices and educate their discursive imaginations (Bogdan 1990, 1992a; Hunt 1990b; Straw 1990b). The move from a notion of determinate, text-based meaning to that of reading as meaning making in the presence of text suggests that many of the traditional vehicles for teaching literature may be in conflict with mature reading. If reading really is transactional and constructive, then transmission teaching methods— methods that assume determinacy of text, that assume the communication of knowledge from author/text (and by proxy, from the teacher) to reader, that deny the construction of meaning on the part of students— are at odds with the goals of our reading programs. As David Bleich (1980) states: "When knowledge is no longer conceived as objective, the purpose of pedagogical institutions from the nursery to the university is to synthesize knowledge rather than pass it along" (159, quoted in Tompkins 1980, xxi). Tompkins expands on this notion by stating that "[Bleich] substitutes for the paradigm of teaching and learning the paradigm of 'developing knowledge,' replacing the idea of education as an activity in which there are agents and patients (teachers and learners) with the idea of education as a communal pursuit in which all parties are engaged on an equal footing in deciding what counts as true" (xxi).

Implicit in these notions of transaction and construction is the idea of the social construction of knowledge—education as a communal pursuit. Building the negotiations between reader and text is a process that is never undertaken in isolation of the social circumstances in which learning and reading take place. One of the most powerful arguments for the reconceptualization of reading as construction comes, it seems, from "social pragmatists" (Hunt 1990b), who suggest that meaning making is learned through the social interactions that readers have, especially when they explore texts in groups. This notion of the social or dialogic imagination provides a built-in corrective to the slippery slope of relativism or solipsism in literary response. Stanley Fish (1980), for example, suggests that reading (at least in terms of literary reading) is the employment of particular interpretive strategies. These strategies—these ways of "constructing meaning"—are learned through social interaction; particular social communities employ particular methods for making sense out of the world and out of text, and they use particular interpretive strategies to make meaning. These strategies are socially mediated, learned through a process of socialization into particular discourse communities (see Clark 1990).

In many ways, this point of view comes from the sociopsychology of Vygotsky (1978), and has been more recently associated with researchers in metacognition both within and outside reading. Vygotsky suggests that the ways in which we think are learned primarily through our social interactions and, in particular, that the ways in which we learn, use, and comprehend language are developed as a result of our use of language in social circumstances. What we learn about language and its use comes from our observation and participation in social interactions around us. We therefore take on the thinking and meaning patterns of our social groups. In this way Vygotsky accounts for the great similarities among the thinking patterns of particular cultures and social groups within cultures. This notion of social mediation in the construction of meaning is hardly new, but researchers are now investigating how readers take on thinking patterns from social groups, particularly instructional groups, and how they employ those patterns in constructing meaning during reading. (See Straw 1990c for a survey of the research in cooperative and collaborative instructional models.)

If the mature, independent reader is involved in active construction of text, in active negotiations of meaning, and if those negotiation strategies are primarily learned through students' social interactions both with us as teachers and with other students, then we as teachers cannot encourage mature, independent reading by merely telling our students what particular texts mean, nor by having students read and respond alone, nor even by asking questions of students that lead them to infer a particular meaning; we cannot assume that "the poem" (as that term is used by Rosenblatt) will ultimately be the same for every reader. Transactional and constructive theories of reading assume that within the context of social construction, meaning in literature is arrived at through the negotiation of the reader with the text based on previous social interactions—a meaning-making process rather than a meaning-getting process. Instructionally, what we really want to do as teachers, we would argue, is to teach students to become active negotiators in the act of creating meaning during and after reading—to help students become part of the active conversation that *is* reading, the conversation between reader and text, between text and community, and among readers. This argues for socially based classrooms, classrooms that lead students to the negotiations that are the heart of meaning making in the act of reading.

With the rationale of increasing social interaction, along with teaching transactional and constructive reading, teachers and researchers have searched for means by which to achieve the combined goal of helping students negotiate meaning both with text and with members of different interpretive communities. Learning situations that require students to work in groups, to identify their own background knowledge, to use that knowledge in constructing meaning, to take on other communities' interpretive strategies, to explore how other interpretive communities come to make meaning with literature, to take on alternately the roles of authors and readers, to negotiate the interpretive strategies with one another, appear to result in students with the most highly developed and educationally discursive imaginations.

In the rest of this introduction, we attempt to show how each of our authors offers a valuable contribution to the discussion of the implications of these learning situations, opportunities in the classroom for "teaching beyond communication." Taken together, our chapters present what we might call a *pragmatics* of constructive reading. In other words, the theoretical underpinning of "teaching beyond communication" originates in the teaching practices themselves and in the conceptual stances informing them. As editors, we found that two main topics came to the fore as organizing principles for the articles: (1) constructing reading among students and teachers and (2) critical theories in the classroom. We have therefore grouped the articles into those two sections. Although both sections deal with reading and literary theory, the first focuses primarily on classroom implications of the actualization model, the second on the ways in which literary theory is used in a deliberate way to shape pedagogy.

In "Beyond Actualization," John Willinsky provides an appropriate first chapter by situating the issues of the present volume against the backdrop of *Beyond Communication*. His main concern is to extend the actualization contract from the focus on authenticity of the individual self to "the authenticity of shared meanings, the actualization of a common ground . . . that can be embraced, denied, resisted, undermined" (17). By emphasizing the importance of participation in "the common stock" of shared linguistic meanings, Willinsky wants to get beyond the "private" sphere of the single experience of self-actualization in literary reading to the meanings students share with one another. This orientation toward social construction argues for a conception of literacy that tempers the individualistic, liberal bias of reader-response theory with its social goal of instilling in students awareness about the conditions underlying the linguistic constructions of their reading experiences. In making his case, Willinsky paints with a broad brush the landscape of this entire book: from his vignettes of students responding to texts orally and in writing, to the social and political implications of poststructuralist theory and its relevance to constructive reading, to the part played by the writing process in meaning making and the actualization of voice. His "search for the grounds of permanent intellectual upheaval" (18), which he believes should inform the teaching of literacy, underscores the classroom in its "historical, ideological, [and] vocational" role as purveyor of the "public meanings" (28) that educate students' discursive imaginations.

Trevor Gambell continues the theme of bringing together the individual and social purposes of the actualization contract in "From Experience to Literary Response: Actualizing Readers Through the Response Process." Gambell stresses the importance of "teaching beyond communication," for both students and teachers, of "living literature," that is, the process or action that takes place when "readers initially respond to literature with which they have engaged through internally derived purposes (32). More sanguine than Willinsky about the educational benefit of the single literary reading experience as a vehicle for cognitive growth and behavioral change, Gambell values the phenomenon of empathic, identificatory reading on the part of individuals, reading that, he points out, includes previous, cumulative literary experience as well as the personal history of the reader. Social and cultural assumptions about literature, however, also form an integral part of Gambell's approach to literary response in the classroom. Insisting that "personal response, which is by nature idiosyncratic, does not exist apart from the cultural milieu" that helps shape that response (38), Gambell draws on the work of Marnie O'Neill, highlighting the categories she advocates for reflection upon literary response: structure of the text, voice of the narrator, construction of character, position of the reader, coherence or consistency of response, and compatibility with cultural values. Gambell borrows from another Australian, Bill Corcoran, in suggesting what might characterize the actualized teacher of literature. Finally, he suggests ways in which teachers can help students move "from experiential response to reconsidered response" (43) through a rich array of imaginative re-creations and multiple revisitings of the text.

In the next two chapters, we feature empirical studies that flesh out some of the assumptions underlying "living literature." In "That Reminds Me of the Time . . . ": Using Autobiographical Writing Before Reading," Michael W. Smith and Brian F. White present the results of their studies investigating the positive influence of writing within an autobiographical mode before student readers even approach a work of literature. These authors build on Rosenblatt's transactional theory but with an attitude of caution about the cognitive benefits of freewheeling associative responses. For Smith and White, all personal responses are not equal, not just in literary terms, but as they affect learning about "life"; the "retrieval and application of personal connections" (48) must be counterbalanced by textual constraints "as a blueprint for the construction of meaning" (49). Centering on students at the grade-nine level, these studies bring to light how the understanding of literature, amplified and intensified by personal writing beforehand, can enhance understanding of related contexts in life. Smith and White contend that actually putting pen to paper before the reading event changes the level of discourse from that of the oral because student readers must continually rephrase the purpose and the structure of what they say. Such writing, they argue convincingly, not only deepens students' grasp of literary characterization but furthers enjoyment, heightens inferential understanding, decreases the incidence of misplaced focus on irrelevant information, and improves their willingness to engage in meaningful class discussion. This last point throws into relief the social relevance of these findings, for it is shown that "at-risk" students in particular are helped by being able to perceive more acutely the connections between their own lives and what they read.

The purpose of David Miall's "Constructing Understanding: Emotion and Literary Response" is to help us further understand the role played by the emotions in the response process. Proceeding from the assumption that literary texts possess certain features that require Rosenblatt's aesthetic reading, Miall's chapter explores the relationship among foregrounding, defamiliarization, and emotional response in arguing for the constructive function of affect in schema creation and literary understanding. While other writers focus on meaning, interpretation, the constructed nature of texts, or the importance of collaborative learning, Miall directs our attention to the registering of significance and its place within the context of the individual reader's preexisting understandings. We might say that his piece conceives of actualization as going beyond the schemata any one reader already has in place. In contrast to John Willinsky, Miall concentrates on the "continual creation of the [individual] self through the work of the emotions" (73), and the function of literature in accomplishing this goal. This goal is broadened and even thrown open to question by our other authors, particularly Jack Thomson, Ursula Kelly, and Judith Millen, who are more concerned with the classroom implications of ideology than with psychology. But Miall's chapter is pivotal to this book in that it addresses a significant though often invisible and unconscious dimension of literary reading. Understanding the complex processes of human interaction at this level can be an important precondition for the social and pedagogical contexts of constructive reading stressed by other authors in this volume. As well, Miall's chapter is perhaps the most focused example in this volume of the bringing together of the empirical and speculative dimensions represented by schema theory and literary theory as they pertain to the classroom treatment of literary response. Not content with theoretical statements about the implications for practice, Miall concludes his chapter with actual classroom strategies.

David Miall and Roy Graham share a common concern: they both underscore the importance to pedagogy of nurturance and a supportive environment and their relationship to student motivation in the task of developing lifelong readers. Establishing self-confidence, creativity, and a sense of autonomy within the individual student is also an objective to which both authors subscribe. Graham's "The Transactional Teacher Under Glass: Refocusing an Ideal" reminds teachers of the significance of nondirective teaching but does so within a particular context—the moral component of the personal transformation at the heart of transactional teaching. In part an answer to John Willinsky's call for literary response as a social enterprise, this chapter looks at the question from the perspective of the philosophy of teaching. Within Graham's formulation, the teacher of reading moves beyond being merely a pedagogue to becoming a moral philosopher with a vision of "the good life." Through the use of Rogerian approaches to facilitating the knowledge exchange between teachers and students, Graham stresses, as does Miall, the interpersonal connection in student-centered learning; but he does so especially by emphasizing trust, empathic understanding, and realness (genuineness) in the one-on-one relationship between student and teacher such that both students and teachers become "strong-sense critical thinkers" (87).

Lorri Neilsen shares with Roy Graham her interest in the ethical/ pedagogical contract between student and teacher and its function in both the implicit and explicit classroom environment. She also shares with him and with Willinsky and Miall a fervor about democratic teaching and its relationship to the negotiation of and reflection on meaning making in reading. Along with Smith and White, she values the reader's personal history in literary response; with Gambell, she believes in the importance of teachers' reflecting on their own reading to the teaching of reflective practice to their students. Centered on her own graduate class, Neilsen's chapter, "Exploring Reading: Mapping the Personal Text," joins company with those chapters that begin with personal response and culminate in carefully wrought considerations about pedagogy in reader response. Specifically, Neilsen considers the connection between teachers' inquiring into their own reading processes and their sense of their role as literacy instructors. Linking the personal with the social and the political, this account emphasizes the reader "as an individual composing the self in relation to others" (97). As an antidote to prepackaged curriculum materials, which, Neilsen worries, are too often accepted uncritically by teachers, the teachers' journals and their own chosen readings become the curriculum for this investigation into graduate teaching. Rather than produce a grand metatheory, this chapter delineates an enterprise in collaborative professional revitalization.

The sense of rediscovering the humanity of reading experienced by Neilsen's students and its power to make interpersonal ties resonates with Willinsky's appeal to the force of language in its more public mode as influencing the intellectual climate of the classroom. Accepting the possibilities afforded by their own language play gave Neilsen's students, who are also teachers, valuable insights into their own teaching. Comprising mainly women, this class also strengthened their sense of voice through an exploration of their own reading subjectivity: delving into memories of early reading experiences and their evocation of maternal nurturance is contrasted with the inhibiting factors of reading as "doing school." Much of this exploration became an unlearning and undoing of "the institutional narrative" (97) of reading as an educational technology. Being able to re-vision their reading helped these students embody themselves as readers and reconceive themselves as teachers by inquiring into their own part in reproducing texts. In this chapter Neilsen poignantly leads us along the path among the personal, the social, and the ideological as readers gradually "expose the broader cultural practices that regulate reading and readers" (106).

Russell Hunt closes the section on student and teacher response in the classroom by addressing the issue of meaning as a social event in "Texts, Textoids, and Utterances: Writing and Reading for Meaning in and out of Classrooms." Beginning from the same theoretical premise of a shared "sociolinguistic competence" (115) as is espoused by Willinsky, Hunt focuses on the ways in which the particular configuration of the relationship among the reader, the text, and the situation informs social context, which, he contends, lies at the heart of verbal meaning. Hunt presents us first with his conceptual framework and then with his sketch of his classroom application of it. In his apologia for meaningful pedagogical contexts in the teaching of meaning, Hunt illustrates the aim of this book by showing the significance of "teaching beyond communication" as precisely that which occurs at the point of instruction when one's classroom strategies directly reflect the actualization contract. Using Bakhtin's distinction between text and utterance, he introduces the concept of "textoid": those texts that, stripped of their contextual enrichment by either the reader or the situation, "*resist* being made into utterances" (118), that is, meaningful meaning.

Hunt even goes so far as to make the somewhat startling allegation that the acontextual nature of educational discourse at all levels tends to breed textoids. In fact, for Hunt, most pedagogical situations virtually dictate that students produce textoids in their effort to engage in what Lorri Neilsen calls "the institutional narratives" (97) of meaningless meaning required by "doing school." Rigid conformity imposed by the exigencies of testing inhibit the acquisition of a "powerful pragmatic imagination" (121) so essential to the meaningful production of meaning in both writing and reading. For Hunt, this normalization of the absence of meaning engendered by schools impedes the kind of metacognitive awareness that real literacy tasks would encourage.

Setting the stage for the authors in the second half of the book but also redolent of Lorri Neilsen and others in the first half of the book, Hunt follows up his position by detailing an exercise he conducted with his own class. He thus lends practical weight to sound theorizing through a series of pedagogical moves that demonstrate how student work can result in "an authentically functional piece of written text" (125) rather than a textoid. Here he resembles Jack Thomson, who offers a compelling approach to the role of literary theory in "teaching beyond communication." "Helping Students Control Texts: Contemporary Literary Theory into Classroom Practice" details Thomson's goal—making students aware of literary texts as constructs. Beginning with Robert Scholes's distinctions among reading, interpretation, and criticism, Thomson's chapter is dedicated to enabling students to interrogate the ideological assumptions underpinning texts, to read against the grain of textual authority. Thomson's attitude to the text contrasts with that of Smith and White, who see it as a legitimate curb on excessive personal emoting or irrelevant divergent thinking. Like Neilsen, Thomson explores the conditions of responses; like Hunt, his theoretical framework spawns a host of classroom activities; like Gambell, he fosters the writing of literature as an appropriate mode of responding to literature.

Thomson's developmental model moves student readers to a high degree of theoretical sophistication at any stage of their reading by teaching them to become aware of "their own constructive reading strategies" (133). In this regard, Thomson shows himself to be a master of *praxis* in that his pedagogical goals are altogether embedded in concrete suggestions for the classroom. Whether it is through students' monitoring their own reading process, writing reading journals, learning textual constructedness, reading resistantly, creating literature through imitation and parody, or breaking down the barriers between literature and popular culture, he brings theory tangibly to pedagogy, to literature, and to life.

Drawing as well on the ideas of Robert Scholes and other current writers who apply literary theory to pedagogy, Deborah Appleman's model also brings theory to literature and to life: but hers is much more explicit than the others in this book in that it presents the students in her college-bound high school classes with four specific theoretical approaches to the texts: reader response, structuralism, Marxism, and feminism. Beginning with a defense of teaching theory in the secondary school, Appleman successfully challenges the skepticism of many educators about the appropriateness of using a "multiple perspective" critical method at the high school level. She then reviews the theoretical positions that have traditionally and invisibly dominated the teaching of literature. Like Thomson, Appleman conceives of literary theory in an instrumental way: it is not taught "for its own sake" but rather to provide student readers with an array of "critical lenses" through which they can view the same text in different ways. The richness of Appleman's study lies, as does that of many of our other authors, not only in its valuable overview of the field of literary theory, but in the expertise with which she adapts definite critical perspectives to actual classroom practices. These lessons, however, are not just exercises, but productive activities in meta-cognition that integrate the creative and the critical in student reader response and writing.

Whereas Appleman's classroom techniques involve several critical approaches to a number of literary texts, Mary Beth Hines concentrates on one approach to one text in "Literature and Social Change: A Feminist Approach to Gordimer's 'The Catch.'" Moved to discover new ways of reading literature that also offer critiques of readers and of the culture out of which they grow, Hines gives an account of one successful teacher who developed a feminist approach to literature "that encouraged students to assess their lives and their worlds as well as their texts" (172) using Nadine Gordimer's "The Catch." Like Hunt, Thomson, and Appleman, Hines prefaces her methodology with "the interplay between educational theory and literary theory that [ultimately] became manifest" in the classroom (173). Hines and the teacher with whom she works pay particular attention to the emotional basis of literary response, an important consideration when dealing with issues of race and class as well as gender, all of which this critical approach embraces. While Hines, like Thomson and Appleman, is concerned with uncovering the ideological biases of text, she is in addition self-consciously aware of fostering in students a sustained commitment to their sense of social responsibility in their textual practices. A highly philosophical critique of the cultural and social order is embodied in this critical method, one that lends fresh import to the meaning of student-centered pedagogy. Abundant in its examples of students' written responses and oral class discussion, this chapter resembles in many ways those of Gambell and Miall, thus illustrating the multilayered overlap of the two parts of this book. Hines shows student readers in the process of examining the conditions of their own responses as they draw "from personal opinion, experience, and history" as well as perform "the more traditional close readings of lines and passages" (181). Ranging widely over the terrains of literary response, ideology, and popular culture, this chapter opens up the myriad possibilities of students' ways of knowing afforded by teaching literature for cultural critique.

The movement into the areas of cultural studies and popular culture is inevitable when a critical, socially based pragmatics of reader response is implemented in the literature classroom. Judith Millen, in her contribution, "Print and Televisual Literacies: Uneasy Companions," extends the expressly sociological aspect of this shift into an exploration of educational assumptions about literacy. Millen not only shows how students' competency in television viewing can be used to advantage in literary study, but also throws open to question some of the most fervently held beliefs about the hierarchies that exist between art and popular culture, and among print literacy and other kinds of literacies. Injecting into the discussion a class- and gender-based analysis of the ways in which teachers can become effective literacy teachers by building on their students' already-in-place expertise about television, Millen echoes Hines and Thomson in their exhortation to teach for cultural critique. This chapter resembles its predecessors in its validation of a student-centered response curriculum but lends a new credibility to what students know. Again, for Millen, like other authors in this section, theory is located in practice, her classroom applications furnishing us with a wealth of strategies for the constructive reading of television.

Our final chapter, "Teaching English: Who's Subject to What?" by Ursula Kelly, provides a counterpoint to John Willinsky's opening chapter in that rather than "apply" any one theory or set of theories to the classroom, it proffers a critical overview of the subject of English studies itself within the context of going "beyond actualization." Kelly's objective is to encourage teachers to historicize our discipline and our own mandate within it, as well as to reevaluate our responsibilities to students in terms of making room for other than canonized voices in the literature curriculum. Hence, the abiding concern throughout this book with *how* to teach "beyond communication" inevitably merges into a concern with *what* we teach (see also Bogdan 1992b). Kelly's form of constructive reading is that of reading the subject, English, as a discipline that constructs, or conditions the formation of, the human subject who is the object of its content. Considering especially the hierarchies of language and values imbedded in the institution of English, Kelly criticizes the "homogenizing process" (207), often barely perceptible, that takes place in the English classroom. If left uncritiqued, the effect of a eurocentric, androcentric curriculum is to normalize the imperialist nature of the canon and, in the end, "reproduce a human subject already privileged in the larger social order ... whose value system is reinforced through and by schooling" (207). Revolutionary in spirit, this chapter provides a context that is especially pertinent to closing a book that seeks to further the theory and practice of response to literature within the social and political context of reader empowerment, broadly defined. In embracing the ideals of critical pedagogy, in which English merges with cultural politics, Kelly reminds us that the logical outcomes of "teaching beyond communication" in terms of the content of the literature class is to supplant The Great Tradition with the study of human beings in terms of "the social order out of which communities of human subjects are formed" (212).

Kelly's chapter recapitulates the themes of the contributing authors while at the same time pushing us to yet another level of critique—that of a metatheoretical scrutiny of our own practices even as we engage in them, what Shoshanna Felman (1987) would call "self-subversive self-reflection" (90) within our profession as a whole. As well as going beyond actualization with Willinsky, Kelly resonates with Thomson in her emphasis on self-reflexivity and the broadening of the concept of ideology from the consideration of the conditions of response as they affect individual students to the construction of the subject English itself. Here she reflects Millen's interest in the hegemonic implications of literacy and Hines's efforts to teach for social justice. Her appeal to reformulate English as a truly liberatory endeavor is a theme we invite you, the reader, to thread through the chapters as you make your own connections to all of our authors and inquire into the conditions of your own professional life. It is, we believe, in the integration of our roles as literary theorists and educational practitioners that we can constructively teach beyond communication.

References

Bleich, D. 1980. Epistemological assumptions in the study of response. In *Reader-response criticism: From formalism to post-structuralism*, ed. J. P. Tompkins. Baltimore, MD: Johns Hopkins University Press.

Bogdan, D. 1990. Toward a rationale for literary literacy. *Journal of Philosophy of Education*, The Journal of the Philosophy of Education Society of Great Britain, 24(2):199–212.

————. 1992a. Literacy, censorship, and the politics of engagement. In *Reassessing language and literacy*, ed. Mike Hayhoe and Stephen Parker. Buckingham, England & Philadelphia: Open University Press.

————. 1992b. *Re-educating the imagination: Toward a poetics, politics, and pedagogy of literary engagement*. Portsmouth, NH: Boynton/Cook.

Bogdan, D. & S. B. Straw, eds. 1990. *Beyond communication: Reading comprehension and criticism*. Portsmouth, NH: Boynton/Cook.

Clark, G. 1990. *Dialogue, dialectic, and conversation: A social perspective on the function of writing*. Carbondale: Southern Illinois University Press. (Published for the Conference on College Composition and Communication.)

Felman, S. 1987. *Jacques Lacan and the adventure of insight: Psychoanalysis in contemporary culture*. Cambridge, MA: Harvard University Press.

Fish, S. 1980. *Is there a text in this class? The authority of interpretative communities*. Cambridge, MA: Harvard University Press.

Hunt, R. A. 1990a. *Educating the dialogic imagination*. Paper presented at 80th Annual Convention of the National Council of Teachers of English, November. Atlanta.

————. 1990b. The parallel socialization of reading research and literary theory. In *Beyond communication: Reading comprehension and criticism*. See Bogdan & Straw 1990.

Hynds, S. 1990. Reading as social event: Comprehension and response in the text, classroom, and world. In *Beyond communication: Reading comprehension and criticism*. See Bogdan & Straw 1990.

Rosenblatt, L. M. 1938. *Literature as exploration.* New York: Appleton-Century.

————. 1978. *The reader, the text, the poem: The transactional theory of the literary work.* Carbondale: Southern Illinois University Press.

Stotsky, S. 1992. Review of *Beyond communication: Reading comprehension and criticism,* ed. D. Bogdan & S. B. Straw. *College Composition and Communication* 43:95–98.

Straw, S. B. 1990a. Challenging communication: Readers reading for actualization. In *Beyond communication: Reading comprehension and criticism.* See Bogdan & Straw 1990.

————. 1990b. *Interaction, transaction, and construction as means of educating the imagination.* Paper presented at 80th Annual Convention of the National Council of Teachers of English, November. Atlanta.

————. 1990c. Reading and response to literature: Transactionalizing instruction. In *Perspectives on talk and learning,* eds. S. Hynds & D. Rubin. Urbana, IL: National Council of Teachers of English.

Straw, S. B. & D. Bogdan. 1990. Introduction. In *Beyond communication: Reading comprehension and criticism.* See Bogdan & Straw 1990.

Tompkins, J. P., ed. 1980. *Reader-response criticism: From formalism to post-structuralism.* Baltimore, MD: Johns Hopkins University Press.

Vygotsky, L. S. 1978. *Mind in society: The development of higher psychological processes,* trans. and ed. M. Cole, V. John-Steiner, S. Scribner & E. Souberman. Cambridge, MA: Harvard University Press.

1

Beyond Actualization

John Willinsky

I recall some time ago asking a class of students to write a biographical statement to include in a book of their poetry from the term. After the class had been working awhile, Jinny brought her book to where I sat atop an empty desk watching the class. She had proven herself one of most engaging poets in this class of eighth-grade students. The class had appreciated her poetry for its bite, the cleverness of her observations, and the flourish she gave to the endings that announced themselves as just that. When I turned to the final page of her book to read about the author, there was a hasty sketch of a house and swimming pool. I went on to read about how this author had grown up and married a rich man who spoiled her rotten, as it were. I was surprised at this from one who seemed to take so easily to making her own point in writing. Self-expression was supposed to lead to other sorts of vision.

I looked up at Jinny and asked in obvious tones of disappointment how, after enjoying her critical acclaim in the class as a writer, she could think of wanting to live in the poolside shade of somebody else's wealth and fame. She laughed off my concern and wandered back to her desk as I took up the book of another student and started to read. It wasn't the first time that a teacher, wanting what was authentic and meaningful from students, recoiled from what was expressed. I didn't think any more about it until the next day when Jinny made a point of showing me that she had erased the swimming-pool version of her life and rewritten it in terms of her own future success as a writer, of which this book was but her first work in all its juvenile charm.

I was impressed by this act of revision. It seemed to symbolize the very change of heart that teachers concerned with the spirit of self-actualization among their students would be proud of achieving. Here was a story I could tell more than once in looking for the moments that make sense out of this line of work. In that way, the exchange took on its own aura of authenticity as the moment came to count for me, if only after its telling. In looking back at this incident, it seems fair enough to conclude that Jinny's two projections of her future did not come from what we imagine as deep down within her but from up out there, from the abiding mythologies that are shared like the common cold by students on the one hand and the teacher on the other. A virtue of her poetry had been its play on less easily spoken myths about tough boys who feared their fathers. She was as much reaching out as she was reaching within to work her variations on common and uncommon themes. But then so was I, as a teacher who was handily imposing his vision onto the work of a young woman and then claiming it as a proud moment in his teaching. Jinny had written her life out in pencil. It meant that she could easily correct it, as most everything in school is subject to correction, to getting it right and getting it scored, the way scissors score paper, leaving a fold that bends without cutting. In this case, the scoring came to count more for the teacher than the student.

Jinny's story retold forms one turning point in my conception of the "actualization model" that Stanley Straw and Deanne Bogdan (1990) describe in their insightful introduction to the book that precedes this one. They situate this "revolution" in reading and literary theory in the liberated autonomy of individualized readers: "The purposes of readers in these conceptualizations are to realize their own potential and meaning within their own unique circumstances" (3). Straw and Bogdan, later in their introduction, distinguish between what they call "transactional" theories and "constructive" theories of actualization. Straw (1990), in his chapter subtitled "Readers Reading for Actualization" documents different concretizations of actualization models, pointing out how we need to account for the fact that "knowledge is socially patterned and conditioned, that coming to know is a result of the social experiences and interactions we have had, and that all knowledge and knowledge construction are essentially social acts" (87). Similarly, "Bogdan is also concerned with textual engagement and aesthetic experience, but . . . problematizes them as part of a humanist ideology with social and political implications" (Straw & Bogdan 1990, 9–10). I want to use this chapter to fill in aspects of literacy that are in danger of being overlooked by many of those who hold to reading as an act of actualization. After some years of modestly toiling away in this revolution, following the inspiring leads of Britton, Rosenblatt, Graves, and the Goodmans, I've begun to rethink the successes and shortcomings, to consider what we are making of literacy when we speak of it in terms of realizing our own meanings, and what we may be leaving out in the cold. The turn to the authenticity of the self, the realization of the student's voice, has been a part of what I have tried to achieve for so long that it has become like a word stared at until the very sense of its spelling falls away. Prompted by poststructuralist questioning of the very possibility of unfettered authenticity, of a realized essence, of an achieved presence on the page, I have grown leery of directing my teaching inward, of seeking to release the truth of each student's life, to overstate it only somewhat.

One alternative appears to be to expand the pedagogical focus outward. In terms of my own work, this has meant introducing the young to more of the historical, economic, political, as well as the legal and moral situations of print as another step on their way toward participation in its pleasure and power. In other places, I have described the elements of this supplement to the actualization model based on fostering students of literacy with the same devotion and attentiveness to history, authorship, and style that we seek from our best students of literature; it has meant taking up historical instances of heroic displays of literacy as well as exploring literature's place within this public sphere of literacy in an effort to understand the ways in which texts work (Willinsky 1990; 1991). It is by no means a coherent program yet, but rather a series of curricular inquiries into the literacy invoked by literary critics and worker poets, billboards and graffiti, emergent writers and pragmatist philosophers, young adult romance novels and conceptual art, intellectual property and literary responsibility.

Yet rather than add another programmatic segment to this curricular perspective on literacy and literature, it seems apt in this setting to look more closely at what Straw and Bogdan claim as a revolution. It is a way of recovering what has led me down this pedagogical side street of cultural materialism and the social history of literacy. My method is to circle back to the work of two students, Jinny and another named Pat, for a deactualized reading of their work, with some support from Margaret (Atwood), Himani (Bannerji), Jane (Rule), and Virginia (Woolf) to lend some authority to this getting beyond actualization as the business of writing. As with Jinny's story, I find the writing side of the literacy equation more revealing than the reading aspect of individual meaning, although I will come to consider what response-centered classes are working on. Writing is the aspect of literacy that would appear most given to actualization; and yet, for me, it brings the limitations of this concept into a particularly stark light. Literacy can be cast, I argue, as engaging the authenticity of shared meanings, the actualization of a common ground, a ground that can be embraced, denied, resisted, undermined. One of the principal gains to be had in this broadening conception of literacy is its encouragement for rewriting the range of possibilities rather than simply realizing the actual, the deeply set. My purpose is by no means a return to prerevolutionary classrooms in which the meaning of texts was fixed at the front of the room and moved from there into the students' heads. Nor am I proposing that this other side to authentic reading and writing is the real or actual truth of literacy. Rather, I want to keep alive the Straw and Bogdan revolution by suggesting that it is ongoing, almost Trotsky-like in its search for the grounds of permanent intellectual upheaval.

In its origins, this revolution is based, as only the best are, on bringing to bear an unrealized truth about humanity that the current regime has suppressed; the revolution promises to put a swift end to an unnatural state, an unnatural state of reading in this case. Many of us have indeed longed to naturalize the time spent with books in the classroom, to take a lesson from the reading we most enjoy, as if the whole class were at home picking up a book for reasons apart from the classroom. In implicitly rejecting the traditional classroom ethos in which individuality of meaning is vanquished, Straw and Bogdan speak of the goals that might guide the reading as coming from within this natural act of reading that differs person by person: "One person, for example, may read history to learn, another may read it for enjoyment. . . . " (3). You can imagine the readers who would serve as models of authentic reading, getting ready for bed, their cares behind them for another day, picking up Gibbon's *Decline and Fall of the Roman Empire* or something lighter. There is always a larger ethos of purposes, pleasures, connections, informing the act of reading; vacuums make poor reading rooms. So it is a reading of history within, perhaps, the context of sleepiness and beds, self-improvement and escape, along with other sorts of interests that leak in from the rest of a day, a life. The deep and abiding mystery of reading is its entanglement of individual lives and the whole of this literate civilization. Between the classroom and the bedroom, the reader navigates the course of a textual life afloat a sea of public meanings.

The authentic, in the sense of original, is not a thoroughly trustworthy concept for the study of language. Readers do find their own way through a piece of fiction; there are long-established versions of self and truth that come with writing things out. The private aspects of reading remain just that, protected by a cranial shield. Response is a public act, as we struggle to make it meaningful, comprehensible, as the success of meaning is often found in the eyes of another. These are the things Jinny's autobiographical parlays were prepared to teach me, as her peers chuckled at her original swimming-pool future and I offered my mock horror. Whose life is this? Ours, always already ours, pieced together out of the meanings and myths within a public domain, not freely chosen certainly, but as we hold out, hold up, hold off, and finally hold onto these mythic states.

My fear is that the constructivist revolution Straw and Bogdan describe can suggest a loss of meaning, since it might be interpreted that readers are mercifully liberated from the tyranny of the text, author, and other readers: "The purpose of reading is to realize the meanings hypothesized by the reader, regardless of the motivations and intent of the author, regardless of the assumptions about the meaning of the text, regardless of the meanings that other readers may ascribe to any particular text" (3). Left at that, this pointed description of reader actualization has an oddly tautological element: we read "to realize" what we "hypothesize," which is to say we will know what we read in order to know what we think when we read. It presumes a singularity of purpose for reading, which Straw and Bogdan had spoken against only a few sentences before in reference to the history readers. But then I'm by no means alone in growing apprehensive with the containment of reader-response theory. In fact, Bogdan and Straw themselves call into question "transactional" (reader-response) theories and suggest that conceptualizations of reading need to be both socialized and politicized. Reed Way Dasenbrock (1991), for one, has recently taken philosophical issue with Stanley Fish's version of this sense that "interpreters do not decode poems; they make them," to quote Fish in a categoric mood (1980, 327). Dasenbrock wonders what we can possibly learn from an endless trail of self-confirming readings. Yet is learning all that is at issue?

The prevailing concept of actualization dominating this revolution in reading is drawn from the top of the psychological hierarchy of individual needs posited by Abraham Maslow (Straw & Bogdan 1990, 3). Maslow more often uses the term self-actualization to designate the confident and contented state of people who have managed to, in effect, find creative, fulfilling work for themselves in this society. In describing this extraordinary level of well-being, Maslow borrows the particular language of Being developed by the philosopher Martin Heidegger to give it a quasispiritual sensibility: "Self-actualization or health must be defined as the coming to pass of the fullest humaneness, or as the 'Being' of the person" (Maslow 1962, 137). There is a belying passivity to this humaneness. As Bogdan (1990) points out in her contribution to *Beyond Communication,* Heidegger promoted an openness or "unconcealedness of being," which, as she describes it, is "the antithesis of self-assertion" (190). This openness, which Heidegger believes the poet is especially effective at naming, is an openness not to others but to a form of being that is no longer concealed, that is realized as a poetic truth about ourselves, in what becomes the authentic moment of actualization. The experience of this moment in which Being is named or felt or known needs to be tempered, I am suggesting, with an equal openness to how it has been constructed through language, how it is an effect that we are in danger of mistaking for an essence (of being in the world). No one is more aware than Bogdan of this, as she identifies "the painful contradiction that connectedness of this sort entails" (191). How far this painful contradiction is realized in

Heidegger has become a point of controversy for consideration by those interested in the roots and realization of actualization models.

Although it is more than can be fairly dealt with here, a number of commentators on Heidegger have recently pointed out that "Being" in this sense has an uncomfortable history in the German philosopher's work and life, especially as he wrapped it tightly in concepts of racial origin, destiny, and essence (Ferry & Renaut 1990; Lyotard 1990). In fact, the better part of the poststructuralist theoretical effort that has come to dominate the current intellectual scene could be said to be directed against the misleading elements of "essentialist" thinking that are in danger of informing, among other things, the actualization revolution (Kaplan 1988; Smith 1988). The point of caution is that whether applied to the act of reading or to the nature of a person, to speak in terms of essences is to unduly privilege one or another state of Being. This at best poses a threat to the otherwise endless human conversation about the possible, and at worst is tantamount to defining those who are not open to this form of Being in the world as falling outside what it is to be fully human, in Maslow's terms.

Beyond these philosophical peregrinations, I propose a more modest sense of purpose to revolutionize what classrooms do with texts. It does not require an identification of reading's essence and natural state nor of a reader's needs and wants, which seems to me a thoroughly misguided quest. After all, the revolution is about changing how the way time is spent in reading lessons, curtailing the enormous amount of time spent dredging up answers to questions that have little other purpose than to prove that the text has been read. It would be better, then, to revise and expand Straw and Bogdan's statement of reading's purpose to say that readers should be encouraged to hypothesize about, share, and otherwise explore the variety of meanings to which texts can give rise. Within this proposal, students are welcomed to explore the personal associations of the actualization model, as well as the intentions of the writer's project. They can set the text in relation to other works, in other places or times. Let us, by all means, release the play of meanings. Let us take up how texts operate on the making of the world. But let us be wary of what can become, of itself, the tyranny of the authentic in the author or the reader, in its singular and insular pursuit of the original and the pure. The search for the authentic and heartfelt response to literature needs to be set among the large number of approaches that texts afford, with more than a few of them providing a segue to an appreciation of literacy as a form of participation in culture, economy, and state.

One such approach is to address the social categories of meaning that transcend personal response. As it turns out, Straw and Bogdan introduce this approach amid discussions of the unique meanings of the self in their introduction to the actualization model. In one instance, they speak of how we might expect that Moslem, Christian, and atheist readers would arrive at markedly different readings of the Book of Revelations (5). Their point about individual difference turns out to be much more about the influence of broad cultural distinctions on our experience of texts. With this example, they have indeed hit on what the schools have for so long suppressed. What the prerevolutionary teaching of reading and literature did systematically exclude from English classes, no less so than in other subjects, was various social categories of meaning. This I take to be the pedagogical point of the enormous wealth of feminist (Kaufman 1989), African-American (Baker & Redmond 1990), and post-colonial literary theory (Ashcroft, Griffths & Tiffin 1989). The challenge to the classroom represented by this diverse body of work, if I can group it together for a moment, is not about the exclusion of individually unique meanings; they are rightly incensed by the way the schools have closed English classrooms to the literacy experiences of whole categories of experience, including to large measure Islamic culture, to return to the example. Bernardo Ferdman (1990), for one, has argued persuasively for setting the development of literacy within the context of cultural identity. Yet a danger must be acknowledged in treating these categories as in any sense categorically pure, as Kwane Anthony Appiah (1991) would remind us in his discussion of postcolonialism in Africa: "If there is a lesson in the broad shape of this circulation of cultures, it is surely that we are already contaminated by each other, that there is no longer a fully autochthonus echt-African culture awaiting salvage by our artists (just as there is, of course, no American culture without African roots)" (354).

In traditional literature classes, students have been asked to learn a narrow band of critical responses applied to an uncontaminated canon, and what is perhaps worse, they have been asked to regard the experience that is represented on the page, the unique and private sentiments, not only as transcendental but among the best that has been thought and felt. Instead of immersing themselves in this noble bathos, students might well consider for a moment or two how this prized literature tends to make up the meaning of what it is to be a hero, a despondent lover, an aging king, a woman. The literature class's cultural work on behalf of patriarchy and colonialism is well documented in the works cited above. One form of response to this sustained critique on literature, set amid notable contro-versy, has been the institution of programs that open the canon to a new range of works at, for example, such venerable institutions as Stanford University.

While traditional classrooms have made it their business to exclude what I am terming social categories of meaning from the classroom, they have always had plenty of time to espouse themes of liberal individualism. In this, I fear that the sense of revolution over individual meaning and response is misplaced. Consider the degree to which the schools are

dedicated to individual demonstrations of competency and accomplish-
ment, whether with the conventions of standard English or literary appreciation. The traditional teacher only asks, after all, that the students
make the lessons their own. The schools also go to enormous lengths to
measure individual differences, often to one part in a hundred, in the
spirit of equal and individual opportunity. In this sense, at least, reading
and writing in the school do not want for a language of individual actualization; the school has as its resplendent goal the development of individual potential. For some time, individualism has been everyone's favorite
educational theme, or as John Meyer (1986) goes on to develop at some
length, "It is impossible not to notice the chronological and functional
links among modern notions of individual personality, its social construction by education, and late nineteenth century expansion of the state and
the economy in the centers of the modern world" (208).

   Yet, there is no denying that the actualization revolution boldly
invites the expression of new realms of response in the classroom, rich in
personal associations. It has meant that otherwise excluded categories of
meaning have a chance to arise in the selection of texts and the discussion
of them (Borovilos 1990). As I have seen it working in response-centered
classrooms, a young woman tells the other members of their group that
the wife in a story was not given a chance to find her own place on the
farm; another student speaks up about the blatant racism demonstrated
by the police characters in a play; a third relates a short story to one read
a previous year in school (Willinsky 1991). But just as often, the students'
personal responses to the text fall within the range of a common literary
education, as they note character contrasts, author's point of view, the
symbolism of bird and beast, as if to reflect that they draw their "personal" responses from the font of previous literature classes that dwell
deep within them.

   It would seem that the authentic is not easily arrived at by students.
The results from a large and systematic study by Benton et al. (1988) of
young readers responding to poetry suggest that it requires some skill to
represent what one experiences as reading, as if it takes the kind of
focused practice used with literary appreciations to get students beyond
banal observations—"So this is a happy poem because I can relate to the
man" (49). The endless student transcripts make it apparent that the goal
is to solve the heady puzzle of what the poem is "about"—"I don't know
what problem the man has but he obviously has got some problem" (50).
The uniquely personal does not spontaneously arise as a rule among students confronted with a bit of verse. It may be due to the continuous suppression of the personal in other classes, yet I'm inclined to see the lack
of the authentic to be absent because it is a form of response that requires
as much careful cultivation as the rosebush. Is it fundamentally less
"authentic" for this nurturance, as the best of the young critics learn to

seek out a response plausible in its association with the text while appearing slightly fresh amid a crowded classroom of ideas?

Patrick Dias (1987), after listening to countless response groups make sense of poems handed out in class, has found it helpful to categorize students into four types of respondents, after the manner in which they interpret the poems they read. He divides these young readers of poetry into "paraphrasers," "thematizers," "allegorizers," and "problem-solvers" (56). The students appear to be, for the most part, too busy teaching themselves what the poem is about to begin speaking in terms of their own purposes, their own needs and wants, as suggested by the actualization model. Instead, they tend to respond to the poems in what must be regarded as a pretty traditional sense—by paraphrase, theme, allegory, or problem. If this general manner of responding, in one form or another, is the basis of a self-actualization, insofar as the students take over the teacher's role, we might speculate that there exists a number of latent educators among our students. They are finding in themselves what they would have found in most English classrooms from their teachers, which is to say that the students have learned how to respond in the traditional manner of English classes. To articulate the poem's relationship to their own experience is something most of them have not learned to do.

Yet what about those times when reader response really seems to work, when the students, in facing a literary work, do not fall back on what they simply know about reading poems in classes? In an eleventh-grade class last year, I sat in on a response group of four students that had gathered to read through the first scene of Allan Uhry's *Driving Miss Daisy* (Willinsky 1991). Pat, who was the only one of us to have seen the movie, complained that nothing really happened in it. Such was the beginning of her response. The end point turned out to tell a rather different tale, one that spoke forcefully about the potential for individual engagement and meaning:

I saw this play in the movie theatre when it came out with my grand-mother while I was in Ottawa. When we came out of the theatre, ladies were crying, mascara running down their faces. We looked at one another both wondering what was so sad. We knew that it was all a part of life and age. We had lived the story only a year earlier.

Reading the play in class brought back many pictures from the movie, pictures of my great grandmother. Daisy reminds me so much of her it's extraordinary. My great grandma is an amazingly strong person. She lived in a big old Victorian house all by her self. . . . We visited her every other summer. It was always the same. She served us ginger ale in the sun room and talked to my parents. My sister and I searched the house for hidden treasure, and when we left we received a stiff hug and a wet kiss. . . .

Then one day last spring she fell and broke her hip, the doctors
didn't think she would live the night. The doctors didn't give my great
grandmother much credit, she lived. . . .
When I found out they were going to sell the house, I was a wreck.
It seemed so strange to sell the house with her still alive. I know how
Boolie felt. I think the thing that hurt the most was the fact that the last
trip we'd taken I didn't go see her. I can't even remember what I was
doing when the rest of my family went. I almost missed my last chance
to see her.
I saw her this spring in the nursing home. She looked the same.
Couldn't hear as well, but the same. She wasn't crying though she had
tears in her eyes. I was afraid she would forget who I was. It seemed as
though all the power she had commanded had died and left her empty.
I miss her house. I want things to go back to how they were. It all seems
so strange and scary. In a way I'm lucky; most kids don't ever get to meet
their great grandmother, but I don't want to see what's happening to her
happen to my grandmother, or my mother or myself. What a vicious circle.

I was astonished and moved on reading Pat's working of the play,
as one response leads to another. It is a long way from Jinny and my
fantasy lives of the rich and famous. It surely reflects the uniquely
personal moment of self-actualization. Yet, even with this rare
instance, I want to balance the welling up of the personal with the
tapping of the public found in the remarkable quality of the writing,
the courage of building to a conclusion that both complements and
denies its complacent, knowing opening. The wonder here is not simply in what Pat found in her response to the play. It is the rendering
of response and the unmistakable sense that rendering it drove Pat to
the irrevocable conclusion of the final sentence, as a car skidding on
ice finds its snowbank. This work in language, we might say, shapes
the meaning of experience as much as vice versa. I want to argue for
the importance of the way she also reaches out to the resources
within the language and this public forum that compelled her to
write, not for her own purposes, not as a coming to pass of her Being,
but as something made public out of personal experience and a shared
language of literary themes. The authenticity is better thought of as
achieved and constructed out of language, rather than as a secret,
private meaning realized or released from within. In teaching, this
means giving the public project of reading and writing its due.
What Pat achieved with her response also points to a confusion
between, or a fusing of, response and expression. In assessing students' responses we are still examining their writing skills. We want
to enhance those skills, finding incentives, topics, approaches, texts,

that facilitate student work with language. Yet we do not want to judge the quality of their Being, or pretend to gauge the depth of their experience and meaning by the awkwardness they bring to this form of expression. They are simply learning to make something out of texts, as they have already learned to make small talk, if often very small talk, out of rock groups, fashion trends, and ball games, turning public events into a common currency of exchange. This cultural engagement actualizes, if you wish, friendships and, more generally, a sense of participation in the commonweal. Literature classes could assist in this articulation process, providing practice in the art of cultural criticism and, as in Pat's case, the craft of empathetic response.

Let me, in a final instance of moving beyond actualization, look across texts and into the eyes of those who write them. One highly relevant area of concern for this question of meaning and authenticity comes from the realm of those whose life is writing. The producers of texts, too, are wrestling with what can pass as the authentic in their art and where the domain of their unique reservoir of meanings extends. In Canadian publishing, the issue has recently made the news with a number of authors standing accused of exploiting those whose voices they took up in their work, whether sympathetically or in supposedly innocent fun. There was an irrevocable split among members of Women's Press in Toronto over the legitimacy of white women assuming the voices of other than their own (Maracle 1990), while in separate incident vehement critical attacks were launched against William Kinsella's *The Miss Hobbema Pageant,* in which the author mimics and mocks voices from an actual Native community that lies in northern Alberta (Harper 1990).

In these cases, the issue of the authentic voice is defined by social categories of experience in the representation or, as some would have it, appropriation of the voices of struggling blacks, women, and native writers. In response to this question of representation, Libby Scheier, Sarah Sheard, and Eleanor Wachel (1990) have assembled a collection of essays by Canadian women writers on the topic on writing and gender, *Language in Her Eye.* The book takes up this issue head on, arriving mostly on the side of the writer's right to freely represent the world in whatever guise desired.

Margaret Atwood's (1990) contribution to the collection, "If You Can't Say Something Nice Don't Say Anything at All," provides a litany of the precepts about language and behavior that women were held to when she was young, beginning with the adage that serves as her title. It meant a broad band of silence, which Atwood had to break out of in order to write: "Any woman who began writing when I did, and managed to continue, did so by ignoring, as a writer, all her socialization about pleasing other people by being nice, and every theory then available about how she wrote or ought to write. The alternative was silence" (18). The issue, as Atwood casts it, is not primarily in achieving the authentic, true voice within her as a writer, for surely that voice would have borne too many traces of her socialization; the issue is overcoming the circumstances that militate against writing to create the very space where that voice can come to exist. To turn in this way against the image of a proper woman is itself to engage in the public sphere, if not quite to the extreme—"ignoring, as a writer, all her socialization"—suggested by Atwood's dramatic statement. Her writing becomes an act of engagement, of the voice recovered and, more important, actually made in this public act of defiance (which the writer may identify as "self-actualizing").

Atwood also comes at the question of the authentic by directly addressing the publishing controversy mentioned above: "Some have claimed that a writer should not write about anyone other than herself, or someone so closely resembling her that it makes no nevermind. What was previously considered a weakness in women's writing—solipsism, narcissism, the autobiographical—is now being touted as a requirement" (22). These supposed weaknesses have also become something of a requirement in the actualization revolution Straw and Bogdan have outlined. The reading process is described as a matter of gazing into one's own unique realm of meaningfulness, into the realm, as it were, of solipsism, narcissism, and the autobiographical, with the implication that this is where English classes should dwell. In taking a stand against this required fidelity to personal meaning, Atwood goes on to name a long list of distinguished women writers who have taken on other persona in their writing, from Emily Brontë to Toni Morrison. Again, the issue is one of social categories of experience to which the writer presumes to give individual form. Writers do many voices, and, for them above all, voice is a craft that invokes authenticity.

For young readers, it would seem important to consider what can be gained in thinking through the lives of others as well as what is risked in acts of misrepresentation. In sharing the possibilities of meaning with others in the literature class, they should be prepared to challenge these acts not only by turning inward to their own experience but by looking out for when the assumed voices of others seem betrayed and exploited, when the laugh is at the expense of the defenseless, when missing voices are crying to be heard. For the reader and the writer, the realm of the un- and misrepresented, the silenced and distorted aspects can be sought. It is a challenge that cannot proceed as easily only from within self-actualization, as readers and writers are protected by their claims to an unassailable realm of individual meanings.

Complementing Atwood's contribution to *Language in Her Eye,* Himani Bannerji (1990) has written movingly about the differences that set her apart, not out of her uniqueness, but from within a group "writing in English as Asian women in Canada" (29). She asks of them and herself the basic writer's question that warns against an easy path to self-actualization: "Are you also struggling with the realization that you are self-alienated in the very act of self-expression?" Again, the problem is one of the social categories of meaning: "Conversely, our 'otherization' becomes much easier as we do carry different sign or meaning systems which are genuinely unrelated to Western capitalist emotional, moral and social references" (31). Literature can help students locate themselves within and outside those sign systems. Here Bannerji's metaphor of having to translate herself as well as her language throws some light on the difficulty that students have in sharing experiences in literature class, as they are encouraged to connect their lives to literature and, in the process, make something worth sharing out of what has been read. Emphasizing the sense of craft required, Jane Rule (1990) uses her turn in *Language in Her Eye* to suggest that authenticity is the success of word-ly fabrication: "A believable or authentic character is a plausible composition made out of words" (228). The search in English programs for a plausibility of meaning, as modest and unrevolutionary as that goal may seem, can be directed at how texts operate beyond the individual realms of author and reader.

The plausibility of Jinny's and Pat's works does not lie principally in their fulfillment of a purpose that came only from within. They took up what was common, fanciful, and nostalgic, giving it their own personal twist, the part we celebrate, but not, I hope, at the expense of removing it from the realm of the shared language we live by. Taking charge of the common and making a small part of it their own is certainly what Abraham Maslow had in mind by the term "actualization." But the key is as much the sense of participation in that common stock gained from trading in the coin of the written word. The actual resides in the words and works, in what comes to hand, given this demand on students to create their own cultural artifacts in response to texts, artifacts shared in the circulation of meanings in the classroom and occasionally slipping into other realms.

The self-actualization that I want to get beyond, without letting it go, is one that we imagine determines the "real" meanings. The primary question for teachers is not, then, one of actualizing the authentic response of individual students; rather it is to explore with students the powers and pleasures that lie with texts, the life that is not so much deep within us as the life that is there, on the page, arising from the time spent with someone's book, reading it, talking about it, writing on it, just as it is with a book of one's own. The classroom can become a forum for speaking about not only the private moments of art—for reader, writer, character—but about its public work—historical, ideological, vocational. Let us find the conditions that have fostered these expressive and receptive acts of language and then see if we can do as much during a school day divided into fifty-five minute periods.

The mystery and wonder to be found in tripping across our uniqueness may arise in these classes like the sparks set off in experimenting with electricity, but in trying to better understand how it is that people come to read, write, and find meaning on the page, we would do better, I have come to conclude, by attending to the social situation of literacy. It is still very much a literary question, as Virginia Woolf (1929) pointed out. When asked to speak on women and fiction, Woolf did not hesitate to tell the young women assembled at Girton College, Oxford, that they had better come face-to-face with the material facts of literary endeavor, against their predilection for taking up its metaphysical concerns: "All I [can do is] to offer you an opinion upon a minor point—a woman must have money and a room of her own if she is to write fiction; and that, as you will see, leaves the great problem of the true nature of woman and the true nature of fiction unsolved" (4).

References

Appiah, K. W. 1991. Is the post- in postmodernism the post- in postcolonial? *Critical Inquiry* 17(2):336–57.

Ashcroft, B., G. Griffiths & H. Tiffin. 1989. *The empire strikes back: Theory and practice in post-colonial literatures.* London: Routledge.

Atwood, M. 1990. If you can't say something nice don't say anything at all. In *Language in her eye: Writing and gender,* 15–25. See Scheier, Sheard & Wachel 1990.

Baker, H. A. & P. Redmond, eds. 1990. *Afro-American literary study in the 1990s.* Chicago: University of Chicago Press.

Bannerji, H. 1990. The sound barrier: Translating ourselves in language and experience. In *Language in her eye: Writing and gender,* 26–40. See Scheier, Sheard & Wachel 1990.

Benton, M., J. Teasey, R. Bell & K. Hurst. 1988. *Young readers responding to poems.* New York: Routledge.

Bogdan, D. 1990. Reading and "the fate of beauty": Reclaiming total form. In *Beyond communication: Reading comprehension and criticism.* See Bogdan & Straw 1990.

Bogdan, D. & S. B. Straw, eds. 1990. *Beyond communication: Reading comprehension and criticism.* Portsmouth, NH: Boynton/Cook.

Borovilos, J. 1990. *Breaking through: A Canadian literary anthology.* Scarborough, ON: Prentice Hall.

Dasenbrock, R. W. 1991. Do we write the text we read? *College English* 53(1): 7–18.

Dias, P. 1987. *Making sense of poetry: Patterns in the process.* Ottawa, ON: Canadian Council of Teachers of English.

Ferdman, B. M. 1990. Literacy and cultural identity. *Harvard Educational Review* 60(2):181–204.

Ferry, L. & A. Renaut. 1990. *Heidegger and modernity.* Trans. F. Philip. Chicago: University of Chicago Press.

Fish, S. 1980. *Is there a text in this class? The authority of interpretive communities.* Cambridge, MA: Harvard University Press.

Harper, H. 1990. Whose story is Kinsella telling? *Journal of Educational Thought* 24(3a):121–23.

Kaplan, A. E., ed. 1988. *Postmodernism and its discontents: Theories, practices.* London: Verso.

Kaufman, L. 1989. *Gender and theory: Dialogues on feminist criticism.* Oxford: Basil Blackwell.

Lyotard, J. F. 1990. *Heidegger and "the jews."* Trans. A. Michel & M. Roberts. Minneapolis: University of Minnesota Press.

Maracle, L. 1990. Native myths: Trickster alive and crowing. In *Language in her eye: Writing and gender,* 182–87. See Scheier, Sheard & Wachel 1990.

Maslow, A. 1962. *Toward a psychology of being.* New York: van Nostrand.

Meyer, J. 1986. Myths of socialization and of personality. In *Reconstructing individualism: Autonomy, individuality, and the self in Western thought,* ed. T. C. Heller, M. Sosna & D. E. Wellerby, 208–21. Stanford, CA: Stanford University Press.

Rule, J. 1990. Deception in search of truth. In *Language in her eye: Writing and gender,* 225–29. See Scheier, Sheard & Wachel 1990.

Scheier, L., S. Sheard & E. Wachel, eds. 1990. *Language in her eye: Writing and gender.* Toronto: Coach House Press.

Smith, P. 1988. *Discerning the subject.* Minneapolis: University of Minnesota Press.

Straw, S. B. 1990. Challenging communication: Readers reading for actualization. In *Beyond communication: Reading comprehension and criticism,* 67–90. See Bogdan & Straw 1990.

Straw, S. B. & D. Bogdan. 1990. Introduction. In *Beyond communication: Reading comprehension and criticism,* 1–21. See Bogdan & Straw 1990.

Willinsky, J. 1990. *The new literacy: Redefining reading and writing in the schools.* New York: Routledge.

——— . 1991. *The triumph of literature/The fate of literacy: English in the secondary school curriculum.* New York: Teachers College Press.

Woolf, V. 1929. *A room of one's own.* Toronto: McClelland & Stewart.

2

From Experience to Literary Response: Actualizing Readers Through the Response Process

Trevor J. Gambell

Here's a little quiz on reading. It's quite simple. All you need to do is answer each statement with a yes or no or maybe/sometimes.

1. You enjoy giving yourself up to a book; leaving behind (or at least putting into suspension) your prejudices, skepticism, resistance—to be drawn into the world it conjures up, taking on the attitudes demanded of you.

2. However, you still realize that it is not good enough simply to be a passive reader, but that you must retain enough of your own being to participate in creating meaning from what you read.

3. In order to do this you draw on experiences from your own literary and cultural repertoire, you "imagine" the events, create a mental picture of them . . .

4. . . . and are able to associate your own feelings (and those of your "implied self") with the images you create, while simultaneously comparing the two.

5. You love puzzles; to be challenged to discover things for yourself and to formulate your own meanings; to become a sort of collaborator or coauthor.

6. You do this creative reading by—
   a. looking at the significance particular details, events, et cetera, have on the whole;
   b. connecting them with other episodes;

    c. modifying interpretations of earlier events;
    d. making predictions about what direction the novel will
        take.

7. You are able to reflect on your own process, and recognize that
    various influences are at work (both within and without the text)
    shaping your perceptual strategies.

Now give yourself five marks for each yes, two marks for each maybe/
sometimes, and zero marks for each no. If you scored at least fourteen you're probably an actualized reader.

The eleventh-grade student who made up this quiz (in Morgan
1990, 19–20) is most definitely an actualized reader. She knows that
the central purposes of reading are internal to and generated by the
reader, and these purposes are to realize her own potential and meaning within her own unique circumstances. I only wish that I had been
so aware at such an age that the reading process was a movement
from communication to actualization as its central purpose (Bogdan
& Straw 1990).

But what of the seventh and final statement in this readers quiz,
particularly the ability to recognize that various influences are at
work both within and outside the text? The ability to recognize influences within the text suggests that the writer makes a contribution to
the meaning generated by the reading process. Then, too, recognizing
influences outside the text contributes to the meaning. Both influences within and outside the text hint of the social nature of actualized readers and actualized meaning. The reader's initial response to
a text is an individual one but before the concept of the "poem"
(Rosenblatt 1978) is realized, response must become a social act
embracing other readers and their responses, as well as the writer
(through the text).

Throughout this chapter, I use the term *response* to refer to various aspects of the response process: personal response, which is the
registering of an individual's initial reactions to a piece of literature;
response in terms of accepting the pedagogical invitation to frame
one's reactions within a certain mode, such as rewriting the ending of
a story; and finally, the entire spectrum of reactions and activities
that make up the movement from the personal to the social within an
educational context.

I suggest that realizations outside the text may come about in
two ways. One of those ways is the sharing of meanings among readers of the same text, which is what happens when students/readers
share their individual responses to a text in open discussion. The
other occurs when teachers posit a particular way of approaching the
text, such as when they ask students to reexamine the text in light of

CONCORDIA COLLEGE LIBRARY
BRONXVILLE, N.Y. 10708

its narrative structure, characterization, symbolism, imagery, or use of language. Both types of influences are outside the text, and both shape the strategies and meaning of readers.

Straw and Bogdan (1990) have suggested that the central and initial purposes of reading are "internal to the reader and are generated by the reader" (3), but there are also purposes for reading that are external to the reader and that also contribute to students becoming actualized as readers. In this chapter, I propose that external purposes of reading are essential to the actualizing of readers, and that the role of the teacher is pedagogically to blend internal purposes for reading with external purposes for reading or rereading the text through the social act of shared response and reflection.

Living Literature

Literature (text) comes alive for readers when they generate their own purposes for reading. *Living literature* is the term I use to express what occurs when readers initially respond to literature with which they have engaged through internally derived purposes. The word "living" in this context as a word of action implies that readers have made literature a part of their lives. Let's view this act of "living literature" from three perspectives. One is that of two eleventh-grade students, another is that of secondary English teachers, while the third is that of a graduate student in language arts education who also teaches English language arts and drama courses in an Aboriginal and Métis teacher education program.

Harper Lee's *To Kill a Mockingbird* is a commonly used text in Canadian and American high school English classrooms. Two eleventh-grade students voiced their experience with this novel assigned in their English class by creating a poem that was printed in the school newsletter.

TO KILL *TO KILL A MOCKINGBIRD*

Let's talk, you and I.
Let's talk about English teachers,
and how to kill TO KILL A MOCKINGBIRD
grade elevens,
open your books
to the first page
now
"When he was nearly thirteen, my brother Jem got his arm badly broken at the elbow."
WHAT CAN WE LEARN FROM THIS SENTENCE?
what is the author telling us?
is there any new vocabulary in this sentence?

other comments?
well then
we now know the brother's name, Jem,
and age, 13.
we now know about an accident
but we don't know what the accident was
we want to know what the accident was
and this is called a narrative hook.
now
"When it healed, and Jem's fears of never being able to play football . . ."

> —Patrick O'Keeffe and Dave Scaddan
> (*Aden Bowman Collegiate Newsletter,*
> November/December 1988)

These two students have chosen satire to express that this novel has been treated as a literary artifact by their English teacher. They imply that the novel has ceased to live for them because it has been treated as an archaeological text, sifted through for evidence of literary artifacts. What is interesting is that their response to a literary text is through the medium of a literary text: they wrote a poem. Further, in the opening two lines of their poem are the artifacts of other literature, namely the opening of T. S. Eliot's "The Love Song of J. Alfred Prufrock." Literature lives through other literature, and literature begets other text. The text became living literature for these students despite their teacher's approach to it as a burial ground of literary artifacts ready for discovery by apprentice archaeologists.

In 1983 in South Australia a group of secondary English teachers on an English curriculum committee were given the chance to reflect on their own experiences as readers, to remember through anecdotes, to become aware through reflection of their own behavior as child, adolescent, and adult readers. They were invited to follow three steps in this process of remembering their experiences.

First, think of a piece of literature . . . which made a profound impression on you at some time of your childhood or adolescence. As a faculty, share these, explaining how you came across them and why you think they remain unforgettable.

Secondly, think of a piece of literature you rejected, either in childhood or adolescence or more recently. Again share information explaining your reasons for rejecting it, and what you did with the piece.

Thirdly, think of a piece of student writing you will never forget. Again, as a faculty share stories of the writing and why you remember them, or share the writing if you still have it. (Education Department of South Australia 1983, 9)

After considerable discussion over their shared accounts, these English teachers arrived at six major conclusions about living literature:

1. that the essential prerequisite for reading literature is a drawing on the experience of living and on the cumulative experience of literature;

2. that literature expands individual perspectives on living in the world;

3. that autonomous readers exercise choice over when, what, and how they read;

4. that readers often (but not always) feel compelled to share their responses to literature;

5. that some literature, through its intensity and permanence, remains unforgettable; and

6. that there are some effects of literature that elude exploration. (Education Department of South Australia 1983, 9–13).

Teachers almost never have the time to sit and reflect on their experiences of reading literature in such a way as to inform their own teaching. Some teachers, such as those in South Australia, are able to reflect on and bring to consciousness their understandings of how readers (themselves) and texts interact in the actualizing of meaning. Lon Borgerson was one. He did it through graduate study; course readings and discussion on literature and response provided the window through which he was able to reconstruct his own experiences with literature as a student. Lon Borgerson was about thirteen years old when he met this significant piece of living literature entitled "Larry Malone."

> ... to his horror, Larry saw that his father lay face down, astride the beam upon which he had been working. A blow from the runaway girder had laid him senseless. But, worst of all, the blow had, in addition, loosened one end of his beam, which was now almost separated from its bed flange in the corner-post. The runaway girder was swaying and banging in the wind ... and should it chance to strike the loosened beam again, this would surely be wrenched from its other socket, and Peter Malone be hurled straight to a dreadful death.... (Traymore 1939)

It had been twenty-four years since Lon Borgerson had first met Larry Malone in his eighth-grade reader, but the images and the tension in that piece still remained for him. Strange, though, he thought, that it should have had such appeal for a prairie boy, far from London and high-rise buildings and steel girders and such. Maybe it captured those teenage nightmares about falling, or the strange mixture of terror and exhilaration he had felt at reaching the top of their farm windmill for the very first time. (Ironically, that was the same year that his buddy, Cameron Schnell, finally dropped out of school. Cameron Schnell, who a few years later would fall to his death from the eighth-floor girder of a Winnipeg high rise.)

Lon Borgerson retrospectively knew that his first reading of "Larry Malone" was certainly not an efferent experience, to use Louise Rosenblatt's (1978) term for reading to gain information or knowledge that one takes away from the text. He concluded this in spite of the eight years of traditional literature training that, in his own words, "had already been inflicted on me." He had no memory of the "Helps to Study" questions that most certainly followed the class reading of the story. He and his classmates had been asked to select all the technical words used in the story of Larry Malone and his father, to look them up in a dictionary, to write down the definitions, to think of three or four words to describe different aspects of the character of Larry, the character of the foreman, of the other workmen. No discussion, and no talk of dreams and windmills and prairie landscapes. No bringing to life a literature; no imaginative re-creation.

These three perspectives of contemporary and reflective thought about what happens when the reader meets literature—eleventh graders, Australian English teachers, and Lon Borgerson—point to one particular conclusion: the essential prerequisite for reading literature is being able, and being permitted, to draw upon one's experience of living. When literature lives, one's experience of living includes the cumulative experience of literature. Part of becoming an actualized reader and bringing internal purposes to reading means beginning with personal experiences, our storehouse of life experiences, which we can apply, hence engaging memory, to that which we read. Then we move, or are moved, to response, blending our experience with that offered by other readers and in the literary work itself.

What happens when readers draw on their experiences as they transact with literature? Readers meet situations and people in texts that trigger long-forgotten memories. That is, they see themselves and people they know in the characters that appear in works of literature. They relive or re-create situations that have engaged or embodied them in real life and that now return for conscious reinterpretation through the medium of literature. Readers relive real life events when they find similar events in literature. They develop empathy with some of the characters they meet in literature. Readers also match their own experience against the created experience, gauging its authenticity. They, too, recognize aspects of themselves in a work of literature. This can be a profound realization, and has the potential for changing behavior because literature can provide readers with possible consequences of unexamined behaviors.

When we allow students to bring their own experiences to literature as a legitimate part of their classroom response, we open the door for them to develop a sense of ownership of a piece of literature. Ownership of a work of literature is built upon three critical factors: (1) choice over material and response to it, (2) the life experience brought to the work, and (3) the cumulative experience of literature brought to the work (Education Department of South Australia 1983, 18).

One way in which students can become actualized readers is through exercising their own choice of literature and mode of response. Not every piece of literature will, or should, elicit classroom reader response. When many students read the same piece of literature, some means of response will feel more comfortable to the student than others. Students can exercise choice not merely about whether to respond to a piece of literature, but also how to respond (the mode of response). Young readers often prefer to dramatize events and characters they meet in literature. Other modes of response include writing from different perspectives, imaginative interviewing of characters in literature, and creating media productions where characters are interpreted through voice, movement, and action.

Literature lives through the reader. This point is iterated by Iser (1978), who avers that fiction is about reality, not the antithesis of reality. In other words, readers create their own reality through their engagement with literature in the act of reading. Iser argues that the difference between language in literature and language in everyday speech lies in the situational context. Fictional language seems to be made without reference to any real situation, whereas language in ordinary speech presupposes a situation in order for communication to occur. Iser states that the reader must therefore work to build up the situation in his or her mind and does so through building a response to the details in the text. This certainly helps to explain how and why different readers create different situations and contexts for literature. It also implies that any unpredictable situation can become acceptable given sufficient details in the text. This type of interaction between reader and text has the dynamics of an event and creates the impression that readers are involved in immediacy—something is happening—and "happening" is the stamp of reality. It is the immediacy of the reading experience that lively teachers draw upon for the sake of their own teaching as well as for the sake of the readers in their classes (Deakin University 1986).

As humans interacting in a social world, we are constantly trying to fill the gaps that occur in interpersonal relations because of the differing perspectives and experiences people bring to relationships and interactions. So it is with reading. As readers, we constantly reaffirm our relationship with the text—and the writer—by filling the gaps in the text, by interpreting, by guessing, or by drawing on our life experience. We do this in our interpersonal relationships and we do it when reading too (Deakin University 1986).

Social and Cultural Assumptions About Literature

When readers generate their own purposes for reading texts, it suggests that they also have assumptions about literary texts, and these assumptions about the act of reading and the text itself will be brought to the experience of reading. It is not simply a matter of personal experiences that shape the reader's response, but those expectations of text that determine how readers approach a work of literature. Probably very few teachers bother to ask students what they expect to experience when they first approach a text. We do know that the title and author's name are powerful prereading influences. Publishers know that cover pages profoundly influence a reader's expectations of a book. Writers, too, exert an influence on readers through the textual choices they make. Not only do writers make choices regarding characters, settings, times, and events, but they also consciously or subconsciously make ethical, moral, political, and ideological choices. Part of the role of English teachers is to make students aware that texts are not "pure" or "innocent"; some texts have agendas that need to be brought to the surface and made explicit in the encounter.

Teachers assume certain things about a literary text, as do students. It is especially important that teachers be aware of students' assumptions about literary texts so that they can pose questions in student response and discussion groups that have students probe and question their implicit assumptions. O'Neill (1989) has examined some assumptions about literary texts harbored by secondary students:

- Structure of text: If the narrative is not presented sequentially, the writer will clearly signal shifts in chronological order, and such shifts are a deliberate part of the writer's design.

- Clarity of narrative voice: Generally speaking, the narrative voice will be consistent and reliable. If not, the writer will clear up the unreliable narrative voice early and offer an "explanation." Students see the narrator as fixed in time, space, and motion; the narrator, unlike other characters, does not change. In other words, there's a logical consistency between character development and plot development.

- Unity of character: The behavior of characters is consistent, as is the behavior of other characters toward them, and their behavior can be judged on cultural norms. If characters do "grow" or "develop," students can attribute the changes logically to their experiences within the narrative.

- Position of reader: The text offers a preferred position from which it is to be read and a "right response" is engendered by accepting that position.

- Coherency or consistency of response: A "mature" critical response is one that gives a "unified" reading of the text, explaining any gaps, silences, and inconsistencies satisfactorily, rather than highlighting them as problematic.

- Compatibility with cultural values: "Making sense" of a text entails being able to place it within the cultural framework of the reader. If cultural values are held up for scrutiny or question, in the end there will be a rapprochement with or a minimal modification of the reader's social construct. Students are rarely expected to take issue or disagree with the values presented by the text; part of the procedure for selecting texts is that they will provide sound moral and cultural values.

Personal response, which is by nature idiosyncratic, does not exist apart from the cultural milieu in which the response is shaped. Thus, the assumption that texts are neutral or lifeless objects from which the reader is free to make meanings that are totally individual seems untenable. O'Neill believes that a student reader's response in a classroom is never likely to be entirely or purely original. The process of sharing and modifying response opens the possibility that a dominant reading will prevail; alternative readings may be dismissed.

Yet it seems that striving for consensus is a characteristic human trait because we exist not individually but as members of groups that organize themselves socially, that develop a society. There are certain elements of a literary work about which most readers, if not all, will be in agreement. At the same time that readers may all agree that Hagar Shipley (in Margaret Laurence's *The Stone Angel*) is a proud, independent, and determined woman, they will have different reasons for why she is so. Personal responses will both converge and diverge on elements of meaning. O'Neill argues (17–18) that the teacher should encourage students to see that:

1. A text is a construction, not a reflection of reality that is "true."

2. Texts have constructed in them assumptions about, for example, race, gender, or class, which a reader might challenge rather than accept.

3. Gaps or silences in a text might be treated as problematic; filling them in different ways produces different readings.

4. The ways in which readers fill gaps may not be idiosyncratic but arise from cultural or social values.

5. While texts may offer the reader a particular position from which to read, the reader does not necessarily have to accept that position.

6. Texts offer possibilities for conflicting or competing meanings rather than consensual responses.

7. Resistant or culturally critical readings offer more opportunity for equity of participation.

The astute teacher is able to provide opportunities wherein the sharing of responses potentially frees the student to pursue his/her personal response while becoming aware, at the same time, of how the writer may subtly influence the response, and of how subconscious social and cultural values condition and shape response. Yet the reader may not be free to respond fully at all.

The Liberated and Actualized Reader and Teacher

Personal responses within a sociocultural milieu allow readers to realize their own potential and meaning within their own unique circumstances. The British critic Terry Eagleton (1985) describes this approach to literature teaching as ''The Reader's Liberation Movement.'' This apt term connotes the sense of freedom and empowerment that reader response allows: the reader is liberated from the domination of the text and from the omniscience of the teacher and critic, is actualized as a reader in the process of personal and shared response. But equally important, the teacher is liberated from preordained text interpretation by critics and premanufactured authorial intent. A Canadian Broadcasting Corporation television series on Canadian writers several years ago featured and interviewed Robertson Davies, the internationally renowned Canadian writer. When asked whether he ever wanted to make changes to one of his books when he'd seen it in print, he responded that once his books are published they take on a life of their own. Books exist independent of their authors. He refused to accept any responsibility for the published text. Whatever subconscious intent or conscious meaning that had entered the work as he wrote it no longer existed when the book reached the hands of readers. For Robertson Davies, the book becomes part of the history of the writer, whose experiences, aspirations, and meanings continue to develop, whereas the text remains static, fixed in time. Thus he, as writer, could only approach his own work as reader and respond to his own work from the perspective of contemporary time, experience, and knowledge.

We can, of course, go beyond Eagleton's description and coin a parallel phrase, "The Teacher's Liberation Movement." A personal-experiential approach to literature teaching is a move toward freeing English teachers from the constraints of predetermined interpretation. In this sense they are actualized teachers because their pedagogical role is socially derived through the process of collaborative response rather than knowledge derived. Such pedagogical empowerment offers a sense of freedom for teachers who no longer feel the need to carry the burden of enlightening students about what an author, poet, or playwright meant when he or she produced a piece of literature. Actualized English teachers are no longer the custodians of hidden mysteries of literary devices and their arcane buried meanings.

I have adapted six points from Corcoran (1989) that describe the liberated and actualized teacher of literature:

1. *The essential prerequisite for reading literature is a drawing on the experience of living, and on the cumulative experience of literature.* This latter point, the cumulative experience of literature, is obvious in the borrowing from T. S. Eliot in the eleventh graders' response poem quoted earlier in this chapter. Literature becomes part of the experience of readers and thus expands, broadens, and deepens their experiential base. As literary experience becomes part of the reader's experiential stock, it becomes part of the reader's life; literature lives. Literature becomes a source of vicarious experience, and as students mature socially and cognitively, vicarious experiences may play as important a role in their lives as do "real" experiences.

2. *Literature offers individual perspectives on living in the world.* Literature can explain individual perspectives because writers embed the actions of characters within a cultural, social, economic, and political context.

3. *Autonomous readers exercise choice over when, what, and how they read.* A primary goal of teaching literature is to develop autonomous readers; this implies that readers must be freed from their reliance on authority figures (such as teachers) to interpret their reading for them.

4. *Readers often (but not always) feel compelled to share their responses to literature.*

5. *Some literature, through its intensity and permanence, remains unforgettable.*

6. *There are some effects of literature that elude explanation.* This suggests that English teachers need to be aware that some parts of a text should be left untrammeled. Some literary works or parts of them strike a response that is rooted in the emotional or mystical and evades attempts to verbalize the experience. Sometimes readers need to experience literature as a private, inward experience. For response to be liberating, it must also be permitted its privacy.

Personal experience is the starting point for response to literature, but is it the end point also? How do we as teachers move students beyond their initial but possibly unsophisticated reactions? One way is to teach literature through re-creation exercises. Through such exercises students are able to enter the text, consider it from different angles, and extend their understanding of it without resorting to metaliterary language, that is, the often clinical and passionless language of literary criticism and analysis.

Stratta, Dixon, and Wilkinson (1973) use the term "imaginative re-creation" to describe this process. They describe imaginative re-creation as the process of seeking to re-create imaginatively for oneself the experience of the writer. Students are involved in active response to and exploration of texts by re-creating aspects of the text, probably with some shift of perspective. Examples of some imaginative re-creation exercises are changing the viewpoint of a narrator or character; rewriting incidents from a story in another context; writing a television or film version or translating the text into scripted drama; improvising a scene from the text or improvising a scene with a similar setting, character, or theme; interviewing a character from a text; exploring characterization through writing imaginative diaries or letters from one character to another; rewriting an incident as a newspaper report (New South Wales Department of Education 1985).

Student responses based on personal experiences can begin during the reading of a text; literary response is not solely the domain of postreading activity. During reading, in order to have students make explicit the associations, reflections, predictions, and speculations that mark their initial encounters with the text, they can be asked to keep response journals. These response journals may take the form of response monologues or anecdotal responses. In the process of recording their own active interchanges with the text, students become aware of how their precritical responses (i.e., initially-felt responses) develop over time. These response-journal entries are the seedbeds for further reflection and are the raw data to be tested against the readings of the text by peers, the teacher, and perhaps the critics (Corcoran 1989, 51–52).

McGregor (1989) has his students engage with a text by drawing from their personal experiences as the starting point. He calls this activity "How Would You Like to Be . . . ?" (22–23). First, groups discuss whether or not they would like to live in the settings described in the text. By projecting themselves into such situations as depicted in the text, student readers can explore and clarify their personal preferences. One of the benefits of such a task is that it encourages students to glance back over the text to make sure of the information before they commit themselves to definite responses.

In McGregor's tenth-grade class, after preliminary discussions, students were asked to write a short piece on what they would think and feel if they had to live in Maycomb, the setting for *To Kill a Mockingbird*. The class had researched the town of Maycomb in time and place, with particular reference to the students' knowledge of the southern United States and attitudes towards blacks there and elsewhere. Here is a selection from the students' writings (McGregor 1989, 22), many examples of which were read aloud to the class.

> I couldn't live there as it was a racist town. . . . If you did something wrong, e.g. vote for the wrong person, the town would look down on you as if you were an outcast. This is because the townsfolk conformed to the ways of others. They were afraid to have their own personal identities, goals or ideas. . . . Their way of life is a routine and an imitation of the generations before them. (Tim)

> I'd probably be dubbed a "nigger lover." Not a nice thought at all. If an outsider moved there, he would have to abide by their rules if any peace is wanted. Not complying with their rules could bring many different things, from harmless gossip to harassment from the natives. . . . I think the key word is "privacy." In Maycomb there would be next to none; where I live, privacy is plentiful. I like it that way. Privacy, that's what Maycomb lacks. I think. I could put up with being called a "nigger lover" but I would miss the privacy I have now if I lived in Maycomb. (Andrew)

Andrew's response throws an unintended and unexpected challenge to his teacher: how does one deal with the phrase "nigger lover," which came up here in classroom discussion? This challenge has to be taken up by the teacher; to ignore it is to comply with the underlying and probably innocent and covert attitudes and values that are racist and belittling. On one hand, given the context of the times in which the novel is set and was written, the phrase "nigger lover" would have been in common usage with a distinct derogatory meaning used by racist whites to marginalize other whites. The teacher, directly or indirectly, needs to bring this culturally positioned "reading" to Andrew's response at the point of utterance.

On the other hand, the teacher might ask Andrew why he had used the term in his response. Was it intended to inflame, and if so, whom and why? Equally inflammatory, but likely in a quite different sense, is Andrew's use of the term "natives," not to depict aboriginal peoples or blacks, but entrenched whites in the predominantly and racially intolerant white community. Andrew's covert voice needs to be heard, and it is the teacher's task to challenge Andrew's response so as to raise the issues that such responses lay bare. In some instances, it requires the teacher to provide a resistant reading or response, one that challenges other readings and responses, especially those that are dominant in the group and likely to go unchallenged.

If personal experience signifies the beginning of the literary response process, where does personal response lead? In his study of teenagers' responses to literature, Thomson (1986) develops the idea of "reflexive reading," in which the reader moves from close emotional and personal involvement with the text to a more distanced, reflective detachment. This description of the response process links the growth of identity and personal values with the active engagement of student readers with text. Here is how McGregor (1989) describes reflexive reading:

> Active readers empathize with people described in the text and hold hopes and fears for them. They draw upon their repertoire of personal experiences to make connections for themselves between the literary characters and their own lives, and reflect upon the significance of events and behaviour. This reflectiveness promotes a distanced or critical evaluation of the text. (17)

The movement from experiential response to reconsidered response is that from unbridled engagement to reflective and detached reevaluation. Reflection upon experiential response is gained by distancing oneself from the text over time and by multiple revisits to the text. It is also gained through the sharing of responses with others. As critical evaluation emerges, the reader is able to stand his or her response against those of others—peers, teachers, the critics—and derive a broad, considered, and self-critical meaning that then becomes part of his or her personal and accumulated experience with literature. This is what occurred in the poem by the two eleventh graders quoted at the beginning of this chapter.

Through multiple revisitings of the text, enhanced and encouraged by shared responses and discussions and by re-creation exercises and other mediated response exercises, students and readers can become actualized readers of literature. In order to realize their own potential and meaning students cannot simply stay within their own frames of reference. The process of literary response is first individual and personal, but it needs to become public through shared and mediated response. Finally, readers reconceptualize their purposes for reading and become actualized as their own reconsidered meanings are realized.

The process of actualizing readers through response to literature offers an exciting prospect for English teaching and English teachers. It is actually another way of negotiating the curriculum so that ownership of literature and learning resides with students and teachers. Although the process of making meaning of literary texts begins with personal response, it of necessity must move toward shared response as a social act of re-creation and rereading before meaning in its full sense can be realized. Actualized readers and teachers is the promise of the process of literature through meaning making that goes from experience to response.

References

Bogdan, D. & S. B. Straw, eds. 1990. *Beyond communication: Reading comprehension and criticism.* Portsmouth, NH: Boynton/Cook.

Corcoran, B. 1989. From a single impulse to the connecting conversation: Personal and cultural accounts of developing response to literature. *Language, Learning and Literacy* 1:46–59.

Deakin University. 1986. *Taught not caught.* Text for course ECT 425: Literature and Young People, School of Education, Deakin University Open Campus Program. Victoria, AU: Deakin University Press.

Eagleton, T. 1985. The subject of literature. *English Magazine* 15:4–7.

Education Department of South Australia. 1983. *A single impulse: Developing responses to literature.* Response to Literature Project Team of the English 8-12 Curriculum Committee, Education Department of South Australia. Adelaide: Publication Branch, Government of South Australia.

Iser, W. 1978. *The act of reading: A theory of aesthetic response.* London: Routledge & Kegan Paul.

McGregor, R. 1989. Imagining realities: Values and literature. *English in Australia* 87:16–28.

Morgan, W. 1990. Not works but the play of voices in discourse: Literature in the secondary classroom. *English in Australia* 93:17–33.

New South Wales Department of Education. 1985. *Imaginative re-creation.* English curriculum paper. Sydney, AU: Directorate of Studies, New South Wales Department of Education.

O'Neill, M. 1989. *Molesting the text: Promoting resistant readings.* Paper presented at the International Convention on Reading and Response, University of East Anglia, April. Norwich, England.

Rosenblatt, L. 1978. *The reader, the text, the poem: The transactional theory of the literary work.* Carbondale, IL: Southern Illinois University Press.

Stratta, L., J. Dixon & A. Wilkinson. 1973. *Patterns of language: Explorations in the teaching of English.* London: Heinemann.

Straw, S. B. & D. Bogdan. 1990. Introduction. In *Beyond communication: Reading comprehension and criticism,* 1–18. See Bogdan & Straw 1990.

Thomson, J. 1986. *Understanding teenagers' reading.* North Ryde, AU: Methuen.

Traymore, E. S., ed. 1939. Larry Malone. In *Life and literature.* Book 2. Toronto: Thomas Nelson & Sons.

3

"That Reminds Me of the Time . . . " : Using Autobiographical Writing Before Reading to Enhance Response

Michael W. Smith
Brian F. White

Introduction

The authors who contributed to this volume's immediate predecessor (Bogdan & Straw 1990)

> [draw] similar conclusions about literature and reading education in arguing for techniques that reject the hegemonies of the past and the autocracies of author and text. In one way or another, each chapter celebrates the reader's emergence from the ethos that prescribed very narrow parameters for reading and interpreting literature to one that is emancipatory in its emphasis on empowerment and choice. (8)

With this new freedom, of course, come new responsibilities: readers must understand that it is their role both to choose and to be aware of the range of choices available to them in interpretation. Straw and Bogdan argue that emancipation will mean hard work for readers: "Because the reader will need to have as much skill as—or perhaps more than—the author, all reader knowledge becomes critical to reading. Not only will readers need to have large bodies of knowledge about content and possible meanings, but they will also need to have a myriad of procedures through which to access and employ those bodies of knowledge" (17-18).

Many of the authors who contributed to that first volume (e.g., Beach 1990; Hynds 1990; Tierney & Gee 1990) argued that one "body of knowledge" particularly important to readers comprises their personal constructs and autobiographical experiences. In this chapter, we discuss the results of two recent studies that examined one possible way to help students retrieve personal constructs and autobiographical experiences and apply them to new and unfamiliar texts: autobiographical writing before reading.

The Importance of Personal Connections

A number of researchers have demonstrated the importance of "bringing life to literature" (Hynds 1989, 30). In their study of fifty-eight eighth-grade literature classes, for example, Nystrand and Gamoran (1991) found that students who are personally involved in reading remember texts better and achieve a deeper understanding of those texts. Nystrand and Gamoran call this "substantive engagement" and distinguish it from mere procedural display, that is, simply following the rules of the classroom. They argue that students are substantively engaged in reading to the extent that the text "addresses questions that students deem are important, teaching them new things that they value, and also to the extent that teachers help students relate their readings to their own experiences" (268). Nystrand (1991) writes that teachers who want to promote depth of understanding "[should] take care to help students see relations between the narrative worlds of the works they read and their own individual experiences" (153).

Hynds (1985) also found that students who make connections between their lives and literature understand texts at a deeper level. She argues that students who retrieve from memory a wide range of interpersonal constructs while reading will read with higher inferential comprehension. And Marshall (1987) and Newell, Suszynski, and Weingart (1989) have demonstrated that writing tasks that allow students to draw upon both personal frames of reference and textual evidence can enhance response to literature.

Rosenblatt (1978) provides an explanation for why this might be true. She has argued consistently and convincingly that the personal experiences and responses of readers are crucial to the understanding of texts. She emphasizes the importance of autobiographical experiences when she writes that "the reader's attention to the text activates certain elements in his past experience—external reference, internal response—that have become linked with verbal symbols" (11). The reader does not attend merely to what the words point to in the external world but also to the internal "images, feelings, attitudes, associations, and ideas" that the words and their referents evoke (10). In other words, the act of reading becomes a transaction: as the reader focuses upon the text, the text stimulates the retrieval of that which has been learned, experienced, and stored. "Perhaps one can think of this as an alerting of certain areas of memory, a stirring up of certain reservoirs of experience, knowledge, and feeling" (54). These fruits of previous learning are then brought to bear upon the text.

According to Rosenblatt, each reader will produce a unique reading of any given text because each reader's "reservoir" is unique. Readers will share common referents for the verbal symbols in a text, but each individual will have what Purves (1985) calls "an idiosyncratic association with any word in the text" (59). Rosenblatt explains this phenomenon by saying that readers will bring to the text not only

> publicly accepted content and overtones but also a special personal feeling, tone and significance. There will be a common reference for "home," say. But the individual will have learned this in specific life-situations and in various specific verbal contexts, spoken and written. Hence, the general usage will be embodied for each in a personal matrix, varying from reader to reader. (53)

Both researchers and theorists have stressed the importance of the reader's role in the process of literary understanding. When personal matrixes are applied to texts, readers respond more fully, understand more completely, and remember more specifically. Although previously dominant theories of literary criticism subjected readers' lives and experiences to the intentions of the author and the structure of the text, recent theory and research have been liberating, arguing and demonstrating that a text is "simply paper and ink" (Rosenblatt 1978, ix) until a reader wills to transact with it. A critical part of that transaction is the retrieval and application of personal connections.

Connections That Enhance Response

This new emphasis on the reader potentially offers teachers liberation from a role that has for many been stultifying, the role of being what Scholes (1985) calls an exegete of the "sacred text of literature" (16). But with the celebration of the reader comes a danger, the belief that because a reader plays a crucial role in the construction of a text's meaning, all readers' responses must be celebrated equally. With such a belief would come a belief in its corollary: all personal connections to a text are equally valuable. Holland (1985) articulates this belief:

A story does not "cause" or even "limit" the responses to it. The response comes from the literent. A literent sets up a feedback loop. In reading, I bring to a text schemata from previous literary experiences, from my historical or critical knowledge, my sense of human nature, my values, my preferences in language, my politics, my metabolism—I bring all these things to bear on the text, and the text feeds back to me what I bring to it either positively or not at all. It rewards my hypotheses or, so to speak, ignores them. That is all the text does, for always it is I who am in control. (7)

As a consequence of Holland's theories, he sees teaching literature as helping readers understand what in them gave rise to their response. A teacher's role, then, would be to elicit students' responses and to use them to help students discover, in Holland's words, the "identity themes" (9–11) that inform them.

Such an approach, we believe, does not serve our students well: it pays far too little attention to the role of the text as a blueprint in the construction of meaning. Rosenblatt (1985) clearly articulates this position:

> Like the Rorschach inkblot, a verbal text may be used to stimulate personal, "free" associations and memories of childhood traumas. But this makes the text simply a passive tool in the psychological study of personality. The emphasis is then on free association, whereas—when the text is read aesthetically—emphasis is on selective attention, guided by cues provided by the text. (36)

Iser (1978) makes a similar argument. He explains: "The text mobilizes the subjective knowledge present in all kinds of readers and directs it to one particular end. However varied this knowledge may be, the readers' subjective contribution is controlled by the given framework" (145). And Scholes (1985) writes that "different, even conflicting assumptions may preside over any reading of a single text by a single person. It is in fact these very differences . . . that create the space in which the reader exercises a measure of interpretive freedom" (154).

Note that Scholes points toward a measure of interpretive freedom; the freedom to interpret is not absolute, because it is, he says, "constrained by language: the text's linguistic code. The reader's choices in 'making meaning' are in fact severely limited by the writer's choices of what to put on the page" (154). He explains why accepting these constraints is so important:

> If we simply project our own subjective modes of thought and desire upon the text, our reading will never be sufficiently other for us to interpret it and, especially, to criticize it. . . . Without a serious act of

"reading"—of a book, a face, or a tone of voice—we will never be able
to agree or disagree with another person, since we will have turned all
others into mirrors of ourselves. (39–40)

All of these theorists explain that personal connections must be
constrained by the text if they are to contribute to a meaningful
transaction with literature, a point also made by a number of
researchers. For example, in their study of the effects of reader-based
writing on students' understanding of literature, Newell, Suszynski,
and Weingart (1989) draw a distinction between personal statements,
in which a writer reacts in a personal way to the form or content of a
story, and reflexive statements, in which writers apply personal experience in their attempts to interpret a story. They found that reader-
based writing about literature resulted in richer, more compelling
interpretations than did text-based writing, and they theorize that an
increase in the number of reflexive statements accounts in large measure for that difference.

Hynds's analysis (1989) of the ways students bring their lives to
the literature they read is consistent with that of Newell, Suszynski,
and Weingart. She explains the value of an interactive style of
response: "Such response processes as predicting, extending, general-
izing, connecting, reflecting, and reality testing are sometimes
employed as readers shuttle back and forth from textual to personal
understandings" (55). On the other hand, she found that the reader-
based style of response of some of the students in her study, in which
they focused on personal circumstances or reactions, "often led to
disengagement from the text" (55).

Both theory and research strongly suggest that all autobiographical connections to texts are not equal. In fact, making uncontrolled
personal connections to the text is likely to interfere with having a
meaningful transaction. Beach's research (1990) suggests that control alone is not enough, however. He found that "the extent to which
autobiographical responses are useful depends on students' willingness to reflect on the text and on their own experiences" (233). When
students elaborated their experiences and treated them, at least to
some extent, as a literary story by adopting a point-driven perspective
(Vipond & Hunt 1984), clarifying their own perspective, employing
narrative strategies, and considering the significance of their experience, they tended to have success both in using their experience to
increase their understanding of texts and in using texts to increase
their understanding of their own experience.

Examples of students' think-aloud protocol responses to John
Collier's story "The Chaser" (1961) provide an indication of the benefits of making controlled connections—and the potential problems

caused by making uncontrolled connections. "The Chaser," told in the third person, is a story of a young man seeking to buy a love potion. The old man who created this potion shows the young man his wares, including a poison "quite imperceptible to any known method of autopsy," a potion for which the old man charges $5,000 a teaspoon. The young man is horrified, both at the poison and the price, but the old man reassures him that the love potion would not be so expensive. The old man goes on to list the effects of the love potion. After explaining how terribly jealous and eternally vigilant the potion would make the young man's love, the old man explains that for this extraordinary love potion he charges but a dollar. The young man leaves with the potion and says good-bye to the old man. "Au revoir," the old man replies. The story turns on the conflict between the young man's naive view of love and the old man's cynicism. Readers are invited to understand that the old man will indeed see the young man again after he tires of his love and comes back for the other potion.

Elizabeth, a ninth grader who, according to standardized tests, is reading over two years above grade level, began her protocol on "The Chaser" as follows (her comments about the story appear in brackets):

> Alan Austen, as nervous as a kitten, went up a certain dark and creaky stairs in the neighborhood of Pell Street, and peered about for a long time on the dim landing before he found the name he wanted written obscurely on one of the doors. [Reminds me of, we have stairs in our house that go down to our cellar that are really . . . creaky!] Um, he pushed open this door, as he had been told to, and found himself in a tiny room, which contained no furniture but a plain kitchen table, a rocking chair, and an ordinary chair. [Reminds me of something I saw on TV last night.] On one of the dirty, buff-colored walls were a couple of shelves, containing in all perhaps . . . a dozen bottles and jars. [The shelves remind me of, trying to remember the word "shelves" in Spanish!]

Elizabeth adopts what we have called an association-driven orientation (Smith 1991a, 1992). Instead of using her personal experience to enrich her reading of the text or using her reading of the text to help her reflect upon her experience, she becomes distracted by what Richards (1929) and Squire (1964) call irrelevant associations. Kathy, a senior in an advanced placement class, uses her personal experience in a far different manner. After completing her reading of the story, Kathy says:

> Ooh . . . I like it. I do. God, I don't know if I could live my life with having someone that possessive of me. I don't think I would ever want that, not even for a dollar. That's just too bizarre. To have someone love me,

yes, I can understand. But not jealous, not worried and not terrified, and not . . . I want to say, I guess, almost slavish. No, I would not want that in a relationship. (See Eavenson [1988] for a more complete discussion of Kathy.)

Both Elizabeth and Kathy are "good" readers, and both seem to have made connections between their personal lives and the story. However, only Kathy's connections seem to enhance her understanding of the story. And in so doing they seem to increase her understanding of her life as well. In the terms of Newell, Suszynski, and Weingart (1989), Kathy's statements are reflexive while Elizabeth's are personal. Kathy's statements demonstrate that she has reflected on the significance of her experience and that her reflections have contributed to both her understanding and her enjoyment of the story.

Students must make personal connections to texts if they are to have meaningful transactions with them. However, as Squire (1964) points out and as Anderson and Pearson (1985) more recently argue, many students do not spontaneously make these connections. Further, both theory and research establish that not all connections contribute positively to meaningful transactions with texts. These understandings suggest that if teachers want their students to have meaningful transactions with literature, they must go beyond simply eliciting students' responses. Instead they must help their students reflect on relevant personal experience and construct it in such a way that they will be more likely to use it to increase their understanding and enjoyment of texts. We have found that engaging students in autobiographical writing before they read is an effective way to meet these goals.

Autobiographical Writing Before Reading

Why Writing?

The work of Bereiter and Scardamalia (1987) suggests that writing could be an especially effective way to encourage students to reflect upon relevant personal experience. Because writers (unlike oral composers) must attend to the verbatim level of text (spelling, word choice, etc.), they must also continually reconstruct their text at a higher level ("Now, where was I?"). Such reconstruction is important for "the work of repeatedly reconstructing content units and higher level text representations should . . . lead to more sharply delineated and detailed mental representations of text" (128–29). By its very nature, then, writing requires reflection. And as Beach (1990) has pointed out, reflection is crucial if autobiographical connections are to be useful.

Why Before?

The results of Bartlett's classic study (1932) suggest why having students write about relevant autobiographical experiences before they read might be especially effective. Bartlett demonstrates that readers' prior knowledge and expectations determine to a great extent what they attend to, comprehend, and remember. For example, when college students who had no previous experience in reading ghost stories were asked to read a story entitled "War of Ghosts," the students failed to notice that some of the characters in the story were, in fact, ghosts; in their retelling of the story, the students retold it as a typical war story—no ghosts involved.

When viewed in the light of our previous discussion of the importance of personal connections, Bartlett provides a strong rationale for instruction that encourages students to reflect on relevant autobiographical experiences before they read. His study suggests that if students have these experiences in mind when they approach a text, they will be more likely to attend to the details that relate to their lives, to use their lives to help them understand their reading, and to remember the text when they have finished. It suggests further that instruction that encourages students to make personal connections after reading is unlikely to have the same benefits.

Two Studies of the Effects of Autobiographical Writing Before Reading

A Brief Description

The students in four highly homogeneous ninth-grade classes—two classes from each of two schools—participated in the first study (White 1990). Each class read two short stories. Before reading story A, classes 1 and 3 engaged in a prereading writing assignment while classes 2 and 4 read without having written. For story B, classes 2 and 4 engaged in a prereading writing assignment while classes 1 and 3 read without having written. After each reading, the students participated in audiotaped, large-group discussions of the stories.

The students in four highly heterogeneous eighth-grade classes— two classes of each of two teachers—participated in the second study (Hamann et al. 1991). Each class read two short stories. Classes 1 and 3 engaged in a prereading writing assignment prior to reading story A; classes 2 and 4 engaged in a prereading writing assignment prior to reading story B. As in the first study, audiotaped class discussions followed each reading. Unlike the first study, however, only two of the four classes participated in large-group discussions; the other two classes were divided into small groups for the audiotaped discussions.

In addition, because the first study produced anecdotal evidence that students who write before reading a text like the text better, students responded to an attitude survey twice: immediately after reading the story and immediately after discussing it.

Effects on Understanding

White's study suggests that autobiographical writing before reading has important effects on students' understanding of characters, arguably the most important single component of a meaningful transaction with literature (Perrine 1978).

But understanding characters is especially hard for readers who have not retrieved from memory relevant background knowledge and experiences. Hynds (1985) argues that even able readers who do not bring a wide range of interpersonal constructs to a text "may be limited in their abilities to fully respond to the complexities of characters, and consequently, the complexities of literary works" (388). Unless a wide range of interpersonal constructs is available, readers tend to respond superficially to characters, focusing on information readily available in the text: "physical attributes ('tall,' 'short'), demographic information ('has a daughter'), behavioral descriptions ('takes drugs'), and psychological attributes applied to physical qualities ('has a mean voice')" (389).

According to Beach and Wendler (1987), young adolescents are most prone to such surface descriptions (287). Older adolescents, on the other hand, tend to use the observable, surface aspects in order to make more abstract inferences. Unlike younger adolescents, older adolescents are more likely to focus on what Hynds (1989) calls "psychological constructs, [including] internal states or motivations ('pessimistic') or behaviors which [imply] psychological states ('he wants to get high all the time')" (389). For example, a young adolescent's superficial description of Huck Finn might be that "he tells a lot of lies," while an older adolescent's more abstract or inferential description of Huck Finn might be that "he's devious, crafty, street-smart, clever, experienced."

White's study strongly suggests that autobiographical writing before reading can enhance younger adolescents' inferential understanding, helping them to move beyond surface descriptions and to focus more on psychological constructs. When the ninth graders in his study had written about relevant autobiographical experiences prior to reading, they were significantly more likely to offer abstract, inferential descriptions of characters than when they had not written before reading. After transcribing the audiotaped class discussions, White coded each response to questions about characters as either a describing or an abstracting response. Answers that focused on surface details and information readily available in the text were coded as "describing"; answers that used readily available information to infer characters' attributes were scored as "abstracting." When students had not written before reading, an average of 50.6 percent of their responses were descriptive, focusing on surface information. But when they had written before reading, an average of only 28.2 percent of their responses focused on the surface; an average of 71.8 percent of their responses moved beyond the surface of the text to more abstract, inferential descriptions of characters.

These percentages indicate that students responded much more abstractly after having written before reading. In order to determine whether these positive results were due to the teachers, to the stories, or to the writing before reading, White analyzed his data using a $2 \times 2 \times 2$ factorial design (Box, Hunter & Hunter 1978). His analysis suggests that these important percentage differences were due to autobiographical writing before reading (estimate, 22.45; standard error, 6.12).

That autobiographical writing before reading seems to have greatly enhanced young adolescents' inferential understanding is certainly an important finding. If the study of literature does indeed offer "an unparalleled opportunity to observe human nature in all its complexity and multiplicity" (Perrine 1978), then autobiographical writing before reading can help more of our students take advantage of that opportunity.

Effects on Students' Attitudes

One possible reason that students' understanding increased in White's study is that they liked the texts better after having written before reading. It is clear that interest plays a crucial role in learning. "Individuals interested in a task or activity have been shown to pay more attention, persist for longer periods of time, and acquire more and qualitatively different knowledge than individuals without such interest" (Hidi 1990, 554). But what promotes interest? Hidi refers to the work of Renninger who "emphasizes that individual interest always involves stored knowledge and value and may or may not be a psychological state of which the individual is reflectively aware. Here knowledge refers to cognitive representations stored from past experience. . . . " (554). If, therefore, teachers can help their students retrieve from memory relevant stored knowledge, students' interest should increase and they should be more engaged in the learning of subject matter. Dewey (1964) calls such engagement *wholeheartedness*, chief among the attitudes teachers need to cultivate in their

students. Because we are convinced of the importance of students'
interest and share Dewey's belief in the importance of wholeheartedness, we looked in our studies for the effects of autobiographical writing before reading on students' attitudes.

Off-task and Contentless Remarks

One measure of wholeheartedness is the number of off-task and contentless (e.g., "I forgot") remarks in classroom discussions. If students
are genuinely enthusiastic about a story, there should be few such
remarks. In his study, White discovered that classes that had engaged
in autobiographical writing before reading made an average of 7.6 percent off-task or contentless responses in their discussions, while students who had done no writing made an average 20.6 percent off-task
or contentless responses. On its face, this seems to be an educationally
significant finding. If one fifth of students' responses are off-task or
contentless, students will likely have difficulty learning from a discussion. Dewey notes that using mental energy to hold one's mind to the
subject lessens that which is available for the subject itself. To sort out
the effects of teacher, story, and treatment, White again used a
$2 \times 2 \times 2$ factorial design. The analysis revealed that writing before
reading significantly reduced the percentage of off-task and contentless responses (estimate, −13.025; standard error, 5.37).

This makes sense. According to Ausubel (1965), verbal learning is
most likely to occur when the material is potentially meaningful and
when the learner purposefully relates new material to old. As the
theorists and researchers we discussed earlier explain, the old material that is most germane to an understanding and appreciation of literature is the personal experience of the reader. Nystrand and Gamoran's results (1991) are consistent with this proposition. Their
research strongly suggests that genuine engagement (as opposed to
mere procedural display) is increased when teachers help students
relate literature to personal experience. It appears that autobiographical writing before reading may help produce these salutary effects.

Liking of Stories

White's research focused on homogeneous ninth-grade classes. However, as Applebee (1989) argues, the greatest challenge our schools
face in teaching literature is to revitalize instruction for those students not on the academic track, the students who too often remain
on the margins of the classroom community—nonwhite and "at-
risk" students. These students are the least likely to perceive the connections between their lives and the literature they read, especially

the canonical literature. Theoretically, autobiographical writing before reading should be most effective with these students because it should help them realize connections they might not readily perceive and because it validates the importance of their experience.

To test these assumptions, in a follow-up study we worked with two classes of each of two teachers in a school that serves an economically and racially diverse student body. (See Hamann et al. [1991] for a more complete description of the school.) In this study we used students' responses to an attitude survey and their evaluations of the stories they read as evidence of their engagement. The attitude survey has twenty-five items: seven items relating to the features of a story, ten items relating to the experience of reading, and eight items relating to the effect of reading. The survey was piloted with 118 ninth through twelfth graders who used it to respond to one of four stories. The stories were randomly assigned to students after they had been nested by class, sex, and ability. A Rasch analysis of the pilot results suggests that the survey implements a single variable well enough to use it as a measure of students' attitudes toward particular stories (Smith 1991b).

The students in the study responded to the survey both immediately upon reading the stories and then again after they had discussed them in large or small groups. A Rasch analysis of their responses revealed some interesting results. (See Wright & Masters [1982] for an explanation of Rasch analysis.) When we compared the responses that individual students made immediately after reading the stories to those they made after discussing the story in large or small groups, we found no significant difference between prediscussion and postdiscussion attitudes of the students who engaged in autobiographical writing before reading (t, 1.143; p, .258). However, students who had not engaged in autobiographical writing before reading liked the stories significantly less after discussion than they had immediately after reading them (t, 3.609; p, .001).

What might account for this distressing result? Certainly we assume that discussion increases students' liking of stories. But this assumption does not take into account the potentially alienating effects of discussion. On the one hand, students could get turned off to stories because they are annoyed by others' off-task remarks. On the other hand, a discussion could reveal to students that their understanding is not as great as their classmates' or that others are able to connect to text in ways they cannot. The results of our follow-up suggest that these or other alienating experiences are less likely if students engage in autobiographical writing before reading. This too makes sense, for as we explained above, engaging in autobiographical writing before reading reduces off-task responses, increases students' understanding of complex issues, and helps students perceive connections to texts that might not otherwise be apparent. In addition, when we examined the written responses to the discussion guide students used for their small-group work, we found that students were three times as likely to say that a story was good when they had engaged in autobiographical writing before reading as when they had not.

Personal Investment

Another measure of interest is personal investment, the willingness to become personally involved while interacting with subject matter and classmates. Personal investment is perhaps most observable when students engage one another in discussion of a text, when student challenges student, when individuals in the classroom care so deeply about their own ideas and interpretations that they are willing to explain, explore, and defend their positions in the face of "opposition." White (1990) found that autobiographical writing before reading increases this kind of personal investment. In his study he asked students to read and discuss "The End of Something," a short story by Ernest Hemingway in which a young couple end their relationship. As we explained above, some of the classes were prompted to write about relevant personal experiences before they read, while others were not. The prompt was this:

> Please answer the following question as specifically as you can (it has two parts). Most young people want to have dating relationships that are fun, exciting, and long-lasting. First describe healthy, lasting dating relationships that you've been part of or that you've observed. What does a relationship need to be like in order to grow and to last? Why do some relationships really seem to work well? Be specific, and remember to write about relationships that you yourself have experienced or watched. Second, why do some relationships break up? What sorts of things can stop a relationship from being fun and exciting? What sorts of things cause relationships to end? Be specific, and write about relationships that you know about.

When students had not written before reading, they seemed unwilling to engage one another in discussion. Even when opposing viewpoints were expressed, students refrained from challenging one another. On the other hand, students who had written about relevant personal experiences before they read demonstrated much greater personal investment. They were eager to respond, they talked to one another, and they challenged opposing views, as the following transcript reveals (thirty-five lines of discussion preceded the excerpt):

Jon: Well, if it was me I'd never want to see her again.

Teacher: So your, what's your prediction? Jon.

Jon: I would say that they never even speak to each other again.

Marissa: Why? Why was it her fault? He was the one acting like a jerk.

Maria: Even if they saw each other again *(inaudible)* . . .

Jon: Bull! You can see somebody and not talk to them!

Teacher: Okay . . . we want to keep it together here. We'll take them one at a time. Marissa's got, I think she's got something to say over here.

Stacey: She is mad at you, Jon.

Marissa: Why would it be her fault? Why wouldn't he ever want to see her again? He was the one who was acting like a total jerk.

The discussion of this question proceeded in a similar fashion for over fifty more lines. But even the brief excerpt we've presented demonstrates that the students were genuinely engaged. A look at what Marissa wrote before reading suggests how the writing before reading contributed to that engagement in discussion:

> I was going out with a guy for 2 years. At first it was going great. We were honest, trustworthy, and pretty much spent all our free time together. I think those are the things you need to have a lasting relationship that works well. Then it started to go down hill. There started to be jealousy, and thinking that we weren't being faithfull, and dishonesty. I think those were the biggest reasons for breaking up. Then it wasn't fun anymore. We started fighting, and then Suzanne came into the picture. He didn't really like her, but she kept nagging. I guess we were just hurting each other with all the jealousy and fighting that we decided it was better if we just saw other people. To this day I still have a lot of feelings for him. After all, it was 2 years of being together and now I realize the stupid things we use to fight about and get jealous over. But I guess my motto holds true: "You can never make mistakes, you can just learn lessons."

What Marissa seems to have learned is that relationships don't end without cause. She has learned, too, that accepting responsibility is a painful but important part of understanding why they end. Perhaps that is why she responds so forcefully to Jon's suggestion that "if it was me, I'd never want to see her again." Students in the classes that did not write before reading had certainly had some experiences with "breaking up," yet none of them responded with Marissa's intensity, perhaps because their experiences were unavailable to them as they read.

Transcripts from the second study reveal similar results. While the students who had not written before reading generated comparatively empty and boring discussions (Hamann et al. 1991), the students who had written before reading engaged in fast-paced, thoughtful give-and-take.

Taken together, our two studies strongly suggest that if teachers want to cultivate wholeheartedness in students' responses to literature, they should consider engaging students in writing about relevant autobiographical experience before they ask them to read. When students in our studies had written before reading, they offered significantly fewer off-task and contentless remarks, they liked the stories better, and they seemed to be more personally and substantively engaged both in the texts and in class discussions of those texts.

Conclusion

Like the authors who contributed to this volume's predecessor, we celebrate the freedom readers have to make personal connections between their lives and literary texts. Our research and our classroom experience both suggest that such personal connections can increase understanding, engagement, wholeheartedness, and enjoyment. However, we do not believe that all personal connections are equally constructive or that all connections should be celebrated equally. Our research and our experience as teachers lead us to believe that some personal connections actually serve to disengage readers from texts. In our research and in our classrooms, we have found that autobiographical writing before reading is an effective way to foster the sorts of connections that enhance students' responses to literature.

References

Anderson, R. C. & P. D. Pearson. 1985. A schema-theoretic view of basic processes in reading comprehension. In *Handbook of reading research,* ed. P. D. Pearson, 255–91. New York: Longman.

Applebee, A. 1989. *The teaching of literature in programs with reputations for excellence in English.* Tech. Rep. No. 1.1. Albany: University at Albany, State University of New York, Center for the Learning and Teaching of Literature.

Ausubel, D. P. 1965. In defense of verbal learning. In *Readings in the psychology of cognition,* ed. R. C. Anderson & D. P. Ausubel. New York: Holt, Rinehart, & Winston.

Bartlett, F. C. 1932. *Remembering: A study in experimental and social psychology.* Cambridge, UK: Cambridge University Press.

Beach, R. 1990. The creative development of meaning: Using autobiographical experiences to interpret literature. In *Beyond communication: Reading comprehension and criticism,* 211–36. See Bogdan & Straw 1990.

Beach, R. & L. Wendler. 1987. Developmental differences in response to a story. *Research in the Teaching of English* 21:286–97.

Bereiter, C. & M. Scardamalia. 1987. *The psychology of written composition.* Hillsdale, NJ: Lawrence Erlbaum.

Bogdan, D. & S. B. Straw, eds. 1990. *Beyond communication: Reading comprehension and criticism.* Portsmouth, NH: Boynton/Cook.

Box, G. E. P., W. G. Hunter & J. S. Hunter. 1978. *Statistics for experimenters: An introduction to design, data analysis, and model building.* New York: John Wiley & Sons.

Collier, J. 1961. The chaser. In *75 short masterpieces: Stories from the world's literature,* ed. R. Goodman, 46–49. New York: Bantam.

Dewey, J. 1964. *John Dewey on education: Selected writings.* Ed. R. Archambault. Chicago: University of Chicago Press.

Eavenson, R. 1988. *A comparison of the processes of good and poor high school readers while reading a short story.* University of Chicago. Typescript.

Hamann, L., L. Schultz, M. Smith & B. White. 1991. Making connections: The power of autobiographical writing before reading. *Journal of Reading* 35:24–28.

Hidi, S. 1990. Interest and its contribution as a mental resource for learning. *Review of Educational Research* 60:549–71.

Holland, N. 1985. Reading readers reading. In *Researching response to literature and the teaching of literature: Points of departure,* ed. C. Cooper, 3–21. Norwood, NJ: Ablex.

Hynds, S. 1985. Interpersonal cognitive complexity and the literary response processes of adolescent readers. *Research in the Teaching of English* 19:386–402.

———. 1989. Bringing life to literature and literature to life: Social constructs and contexts of four adolescent readers. *Research in the Teaching of English* 23:30–61.

———. 1990. Reading as a social event: Comprehension and response in the text, classroom, and world. In *Beyond communication: Reading comprehension and criticism,* 237–56. See Bogdan & Straw 1990.

Iser, W. 1978. *The act of reading.* Baltimore: Johns Hopkins University Press.

Marshall, J. D. 1987. The effects of writing on students' understanding of literary texts. *Research in the Teaching of English* 21:30–61.

Newell, G., K. Suszynski & R. Weingart. 1989. The effect of writing in a reader-based and text-based mode on students' understanding of short stories. *Journal of Reading Behavior* 21:37–57.

Nystrand, M. 1991. Making it hard: Curriculum and instruction as factors in difficulty of literature. In *Difficulty in literature: A symposium*, ed. A. Purves, 141–56. Albany: SUNY at Albany Press.

Nystrand, M. & A. Gamoran. 1991. Instructional discourse, student engagement and literature achievement. *Research in the Teaching of English* 25:261–90.

Perrine, L. 1978. *Literature: Structure, sound, and sense*. 3d ed. New York: Harcourt Brace Jovanovich.

Purves, A. C. 1985. That sunny dome: Those caves of ice. In *Researching response to literature and the teaching of literature: Points of departure*, ed. C. Cooper, 54–69. Norwood, NJ: Ablex.

Richards, I. A. 1929. *Practical criticism*. Edinburgh: The Edinburgh Press.

Rosenblatt, L. 1978. *The reader, the text, the poem: The transactional theory of the literary work*. Carbondale: Southern Illinois University Press.

————. 1985. The transactional theory of the literary work: Implications for research. In *Researching response to literature and the teaching of literature: Points of departure*, ed. C. Cooper, 33–53. Norwood, NJ: Ablex.

Scholes, R. 1985. *Textual power*. New Haven: Yale University Press.

Smith, M. 1991a. Constructing meaning from text: An analysis of ninth-grade reader response. *Journal of Educational Research* 84:263–72.

————. 1991b. *Using Rasch analysis to design and interpret a measure of students' liking of short stories*. Paper presented at the Annual Meeting of the American Educational Research Association, Chicago.

————. 1992. Submission versus control in literary transactions. In *Reader stance and literary understanding: Exploring the theories, research, and practice*, ed. J. Many & C. Cox, 211–30. Norwood, NJ: Ablex.

Squire, J. R. 1964. *The responses of adolescents while reading four short stories*. Champaign, IL: National Council of Teachers of English.

Straw, S. B. & D. Bogdan. 1990. Introduction. In *Beyond communication: Reading comprehension and criticism*, 1–18. See Bogdan & Straw 1990.

Tierney, R. J. & M. Gee. 1990. Reading comprehension: Readers, authors, and the world of the text. In *Beyond communication: Reading comprehension and criticism*, 197–210. See Bogdan & Straw 1990.

Vipond, D. & R. Hunt. 1984. Point-driven understanding: Pragmatic and cognitive dimensions of literary reading. *Poetics* 13:261–77.

White, B. 1990. *Writing before reading: Its effects upon discussion and understanding of text*. Ph.D. diss., University of Wisconsin–Madison.

Wright, B. & G. Masters. 1982. *Rating scale analysis*. Chicago: MESA Press.

4

Constructing Understanding: Emotion and Literary Response

David S. Miall

Introduction

The actualization model of reading discussed in this book suggests a rich agenda of possibilities for changing classroom practice. Whether this will be realized and whether it will result in lasting improvements in the teaching of literature depends on many factors, but one central factor will be how well we understand the process of literary response. The ideology of liberation or empowerment that drives the vision of actualization (Straw & Bogdan 1990) will take us a great distance along the road, but such a revolution must be founded on a grasp of the realities of the process it is intended to facilitate; otherwise we will see it swept aside by the next ideological wave to overtake educational practice (relevance, accountability, basic literacy, cultural literacy—our literature classrooms continue to be vulnerable to all of these). A set of practices modeled on an enhanced understanding of the response process, however, would constitute a genuine advance, and one more resistant to external pressures.

An important reason for focusing on literary response, rather than reading in general, is that in this domain a constructive role for emotion becomes apparent. The affective aspects of reading have received rather little attention, and among those who have studied it (Athey 1985; Mathewson 1985) attention has been confined mainly to affective factors that predispose to reading (readers' beliefs and values or various personality variables). I argue that affect plays a central role in the comprehension of literary texts—a view that calls into question the predominantly cognitive theories of the reading process that abound in the research literature.

One of the purposes of this chapter, then, is to outline a model of literary response and show some of the ways in which it has been possible to test it. (I will refer mainly to my own research.) In the second part of the chapter I take up the implications of the model for rethinking classroom practice. The central idea behind the discussion cuts across some existing views of both student learning and reader-response theory. A central implication of my argument is that the learning process in a given subject (here, literary studies) should model the relations and dynamics intrinsic to the subject. To apply learning theory or a general theory of reading to developing methods for literary study is rather ineffective because it fails to speak to the experience of literature that is central to the student. The primary task is to understand that experience, to seek information on what may be involved in the process of reading a literary text. Our classroom practices should then grow from that understanding.

As I try to show in the next section, the emotional aspect of response appears to be central—a realization that will play a decisive role in reconceiving the nature of our work in the classroom. The constructive aspects of response, particularly in the moment-by-moment processes of literary reading, appear to be due to several properties of emotion: its role in providing a context at moments of defamiliarization, in drawing in the experience and concerns of the reader, and in enabling readers to track the relationship between the local details of a text and their sense of the text as a whole. Evidence for some of these functions of emotion has been gathered in several empirical studies of literary response.

Literary Response: Testing the Model

Much classroom discussion, especially in more advanced classes, involves relating a text to information about its background, to the history of its period, to other texts, to a given theoretical stance, or to other matters. But assume for the moment that readers require no background information to make initial sense of a text and that such extrinsic questions are not the reader's priority: what are readers actually doing as they read? In particular, what characterizes the first response to a text that is being read as literature? Or, to adopt the terms of Rosenblatt (1978), are readers doing something characteristically different during an aesthetic as opposed to an efferent reading? As Rosenblatt points out, the same text may be read either aesthetically or efferently, but the evidence I put forward here suggests that there are some significant differences in the two reading processes and that literary texts seem to possess certain features that require the aesthetic reading.

Foregrounding and Defamiliarization

One dimension on which literary texts can be distinguished from nonliterary texts is that of their linguistic properties. Whether we are looking at prose or poetry, literary language is distinctive; it deviates noticeably from the norms of language use elsewhere (if we think of the language in a newspaper article, for example, as a norm). A poem may include inversions in normal word order, a high degree of repetition of vowel sounds, or assonance; it may develop its meaning through two or three important metaphors. Much literary prose, especially modernist fiction, shows a similar range of deviant features. Given that features such as those I have mentioned stand out, or seem to attract special attention from the reader, this dimension of literature, following Mukařovský ([1932] 1964), is known as *foregrounding*. Foregrounded features have commonly been the focus of one kind of classroom study, the approach of practical criticism or *explication de texte,* where interpretation of a text is seen to depend on a grasp of the meaning and implications of such features. We have only recently, however, begun to ask whether attention to the linguistic properties of the text is central to the reading process. No doubt, following the generations of students and teachers who learned that literature in the classroom means practical criticism, readers will be inclined to tell us that they find such features important. But are there reasons beyond the effects of this particular social practice for thinking that foregrounding is intrinsic to reading?

Two types of explanation for an intrinsic view of the matter seem available: one empirical, the other theoretical. On empirical grounds, there is evidence that all readers are influenced by foregrounding: when readers are asked to rate the lines of a poem for how striking or important they are, they provide the same rating pattern whether they have no training in literature or have a college degree in the subject (Van Peer 1986). Sensitivity to foregrounding thus seems to be a faculty inherent in knowledge of the language. On theoretical grounds, foregrounding can be explained as the linguistic dimension of the psychology of literary reading. If literary texts exist to change the way we see, think, or feel, then foregrounding is a central tool in initiating the process of change. To the extent that assonance or metaphor captures attention, the reader is more likely to focus on the new or unfamiliar view being offered in that part of the text. Change involves seeing what was familiar as different in some way: thus I call the psychological correlative of foregrounding *defamiliarization,* following here two notable groups of critics, the Romantic poets and the Russian Formalists.

Shelley ([1821] 1988), for example, remarked memorably that poetry "strips the veil of familiarity from the world, and lays bare the naked and sleeping beauty, which is the spirit of its forms. . . . It purges from our inward sight the film of familiarity which obscures from us the wonder of our being" (295). Similar statements have also been made by Coleridge and Wordsworth. A hundred years later the Russian critic Shklovsky commented on the automatic nature of normal perception, which poetry is designed to overcome. In his essay "Art as Technique" ([1917] 1965) he states:

> Art exists that one may recover the sensation of life; it exists to make
> one feel things, to make the stone *stony.* . . . The technique of art is to
> make objects "unfamiliar," to make forms difficult, to increase the diffi-
> culty and length of perception because the process of perception is an
> aesthetic end in itself and must be prolonged. (12)

Like the Romantic writers, Shklovsky also argued for the emotional effect of such devices in literature, although literary theorists have not systematically explored this implication for the process of reading. One hypothesis thus presents itself for examination: that the reader's encounter with foregrounding will be marked by an emotional response.

If defamiliarization signifies a shift in perception, this suggests one way of testing the hypothesis. In a study I carried out with several readers drawn from a class of college students (more fully reported in Miall 1992), I decided to obtain readers' first responses to a set of words and phrases and then see to what extent their responses modified under the impact of reading a poem in which those words and phrases were placed in a defamiliarizing context. The poem I chose was one of the texts analyzed by Van Peer (1986): Roethke's "Dolor."

The result was striking. The readers began by associating various experiences with the words and phrases and rating them for emotion. After reading the poem, they rated the experiences again. In proportion to the amount of foregrounding in each line of the poem from which a word or phrase had been taken, the rating for emotion increased. The higher the rank of the line for foregrounding, in other words, the greater the shift in the ratings: $r(8) = -.647, p < .05$.

Some of the students also provided descriptions of the shifts they noticed. For example, the word "duplication" extracted from line 8, "Endless duplication of lives and objects," elicited this comment: "After reading the poem I felt the sinister effect of many things being the same." For the same reader, "afternoons" was at first seen as having "very pleasant" associations. But in the context of line 11, "long afternoons of tedium," she said, "After reading the poem they are linked with 'long' and 'tedium' and I remember jobs I'd done when afternoons went on apparently forever."

These two comments point to two types of defamiliarization: in one a new aspect of a familiar concept is revealed, in the other an aspect of experience that has been overlooked or forgotten is recalled. In either case, the main sign of defamiliarization appears to be an increase in emotion, and the more foregrounding, the greater the increase. This suggests that the experiences or concepts that readers apply to understanding a text are called into question as they read, and this in itself arouses emotion. But is emotion more than just a side effect of response at such moments? Other evidence suggests that emotion plays a constructive role in the response process.

One reason for thinking of emotion as a constructive response is that emotion is manifested in conditions of uncertainty. This seems a logical outcome: given that the schemata applied to understanding a situation have proved inadequate, emotion allows us to relocate the uncertain experience in a context that will help clarify it. Metaphor provides a succinct example of this process: in understanding a metaphor, we use the feelings of the modifier to locate a context for the defamiliarized subject. For example, referring to a clumsy discussion of a poem, if I assert that a student used the cleaver of common sense to destroy the poem, the emotional resonance of the modifier *cleaver* enables my hearer to create a context for the subject, common sense, in which a normally useful and productive faculty has a destructive, butchering effect. As several writers have noted (e.g., Bower & Cohen 1982), comparisons and similarities can be revealed by emotion that are unavailable by other means. At the moment of defamiliarization, then, emotion serves to reorientate the reader in the face of what is strange or unfamiliar.

The role of emotion in this sense, as a contextualizing agent, was seen in another study of response, this time involving short stories (Miall 1988a). I obtained data on reading times for eighty to ninety segments of a story (a segment consisted of a sentence or a long phrase) from readers who were asked to read the story on a computer; the computer collected the time taken to read each segment. The same readers then rated each segment for affective intensity. The noticeable feature of the data lay in the pattern of correlations between reading times and affect ratings. At the beginning of an episode affect ratings correlated positively with reading times: in other words, where a segment took longer to read (adjusting for the number of words within the segment), this correlated with reported stronger affect. But towards the end of an episode, the reverse relationship was found: the shorter reading times now correlated with the stronger affect. The implication of this finding is that in order to locate a context at the beginning of an episode, the reader has recourse to affect; but once that context has been located, the affect that has been established then enhances understanding and makes reading more efficient (as measured by shorter reading times).

In a study I am currently carrying out with Don Kuiken at the University of Alberta, we have also been examining the relation of reading times to foregrounding. The segments of a story have been analyzed for foregrounded features at the phonetic, grammatical, and semantic levels: our count of such features (converted to standard scores) constitutes an index of foregrounding for each segment. The mean reading times of a group of sixty readers have been compared with the index: the level of correlation we have found, $r(84) = .43$, $p < .001$, is highly significant. While there are clearly several other influences on the speed of reading, this finding shows that readers do indeed take longer to read passages that contain foregrounded features, suggesting that more attention, and hence greater processing, is required for comprehension at these points.

Studies of this kind are informative in establishing a framework for conceptualizing the process of literary reading. While many more such studies will be required, the findings so far provide the basis for a productive and replicable approach to literary response. Such data point to several elementary aspects of the act of reading, which are distinctive to literary response but are arguably features of response that lie beyond the influence of the types of literary training that readers might have received in school (as Van Peer's study also showed).

If readers are sensitive to foregrounding, if they experience defamiliarization at those points in the literary text, and if the main response to defamiliarization is an affective one, are there then typical response processes that readers show as they attempt to develop an understanding of the details of the text? And if affect is the primary response during defamiliarization, what specific role does affect play in the comprehension process?

Constructive Processes in Response

Two other studies I have carried out cast some light on this next stage. First, it can be postulated that the main interpretive work for the reader consists in creating a schema that is appropriate to the evidence of the text—that schema creation, in other words, not schema instantiation (as in some models of reading, such as the story grammar approach) is the goal that is distinctive to literary reading. The view that reading involves exploration and discovery has been supported by several previous studies. Tierney and Gee (1990), for example, who studied readers' responses to three literary stories, found that

> from the very beginning of reading these texts, our readers were hypoth-
> esizing, using a prediction-confirmation process in meaning making.
> Tentative possibilities were later confirmed or discarded as they seemed
> to fit or no longer fit with the reader's new expectations. (199)

The second key feature of literary response, however, which has not been sufficiently examined, is that affect appears to play a constructive role, guiding the process of schema creation.

The response process of readers can be studied by asking the reader to talk aloud while reading. While this undoubtedly interferes with the normal response process, and while the reader cannot be expected to be able to verbalize all aspects of the response process, enough reliable information seems to be obtained to cast genuine light on the process of response. The readers I have studied also told me that although their response was disrupted by the requirement to talk aloud, they did not feel it was radically different from normal reading. The procedure involves presenting the segments of a story one at a time on a computer screen: the reader talks aloud, where this is appropriate, while thinking about what the segment means and how it contributes to the developing sense of the story, before pressing a key to display the next segment. The story I presented in the study (Miall 1990) had already been rated by other readers, segment by segment, for affective response and for the relative importance of the segments; thus it was possible to make some predictions about which segments would be more likely to require interpretive effort. But what kind of effort would readers make?

Three characteristic responses were found. First, segments rated as more important or more affectively significant were treated by the readers as offering a new step in the story, which required more thought. In the terms of Hunt and Vipond (1986), these were segments requiring evaluative effort. Hunt and Vipond identify three types of evaluation: discourse evaluations, which refer to stylistic features, story evaluations, which are incongruous or unpredictable elements in relation to the story, and telling evaluations, which are unusual aspects of the narrative. The readers in my study manifestly expended more thought at these points in the story, developing a framework for the new information. Second, readers worked harder at relating such segments to other segments they had already read: they would refer back more often and offer more speculations on the connections in meaning being built across the story. Third, the readers looked forward more often, forming anticipations about the meaning of the segment for what might happen next. In summary, the affective implications of foregrounding seemed to involve these three constructive processes in response: evaluating, relating, and anticipating.

To make this clearer, here is a short section from the response of one reader, whom I call Emma. The story she is reading is by Virginia Woolf, "A Summing Up" (1944), in which, at a London party, Sasha Latham has been led out into the garden by her old friend Mr. Bertram Pritchard. Sasha is relieved that Bertram can be trusted to do all the talking. "Indeed," the story continues, "if one had taken a pencil and written down his very words. . . . " At this point, Emma's verbatim comment on the last phrase is:

> Why you should write down anybody else's words, his 'very words'—it's an odd word to use, 'very words,' it has this . . . trying to convey that there might have been sense in what he said, somewhere or other, but if you take down every word, you take down anything else but its peculiarness, its . . . it makes you wonder what's coming next. It makes you wonder what on earth she's going to say, it makes you want to look forward to the next image about what his very words will say.

Emma's commentary here shows both evaluation (i.e., the time she spends on the word 'very': she has noted an incongruity in relation to the style of the narrative) and anticipation. The anticipation is both immediate, her wonder about "what's coming next," and more implicit, in that her comment "if you take down every word, you take down anything else but its peculiarness" foreshadows the description of Bertram's speech that is given several lines further on, where the "peculiarness" is specified: "There was a sound in his voice . . . something immaterial, and unseizable, which existed and flourished and made itself felt independently of his words." Above all, Emma's comment as a whole seems impelled by an affective response, reflected in such words as "odd . . . wonder . . . want to look forward."

Similar constructive functions in the response process can be seen in the protocols of other readers: those phrases requiring evaluative effort also tend to be those that involve relational and anticipatory thought; and the phrases that call for this distinctive effort by the reader tend to be those that exhibit foregrounding. Of course, readers do not all invariably attend to all the foregrounding. Another reader failed to register the foregrounded word "very" as he encountered this phrase in the story: he repeated the phrase omitting the qualifier, "written down his words," and then had nothing to say at this point. Nevertheless, his protocol contained the anticipation corresponding to Emma's sense of "peculiarness," albeit delayed by three phrases: at this point he then said "Perhaps more important . . . is how he said it, and, you know, not its content."

The ideas that a reader such as Emma develops during reading do more than locate meanings for the text within her preexisting understanding. While at least some of the work of the reader, as the protocols show, serves to register such meanings, in the sense that the reader must place the story in relation to relevant schemata (such as, in this instance, those for London, parties, typical characters), the foregrounded aspects of the text tend to challenge the adequacy of certain schemata and require the reader to go beyond them in order to formulate a satisfactory interpretation. The last study I cite (Miall 1989a) was designed to examine this process.

Another Woolf story, "Together and Apart" (1944), was chosen for this study, partly because it is very short (readers were asked to read the whole of it) but also because while initially inviting one type of interpretation the story as a whole turns out to elicit something rather different. The opening scene again takes place at a party, where the two main characters are introduced. The opening lines are:

> Mrs. Dalloway introduced them, saying you will like him. The conversation began some minutes before anything was said, for both Mr. Serle and Miss Anning looked at the sky and in both of their minds the sky went on pouring its meaning though very differently. . . .

The characters then begin to talk, in a halting manner; they discover a common interest in the city of Canterbury and become more animated.

Readers were asked to read and then rate the first fifty-six phrases of the story (amounting to about one fifth of the story in length) for importance; they were also invited to make written comments about their understanding of the story so far. Having done this, they continued to read the remainder of the story. At the end of the story they made further written comments, and then returned to the first fifty-six phrases and rated them again for importance. The two sets of ratings and written comments thus reflected readers' views of the story at two different stages. The significant finding to emerge from analyzing the ratings was how the importance attributed to many of the phrases had shifted after the story as a whole had been read.

As the opening phrases I quote above show, the story begins by suggesting a possible relationship between Miss Anning and Mr. Serle. At the same time, a series of references to the sky and the setting of the party have an ambivalent bearing on this primary meaning. Nevertheless, most readers tended to assume that the relationship would be the main meaning developed and rated the phrases that describe this as the most important. By the end of the story, when nʋ relationship has actually developed, readers downgraded such phrases in importance and now saw more significance in the phrases describing the sky and setting. By the end of the story it was apparent that for these readers the latter phrases had a certain symbolic function: as their responses showed, the phrases conveyed the difficulty of making any relationship, the impossibility of revealing anything personal. The sky and setting phrases thus formed one important source for the readers in reconceptualizing their understanding as the story developed. The story, in other words, required readers to go beyond their initial relationship schema and to locate or develop a schema that was more appropriate, picking up the clues offered by the sky and setting phrases. The latter phrases also, it may be noticed (and this can be seen in the second sentence cited above), contain more metaphors: in other words, it is the foregrounded phrases, once more, that are the focus of the interpretive effort required.

The shift in schemata is reflected in the comments of readers. For example, after reading only the first section one reader said, "The story may continue with a more in-depth conversation between the characters, perhaps culminating in the discovery that they have a lot in common." Another referred to the second sentence as showing "affinity 'the together bit' between two people." But after reading the story as a whole the relationship schema was seen by most readers as inadequate, and several commented on the sky and setting phrases: for example, "Moon and sky—awesome, tend to show the unimportance of people's lives. They are not particularly romantic symbols— emotion is stunted and undeveloped."

The last comment suggests one of the types of schema that the story as a whole created in readers: a reconceptualization of the internal states of the characters. For another reader the story was about the impossibility of "'ultimate' communication." From a review of such comments, however, it is also apparent that among this group of readers the final schemata of the readers differed more or less from each other. While a given schema may be adequate or not in accounting for the evidence of the story, a range of different schemata are possible, each of which may be quite adequate. Thus, while readers appear to be responsive to the same textual features, because of foregrounding, and while they exhibit similar interpretive processes— evaluating, relating, anticipating—individual interpretations may vary, sometimes incompatibly, when compared with one another, yet each can be seen as a viable, persuasive interpretation of the text given the validity of its premises (Miall 1988b). The text, in other words, has determining features—the study of foregrounding points to one such set of features—but no determinate meaning. How readers understand a text will depend in critical ways on their prior experience and cultural position. The literary text, viewed from this perspective, is an instrument by which readers are enabled to reflect on, and perhaps reconfigure, some aspect of their experience. It is at moments of defamiliarization that the experience of the reader is engaged (perhaps unconsciously for the most part), through the predominantly affective response that appears to characterize foregrounding.

Emotion, the Self, and Literature

There is evidence that emotion primarily represents self-referential concerns (Bock 1986; Miall 1986), that is, the "current concerns" (Klinger 1978), "strivings" (Emmons 1986), or goals that motivate and guide each individual. Such concerns are probably often implicated in the response process of the reader through the reader's affective response, particularly at moments of defamiliarization. Thus we can see the overall schema that is created by the reader in response to a literary text as a part of the reader's continual creation of the self through the work of the emotions. Given that a text, such as the Woolf story, draws in a reader's ideas and emotions (about relationships at a party, for instance) but works to defamiliarize them and locate them in a different context, we can see that such ideas and emotions are subject to correction, to an altered perspective, to novel contexts, or to new relationships with other knowledge. In this respect the defamiliarizing process of reading works to restructure the reader's anticipations, to feed corrective information back to the initiating emotion. The emotions invoked by texts allow the reader to enact symbolically various implications for the self. The emotional valency of particular schemata may be altered, their relationship to other schemata redefined, and new (possibly more adaptive) schemata brought into being.

If this is correct, then the reading of literature clearly plays an important part in developing the self of the reader: more particularly, it provides a context in which the reader's own experience can be reassessed through constructive reformulation of the meaning and scope of the emotions. Given the constraints both on expressing and understanding emotion in our society, literature (and perhaps the other arts also) thus has a role of considerable significance. Given also the centrality of emotions and their evolutionary place in the human system, it is also clear that literature has the power to engage us at

levels–perhaps mainly unconscious—that are critical for our func-
tioning, even survival. Responding to literature can be seen as a part
of the adaptive system we have, so far rather successfully, devised to
sustain ourselves in an often unpredictable and difficult world, especially within the social system that is so necessary to our support but
that also necessarily places many constraints on our ability to
respond and act. Frequently in daily life an immediate response, a
particular emotion (a sudden joy, a moment of hostility), must be
suppressed in the interests of our social relationships or our own
future concerns: the complexities of human interaction make this
essential; social life would otherwise become impossible. However,
such restraint has an impact on the self-concept, on an individual's
sense of the meaning of the past or on the possibilities of the future.
The emotional implications can be addressed and perhaps reconfig-
ured through the symbolic processes involved in the act of reading.

Recently, however, the teaching of literature has become institu-
tionalized in our culture. The preeminent risk we face as teachers is
that we will limit or negate the self-enhancing, adaptive powers of literary reading for the individual. How can our methods in the literature classroom be redesigned not only to minimize this risk but to
actively promote the self-actualizing powers of literature?

Literature in the Classroom

The theoretical model of reading that we hold will influence our
instructional strategies. The widespread acceptance, for example, of
the schema model has led to techniques for enhancing the cognitive
component of reading. The teacher can work to enhance the reader's
background knowledge or can require the reader to reduce a text to
its gist or summarize each paragraph of the text. Such strategies will
often be appropriate for expository prose, but for the literary text
they are a distraction or, at worst, a barrier to the reader's engagement with a text. As Patrick Dias (1990) argues, classroom strategies
involving such instructional procedures and materials tend to subvert individual response to literary texts, so that the reader is "likely
to cultivate a passive, receptive attitude to text at the expense of an
active effort after meaning" (286). Why is response subverted?
Because an initial and essential feature of literary response is not
cognitive but affective. That is to say, the constructive or generative
dimensions of reading, as the research reviewed above suggests, are
initiated by the reader's affective responses, whereas the schema-
based strategies imposed in the classroom cut across or destroy this
process. Only secondarily does response take on a cognitive (and
hence shareable) pattern.

Motivation

The first issue, following Dias's point, thus concerns motivation. Students whose reading is constrained or predetermined by inappropriate classroom procedures lose motivation: their nascent sense of where the text touches on their own interests or experience is brushed aside in the requirement to answer questions, summarize, or report. The first requirement of the alternative classroom is to cherish and nurture students' first responses and enable them to explore any felt personal relationship with the text as far as they can. Out of such exploration they will produce an agenda of issues for sharing and discussion.

Method

Second, students will require a range of methods for exploring the issues that interest them, whether they work alone, in groups, or as a whole class. The literature teacher should be familiar with a variety of methods, help students acquire them, and be available to give advice to students on the benefits and limitations of each method. In the long run, students are encouraged to devise methods of their own: this is perhaps the ultimate goal of learning, knowing not just how to apply existing methods to a problem but knowing both when it is appropriate to devise a novel strategy that is more effective than an existing method and how to do so. A central issue when considering method, in addition, is to facilitate the work of small autonomous student groups. Students who work together in small groups (I find that four seems to be the optimum size) on a common interest usually report that they learn more from one another than from whole-class discussion, that they are much more willing to contribute in the small-group context, and that they gain a greater variety of different ideas and are more able to engage with the ideas. Thus it is also a part of the teacher's role to be familiar with methods for small-group work and to be able to offer advice to groups that run into difficulties, such as not being able to apply a method, not being able to resolve a disagreement, or not being able to keep one of its members from dominating (collaborative methods in reading and writing are discussed in Bruffee 1984; Golub 1988; Straw 1989).

Reporting

Third, students learn how to share the results of their work: when and how to report and how to make reporting effective for others in the class. In much traditional teaching, of course, a student reports

only to the teacher in the form of written essays: the student never
benefits from seeing other students' essays (at least not 'officially'), is
certainly not invited to comment on them, and because of competitive
grading and fear of plagiarism, is actively discouraged from working
on the essay in cooperation with other students. Thus perhaps the
most constructive work the student does in a literature class remains
private, an unexploited resource for the rest of the class. While essay
work, as a form of reporting, can be made less private and more constructive, other forms of reporting are often preferable: displays, dra-
matizations, debates, class books, journals, peer and collaborative
writing, etc.

Authority

The outcome of such procedures in the classroom is to confer authority
on students' readings of literature. The methods respect the student's
own sources of authority: their preexisting knowledge, experience, and
direct responses to the texts they read, the authority gained from collaborative work. At the same time, such methods provide pathways for
extending that authority outward toward a better understanding of
their own reading processes, the groups in which they work, and the
historical and cultural place of the texts they study.

Classroom Practices

These, then, are four cardinal components of an actualization model
of classroom learning, compatible with the research findings on the
process of literary response that show the important place of emotion
in the initial phases of response: motivation, method, reporting, and
authority (for more extended treatment of these issues, see Miall
1989b). To see how these work out in specific classroom activities,
here are a few of the practices I have adopted in my own classes:

1. At the beginning of a new class, I invite the students to tell me
what they believe the purpose of the course to be and what their
own aims are. From the written comments of the students and
the discussion we then have, we formulate a "Learning Agreement," which is typed up and given to all the students the following session for them to keep on file. The agreement also incorporates any points that I wish to have recorded, or points that are
essential to the requirements or running of the course. The students can then use the agreement as a reminder of what their
personal agenda and that of others is for the course; it can also
be used as a basis for evaluating the course while it is in progress

(formative evaluation being an important tool for enabling students to reflect on their own role and progress during the course): Are we fulfilling these aims? If not, how can we modify our methods to make their fulfillment more likely?

2. Students are asked to make immediate responses to a text (usually a poem or part of a short story) by marking those words or phrases they find most striking. Having then spent some further time on their own trying to work out some reasons why they marked certain passages, they discuss their findings in small groups. The exercise is a way of capturing first responses, often initiated by foregrounding in a text, as an alternative to the (more usual) requirement that students rather quickly develop some interpretive ideas. Students are pleased to find that other students may have marked many of the same passages, but are also intrigued that another student may have a rather different view of what a particular passage may mean. This then leads to a class discussion in which students can focus both on the detail of a text and how details relate to an interpretation of the whole. Starting with the local details of a text is consistent with the view that a text requires the reader to create an appropriate schema during reading: it enables students to gather evidence for the work of creation and discourages foreclosure on an interpretation until considerable discussion has taken place.

3. Given that a text may be concerned with implying, or arguing for, an alternative view of some part of the world, students can (again on their own or in small groups) be set to look for contrasts and opposites. This can be done by having students underline a series of key terms in the text, then asking them to generate a contrasting term. The contrast may appear explicitly elsewhere in the text, or it may alert the student to an alternative domain of meaning that the text points to implicitly. In this way students gain a firmer grasp of the issues that the text is presenting. This exercise also encourages the discovery of relationships across a text: the similarities in pairs of contrasting terms become easier to see, particularly if the pairs are written out separately and students then try to classify them.

4. Students' intuitions about the shape and development of a text can be given definition by asking them to devise structure diagrams for a story or a chapter in a novel (see Miall 1986). How can the text be divided up into sections—say six to eight sections? What would each section be called? What is the key development in each section? Why are the sections placed in this order? What effect would a different order have? In this way the dynamics of a

given text are given graphic form (and, as research has often
shown, information given in images is usually much better assim-
ilated and remembered). Again, students often find the differing
perceptions of other students during this task illuminating.

5. Several of these techniques and others can be combined in a
   more major piece of group work, in which students spend several
   class sessions (or work outside the class) to prepare a presentation on a text. This might take the form of a verbal report or a
   display placed on the wall of the classroom. A display has the
   advantage that students who were not involved in the work can
   spend time examining the report and can thus be better prepared
   to engage in discussions about the outcome.

The relation of these techniques to the model of literary response
presented earlier may not be immediately obvious. What, after all, is
the difference between asking students to summarize paragraphs and
asking them to produce structure diagrams? The important difference
between these and more traditional, teacher-directed activities is that
in the case of each of the techniques I have described above the students are asked to work from their own intuitions about a text (and
those of their peers, where appropriate), and each technique is designed to elucidate and strengthen that original first response. The
structure plan, for instance, is a sketch of what the student perceives:
the student draws up a model that is distinctive to his or her own
reading before interpretations of the text are discussed with other
students or the teacher. In fact, for the most part, the teacher should
refrain from offering any interpretative ideas, at least until the students have developed their own views and are willing to debate and test
their views. Another important feature of the techniques is this: interpretation as such is postponed until students have undertaken extended work on the text both individually and in small groups. Asking
students to say what a text is "about" before such work has been done
pressures the students to make premature formulations about meaning, and this is likely both to distort personal response and to cause
them to overlook evidence in the text that they might have considered.

The Dialogic Foundation

Finally, in addition to facilitating those first, all-important affective
responses, the methods I have been describing come closer to imitating or drawing upon the dynamics of the response process itself. If
literary texts are designed to challenge our ideas and feelings about
the world, to shift our perspective about ourselves or some significant

aspect of our knowledge, as the concept of defamiliarization empha-
sized by Coleridge, Shelley, Shklovsky, and others suggests, then
every text is inherently dialogic, in Bakhtin's term: it is the site of
conflicting ideas, arguments, and debate. We do both our students
and the texts we study a disservice if we insist on imposing our own
interpretations on them from the front of the class, reducing them to
monologic status.

In fact, while Bakhtin does not offer a developed reader-response
view as such, his writing is replete with suggestions both for how we
read and for how this might be reflected in the literature classroom.
As he argues (thinking of the characters in a Dostoevsky novel), consciousness itself is dialogic: "Every experience, every thought of a
character is internally dialogic, adorned with polemic, filled with
struggle . . . " ([1963] 1984, 32)—a resource, if true, that traditional
teaching methods in the literature classroom have overlooked or suppressed in our students. Thus, to adopt another Bakhtin comment
(again about Dostoevsky), the reader who is reading attentively is in
"that extremely complex and subtle atmosphere that would force him
to reveal and explain himself dialogically, to catch aspects of himself
in others' consciousness, to build loopholes for himself, prolonging
and thereby laying bare his own final word as it interacts intensely
with other consciousnesses" (54). It is toward this revealing of the
reader to him- or herself in debate with others that our classroom
methods must be directed.

References

Athey, I. 1985. Reading research in the affective domain. In *Theoretical models
and processes of reading*, 3d ed., ed. H. Singer & R. B. Ruddell, 527–57. Newark, DE: International Reading Association.

Bakhtin, M. [1963] 1984. *Problems of Dostoevsky's poetics.* Tran. C. Emerson.
Manchester, UK: Manchester University Press.

Bock, M. 1986. The influence of emotional meaning on the recall of words processed for form or self-reference. *Psychological Research* 48:107–12.

Bower, G. H. & P. R. Cohen. 1982. Emotional influences in memory and thinking:
Data and theory. In *Affect and cognition: The 17th annual Carnegie Sympo-
sium on Cognition*, ed. M. S. Clarke & S. T. Fiske, 291–331. Hillsdale, NJ:
Lawrence Erlbaum.

Bruffee, K. A. 1984. Collaborative learning and "The Conversation of Mankind."
College English 46:635–52.

Dias, P. 1990. A literary-response perspective on teaching reading comprehension. In *Beyond communication: Reading comprehension and criticism*, ed. D.
Bogdan & S. B. Straw, 283–99. Portsmouth, NH: Boynton/Cook.

Emmons, R. 1986. Personal strivings: An approach to personality and subjective well-being. *Journal of Personality and Social Psychology* 51:1058–68.

Golub, J., ed. 1988. *Focus on collaborative learning.* Urbana, IL: National Council of Teachers of English.

Hunt, R. A. & D. Vipond. 1986. Evaluations in literary reading. *Text* 6:53–1.

Klinger, E. 1978. The flow of thought and its implications for literary communication. *Poetics* 7:1–205.

Mathewson, G. C. 1985. Toward a comprehensive model of affect in the reading process. In *Theoretical models and processes of reading,* 3d ed., ed. H. Singer & R. B. Ruddell, 841–56. Newark, DE: International Reading Association.

Miall, D. S. 1986. Emotion and the self: The context of remembering. *British Journal of Psychology* 77:389–97.

———. 1988a. Affect and narrative: A model of response to stories. *Poetics* 17:259–72.

———. 1988b. The indeterminacy of literary texts: The view from the reader. *Journal of Literary Semantics* 17:155–71.

———. 1989a. Beyond the schema given: Affective comprehension of literary narratives. *Cognition and Emotion* 3:55–78.

———. 1989b. Welcome the crisis! Rethinking learning methods in English studies. *Studies in Higher Education* 14:69–81.

———. 1990. Reader's responses to narrative: Evaluating, relating, anticipating. *Poetics* 19:323–39.

———. 1992. Response to poetry: Studies of language and structure. In *Reader response: The empirical dimension,* ed. E. F. Nardocchio, 153–70. The Hague: Walter de Gruyter.

Mukařovský, J. [1932] 1964. Standard language and poetic language. In *A Prague School reader on esthetics, literary structure, and style,* ed. P. L. Garvin, 17–30. Washington, DC: Georgetown University Press.

Rosenblatt, L. M. 1978. *The reader, the text, the poem: The transactional theory of the literary work.* Carbondale: Southern Illinois University Press.

Shelley, P. B. [1821] 1988. A defence of poetry. In *Shelley's Prose,* ed. D. L. Clark, 275–97. London: Fourth Estate.

Shklovsky, V. [1917] 1965. Art as technique. In *Russian formalist criticism: Four essays,* ed. and trans. L. T. Lemon & M. J. Reis. Lincoln: University of Nebraska Press.

Straw, S. B. 1989. Collaborative learning and response to theme in poetry. *Reading-Canada-Lecture* 7:191–200.

Straw, S. B. & D. Bogdan. 1990. Introduction. In *Beyond communication: Reading comprehension and criticism,* ed. D. Bogdan & S. B. Straw, 1–18. Portsmouth, NH: Boynton/Cook.

Tierney, R. J. & M. Gee. 1990. Reading comprehension: Readers, authors, and the world of the text. In *Beyond communication: Reading comprehension and criticism,* ed. D. Bogdan & S. B. Straw, 197–209. Portsmouth, NH: Boynton/ Cook.

Van Peer, W. 1986. *Stylistics and psychology: Investigations of foregrounding.* London: Croom Helm.

Woolf, V. 1944. *A haunted house.* London: The Hogarth Press.

5

The Transactional Teacher Under Glass: Refocusing an Ideal

Robert J. Graham

We cannot teach another person directly; we can only facilitate his learning.

Carl Rogers

Even within those subjects most frequently studied the focus of the investigation is almost always upon *epistemic* outcomes rather than *transformative* ones—on the acquisition of scientific *knowledge* rather than the development of a scientific *attitude,* on the growth of reading *skills* rather than the cultivation of a love of literature.

Philip W. Jackson

One of the more common features associated with reporting the results of a research project in education, usually found at the end of the report after the procedures and data have been carefully set down, is the section entitled "Implications for Practice." It generally consists of remarks directed to the teacher/reader of the report and designed to spell out how approaches to pedagogy might be altered on the basis of the reported findings. At least one consequence of this convention has been to reinforce in the minds of teachers the particular notion that the relationship between theory and research and the world of practice is or ought to be direct. McKeon (1951) termed this view of theory and practice *logistic,* that is, that theory production and research findings should begin almost immediately to affect the way teachers teach. Now clearly, while in many instances researchers' and theorists' remarks may indeed appear to have some immediately direct implications for practice, the relationship is by no means as clear-cut as might at first appear. For example, what aspects of the findings or the theories teachers choose to attend to, how they are interpreted, and how they get "translated" into specific practices still rest squarely on the shoulders of every teacher, individuals who are situated in real classrooms and work under many different kinds of institutional constraints (Graham 1990a).

When the theory concerns the thorny issue of how readers respond to and make meaning from literature, then the process of drawing implications for practice becomes increasingly difficult. Louise Rosenblatt's (1968; 1978) transactional theory of reading and response to literature has become the object of a great deal of recent teacher talk and writing (Bogdan & Straw 1990; Cooper 1985; Dias 1990; Dias & Hayhoe 1988; Farrell & Squire 1990; Graham 1990a; Willinsky 1990). However, although there is general agreement that Rosenblatt's views do contain some far-reaching implications for practice, implications that challenge many of the assumptions upon which much literature teaching now rests, I want to argue that what has been overlooked and consequently has received much less attention is the figure of what I will call here the "transactional" teacher. For teaching based on a sound understanding of the transactional theory of reading and response to literature is also based on the existence of a certain kind of *teacher*, an individual whose posture in the classroom is grounded in his or her beliefs about the larger purpose of the institutional study of literature in a democracy.

In this chapter I bring the image of the transactional teacher into sharper focus by first of all turning to the work of Rosenblatt herself, specifically *Literature as Exploration* (1968). My exposition is useful insofar as I am able to abstract from her work some notion of the part she envisages teachers of literature must play in creating the conditions for a transactional approach to literature in the classroom. I augment this analysis by showing that the teaching style that best captures the kinds of dispositions, skills, and attitudes required of the transactional teacher can be discovered in the nondirective teaching approach given voice in the work of psychologist Carl Rogers (1951; 1969). I argue, however, that there is a general lack of clarity in teachers' understanding of the nondirective style, a situation that proponents of the transactional approach to reading and response to literature would do well to attend to if they hope to persuade more skeptical teachers to alter their own beliefs and consequently to alter their practices.

Therefore, while I remain convinced that practices derived from transactional theories of reading and response to literature still represent the best chance of redefining more democratically the relation between power and knowledge in the classroom and of ushering in an interpretive "new deal" for our students (Graham 1990b), the objective of this chapter as a whole is to enter several notes of caution into the general debate over this particular approach to the teaching of literature. For, if to teach at all is to "assume moral responsibility for the development of another person" (Tom 1984, 80), then to engage students in the study of literature is to be committed to assisting in a process of personal transformation—a process moral to its core—and one that constantly interrogates a teacher's own beliefs and values and presses hard against years of being conditioned to conceive of teaching in an altogether different light.

With these caveats in mind, let us turn our attention to the figure of the transactional teacher. As we do, and while we agree with Farrell (1991) that the picture that emerges from Rosenblatt's work "seems more like the ideal teacher of English than the one most often observed" (73), this analysis will take us closer to the source of both the difficulties and the promise in putting transactional theory to work in the classroom.

Students and Teachers in the Transactional Classroom

As is well known by now, Rosenblatt's choice of the term "transaction" to describe her view of what happens during the act of reading was borrowed from John Dewey and Arthur F. Bentley's book entitled *Knowing and the Known* (1949). Dewey and Bentley are there concerned with articulating a theory of how we gain knowledge and offer the term "transaction" to designate the *two-way process* in which "the elements or factors are, one might say, aspects of a total situation, each conditioned by and conditioning the other" (Rosenblatt 1978, 17). As far as Rosenblatt's understanding and appropriation of the term to describe the act of reading is concerned, the word *transaction* was chosen to imply not only that both text and reader are active in the process, but that a transactional view of reading also contains a theory of how human beings construct knowledge. Then, as now, Rosenblatt (1978) believes that since meaning is constructed as the reader evokes "the poem" (12) by attending to the fluctuating states of consciousness during the act of reading, no one text can mean precisely the same for each individual, since each person will pay more attention to some aspects of the text and less to others. Consequently, "without accepting the notion of a single 'correct' interpretation, the transactional concept provides the basis for developing . . . criteria for discriminating the relative validity of differing interpretations" (Rosenblatt 1990, 106).

We can see from this approach to the reading of literary texts that not only does it alter our conception of the teacher as the single source of interpretive authority, but that it places many students in the unfamiliar position of having to assume responsibility for their own transactions with the text. In other words, when teachers approach the text "as though it were a neatly labeled bundle of literary values to be pointed out to the student" (Rosenblatt 1968, 58), they are implying that all the interesting things that can be said about the text have already been said by someone else, and that the student's role is to memorize and reel off these informed judgments on a quiz or examination. Under this regime, students can certainly learn to be skillful players of this literary-critical language game; yet as Rosenblatt (1968) notes, "the frame is elaborately worked out, but there is a blank where the picture should be" (61), the picture here connoting the developed expression of the student's feelings and responses to the text.

Although I have described very broadly only the bare bones of Rosenblatt's theory, the description contains sufficient validity to warrant inquiring into what kind of classroom atmosphere might nurture the expression, exploration, and development of a student's personal response to literature. For Rosenblatt herself believes that many of the ways in which literature teaching now proceeds has placed "a screen between the student and the book" (1968, 61). In her chapter in *Literature as Exploration* entitled "The Setting for Spontaneity," Rosenblatt underlines several considerations that not only have implications for practice, but more importantly for us here speak to the role of the teacher in helping to create a psychosocial environment favorable to personal response.

An Environment for Response

Everything that Rosenblatt has to say about her ideal English teacher is premised on the fact that the teacher "values literary experience" (1968, 65) and possesses "a zestful sense of literature as a living art" (66). Because such teachers continually model their own love of literature through such activities as verbalizing personal associations with the text or connecting it to other texts they may have shared with their students, they will ensure that they are not imposing "a set of preconceived notions about the proper way to react to any work" (66). However, this does not mean that the teacher "abdicates his duty to attempt to instill sound habits of reading or sound critical attitudes" (66), but rather that the teacher will help students develop their own understandings in the context of their "own emotions" and their "own curiosity" (66) about life and literature.

In other words, the teacher's understanding of the importance of creating a favorable psychosocial environment is grounded in the belief that providing students with a sense of individual and collective security is a necessary condition for encouraging personal response. In addition, although such teachers realize they can never efface their presence from the classroom (Roemer 1987), they constantly try to minimize getting in between the students and the book, actions that say to students that the most important thing on their part is "an unself-conscious, spontaneous, and honest reaction" (Rosenblatt 1968, 67).

From this brief exposition, it is already clear that creating and maintaining an atmosphere conducive to the free-flowing response and discussion at the center of the transactional classroom is no easy business, certainly not for the personally insecure or faint of heart. Rosenblatt is aware that there is no magic formula for creating the conditions under which students will want to speak out, but she is sure that the teacher must be skilled in the art of "drawing out the more timid students" while keeping "the more aggressive from monopolizing the conversation" (1968, 71). In addition, the teacher must be alert in these discussions to possibilities where students require help in clarifying their ideas; in this, the teacher will be assisted by "his own flexible command of the text and understanding of the reading skills it requires" (71). However, Rosenblatt knows that these familiar routines can sometimes serve to reinforce the image of the teacher as in control of the discussion; "in a more wholesome situation," she states, "the [conversational] ball is passed from student to student, with the teacher participating as one of the group" (72).

Rediscovering the Purpose of Literary Study

It is perhaps easier now to see that the approach of the transactional teacher to making provision for student response is substantially at odds with other models of teaching derived, say, from the familiar features of the Tyler (1949) rationale for planning instruction. For under the transactional approach, as Probst (1991) knows, "it is hard to plan the craftsman-like lesson, moving logically from objective to evaluation, its purpose always clearly evident, and still allow for the uncertainties of response" (655). Likewise, the model of the teacher that is emerging from current research on response to literature runs counter to the dominant model of what Jackson (1986) has called the "mimetic" teacher, an individual "who gives a central place to the transmission of a factual and procedural knowledge from one person to another" (117).

Contrary to this posture, the transactional teacher understands from his/her own engagement with literature that genuine, thoughtful response cannot be made-to-order while working against the clock. Consequently, as Hynds (1989) reports, students who were given both the time and opportunity to respond derived great pleasure in working with teachers "who were willing to act as 'co-learners' in the process of literary analysis" (57). In this respect, then, it is worth reflecting on what Rosenblatt considers the main objective of this approach to the teaching of literature, for it clearly matters that teachers from whom so much is being demanded understand the full implications of their labors.

For Rosenblatt (1968), creating a classroom climate for free discussion and giving students the sense that their ideas are worthy of consideration only means "that the obstacles to real education have been eliminated" (75). Students still need to acquire the mental habits that will lead to "literary insight, critical judgement, and ethical and social understanding" (75). Rosenblatt contends that although an honest response to literature serves to remove some of the "false reverence" (76) for literature that many students have affected in the past, this is still not "an emotionally organized or reasoned approach to literature" (76). The main objective of the study of literature is not simply to respond to literature in a personal way, but to *reflect* on that response. Only when the student "attempts to understand what in the work and *in himself* produced that reaction, and when he thoughtfully goes on to modify, reject, or accept it" (76, emphasis added) will engaging with literature come close to fulfilling its ideal potential.

It is essential to reiterate here how vitally important the consequences are for the transactional teacher's students when a space has been cleared for free-flowing response and discussion. The teacher can now turn his/her attention to having students reflect on the literature and on their own responses to it, a process geared to producing what philosopher Richard Paul (1982) terms "strong-sense critical thinkers," that is, individuals who have had experience in "seriously questioning previously held beliefs and assumptions and in identifying contradictions and inconsistencies in personal and social life" (3). In other words, the politics of the transactional approach to reading and response rests only partially in teachers getting out from between the student and the text; it also rests on helping students develop not only "a readiness to question and to reject anachronistic or unjust assumptions, but a willingness also to accept and build on what is sound in our culture" (Rosenblatt 1990, 106). Expressed in these terms, we must reject the view of the transactional teacher as an individual "soft" on students or motivated by a misdirected sense of the relationship between power and knowledge. Rather, transactional teachers are not only individuals deeply committed to inaugurating changes in the classroom setting where encounters with literature take place, but also individuals who, as Probst (1991) suggests, have gone beyond concentrating exclusively on developing ever more refined instructional methods and moved toward "philosophy," that is, they are clearer about "our vision of the good life, our hopes for our children" (662).

The Challenge of Nondirective Teaching

The figure who comes closest to embodying the admittedly ideal characteristics of the transactional teacher is that of the nondirective "facilitator" made popular in the work of psychologist Carl Rogers. Unfortunately, however, the image that has come to be associated in the public's mind with the Rogerian approach verges on caricature: a completely nonjudgmental, accepting individual whose speech is punctuated by a string of uh-huhs, or one who avoids answering questions by posing another question—"Well, what do *you* think?" Nowhere in Rosenblatt's image of the teacher is there any suggestion that a teacher can or could operate entirely in this manner. What Rosenblatt's views do imply is that a nondirective approach is the *preferred* instructional style. This is also the view taken by educators like Beach & Marshall (1991), Dias (1990), and Probst (1988), who have closely followed Rosenblatt's lead. Only the nondirective style comes closest to creating the conditions whereby the Deweyan model of education as personal growth, upon which Rosenblatt's transactional approach to literature is based, can in fact be realized.

There is a need, then, to reevaluate Rogers's conception of the facilitator and to rescue it from some of its more common stereotypes and caricatures. However, it will become clear from my remarks that the role of the facilitator is not something that Rogers thought would come naturally or easily to many individuals, especially perhaps to preservice teachers for whom class management and the maintenance of "discipline" may appear to be items of overriding concern. Therefore, while recognizing that the style of facilitator is one into which many teachers must *grow* rather than one they immediately assume, the long-term prospect for the teaching of literature grounded in transactional theory is premised on the existence of this kind of teaching and teacher, a fact that of itself warrants some closer attention.

The Qualities of the Facilitator

In both his early essay entitled "Student-Centered Teaching" (1951) and in his important volume *Freedom to Learn* (1969), Rogers took great pains to counter the charge that his approach to learners and learning was "hopelessly unrealistic and idealistic" (1969, 124). The idea of the facilitation of learning as a "constructive, tentative, changing *process*" (105, original emphasis), whose success rested on certain "attitudinal qualities which exist in the personal *relationship* between the facilitator and the learner" (106, original emphasis), was considered by many to represent a quite impossible goal. What precisely Rogers thought these attitudinal qualities were that gave rise to such skepticism will occupy us presently. It is more important to recognize here the passion with which Rogers sought to defend his position and the solidly democratic philosophy on which, like Rosenblatt before him, he based his "solution" to the dilemmas of education. Rogers believed that the only way out of many an educational impasse was through taking to heart the fact that people matter, and that the greatest human potential could be released by "persons, acting like persons in their relationships with their students" (1969, 125). Rogers believed that if we fail to give the strongest attention to the development of the interpersonal side of education, then, as he put it, "our civilization is on the way down the drain" (125).

While Rogers, like Rosenblatt, does not labor under the illusion that schools alone can change society, he does believe that the facilitator is an individual deeply imbued with and committed to democratic principles, principles that he argues lie at the heart of a student-centered approach to education and learning (1951, 387ff.). But what are these personal qualities that the facilitator must possess when the stakes are so high and the consequences so important for individuals in a democracy? Although Rogers employs different terminology on occasion, the three basic qualities a facilitator must possess are "realness," trust, and empathic understanding. As I deal briefly with each of these in turn, I will also comment on the extent to which an appreciation for their importance is crucial in order to construct the kinds of classrooms and procedures required by the transactional study of literature.

Realness

The quality of realness as Rogers describes it is perhaps the most contentious, not only because it seems to beg so many questions, but also because it poses a personal threat to any individual considering teaching in a nondirective style. By realness Rogers appears to mean genuineness, the quality of entering into a relationship without presenting "a front or a facade" (1969, 106). Many experienced and novice teachers alike tend to assume the *role* of the teacher in front of their students, and for some teachers this role may be difficult to set aside even when they leave school in the afternoon. Rogers would counter the tendency toward role playing with the figure of the facilitator, an individual who, because he or she understands and accepts himself or herself, is able to enter into encounters with students person to person. The realness of the facilitator does not make itself manifest in any feigned enthusiasm or interest in students because he or she feels that this is expected; this is the behavior of individuals still trapped in playing the role of teacher. As Rogers states, the facilitator "can like or dislike a student product without implying . . . that the student is good or bad" (1969, 106). Now clearly Rogers discusses the realness that he has in mind only with respect to the characteristics of the teacher, since he has little or nothing to say about the student who deliberately provokes or who unwittingly misinterprets a teacher's expression of his or her feelings. And yet while Rogers knows that "to be real is not always easy" (109), he still maintains that it is basic to individuals who have their minds set on becoming "that revolutionary individual, a facilitator of learning" (109).

From this sketch it is easy to see how quickly some misunderstandings might arise, especially if we take too simpleminded a view and equate realness with a license to emote whenever the teacher feels like it or to express disdain for students or their behavior. The key here is to bear in mind that for Rogers the facilitator must not only be able to live his or her feelings but be able "to communicate them *if appropriate*" (1969, 108, emphasis added). In other words, realness must be tempered with prudence if the classroom climate that exists in such a delicate balance is to be maintained and strengthened.

Trust

Rogers believes that much contemporary education is based on the assumption that teachers can't trust students. Under this assumption it is then the teacher's responsibility to supply everything from motivation to evaluation, since the perception is that students need to be coerced into learning. Naturally, Rogers's approach is diametrically opposed to that: "'You can trust the student'" if "the atmosphere for growth is available to him" (1951, 427). These feelings and this atmosphere of trust are best catered to when the facilitator "prizes and accepts" (1969, 109) the learner as an expression of the facilitator's essential belief in the working hypothesis that when "the threat to the self of the learner is reduced to a minimum" (1951, 391), then one of the major barriers to significant learning has been removed. Not only do we hear echoes of Rosenblatt's earlier argument for setting the scene for spontaneity, but we are also beginning to see how fundamentally important to a student-centered approach to literature an individual teacher's beliefs really are. (I have more to say on the topic of teachers' beliefs in the final section.)

Empathic Understanding

Empathic understanding is "the ability to understand the student's reactions from the inside, a sensitive awareness of the way the process of education and learning seems *to the student*" (1969, 111, original emphasis). This ability, Rogers feels, is so rare that it "is almost unheard of in the classroom" (112). Certainly Rogers wrote that comment in 1969, and many would argue that teachers have indeed come a long way in their understanding of students. And yet this kind of "objective" understanding (developed in teachers through, perhaps, taking courses on the psychology of the learner) is not the kind of understanding Rogers has in mind. I believe the empathy Rogers has in mind relies heavily on memories of previous schooling, the memories about which teachers often suffer a collective amnesia when they make the transition from "student" to "teacher." These are the memories of what it feels like being bored in class, what it feels like having one's work endlessly red-penciled; and, on the other hand, what it feels like to draw applause from one's classmates for a poem well read or what it feels like to realize that a reading period is over and one was totally absorbed in one's novel. The suggestion here is that the more teachers remember these kinds of feelings from the inside, then the more they will be likely to remain sensitized to how students also feel. Although it may prove difficult to communicate this kind of empathic understanding to students, Rogers remains convinced that it "has a tremendously releasing effect when it occurs" (1969, 112).

Conclusion: Problems and Possibilities

I have been stressing throughout that as with Rosenblatt's recommendations for creating an ideal classroom climate conducive to fostering a situation in which students can negotiate meaning in a supportive milieu, Rogers's concept of the facilitator is based on an ideal equally difficult to discover operating in any real teaching situation. Nevertheless, the existence of these ideals always keeps before us the possibility that there still exist moments and opportunities in the classroom where real engagement and genuine change can occur. This search for the transactional teacher has uncovered some residual problems and some distinct possibilities.

I began this chapter by conducting a brief excursion into the real difficulties surrounding commonly held perceptions of the relationship between theory and practice in education. One of the strongest implications of transactional theory is the extent to which it impacts on the *beliefs* teachers hold about themselves and their students, as well as their conceptions of how knowledge is or might be constructed in their classrooms. The importance of emphasizing the potential impact of transactional theory on teachers' beliefs cannot be over-stressed. Under a strategic (logistic) view of teaching, the purpose of educational theory and research is to assist in generating specific approaches to subject matter that will be immediately useful in the classroom. However, if teachers begin to take this too literally, it can lead to disillusionment when certain strategies fail to bring about the desired outcomes quickly enough. While recognizing the complemen-tary need for teachers to *adapt* specific strategies to their own teach-ing situations, the approach that is slower, less certain, yet ultimately longer-lasting is to invite teachers to judge the merits of particular theories or research findings and thereby challenge them to alter the premises on which some of their own unexamined assumptions about teaching are based (Fenstermacher 1986). In other words, just as the most effective role educational theory and research can play is to invite teachers to become strong-sense critical thinkers themselves, so too the aim of a transactional approach to literature and the class-room is to produce strong-sense critical thinkers who are not hide-bound by their own assumptions.

One of the outcomes of transactional theory in particular has been the emergence of the facilitator or nondirective teacher as an individual who best embodies the beliefs and dispositions required to alter approaches to classrooms and the study of literature. The qual-ities of the facilitator are quite simply those that one might expect of reflective individuals who have not forgotten from the inside what the experience of schooling is like for too many of our students. In this respect, then, transactional teachers have looked toward cooper-ative learning (Brubacher, Payne & Rickett 1990; Johnson & Johnson 1990) as one way of addressing the neglected issue of stu-dent voice and feelings, as well as a way of making provision for the dispersal of interpretive authority in the classroom. Notwithstanding the difficulties that are often involved in initiating a move toward more cooperative learning procedures, these procedures not only offer rich opportunities for students to extend and explore their col-lective understanding of literature, but also represent key moments where the qualities of facilitators are employed to best advantage as they move around the room probing, questioning, cajoling, and above all, learning with and from their students.

On the other hand, it is precisely the difficulty many novice and veteran teachers alike experience in adopting or making the transi-tion to the position of facilitator that may impede the general progress of bringing transactional theory to bear more widely in the life of our literature classrooms. That is why a strenuous effort must be maintained by teachers whose beliefs about the nature of reading and response to literature have been altered through their contacts with transactional theory not only to publicize their successes but also to undertake the more threatening task of acknowledging and sharing their own uncertainties and submitting them to public reflection and debate. Therefore, because the implications of transactional theory ask stiff questions of teachers as persons, and because the nondirective approach entails rethinking issues that connect literary instruction with conflicting political agendas over the purpose of literacy (Norris & Phillips 1990), adopting the nondirective style will continue to prove for some a daunting and forbidding proposition.

Rosenblatt herself has recently stated that in her view, "the political indifference of many of our citizens, their acceptance of appeals to narrow personal interests, and their vulnerability to the influence of the media" (1990, 107) are symptoms of a general malaise of people who feel powerless to initiate any meaningful change in their lives or in society. It might be a rash piece of wishful thinking to consider that a transactional approach to the reading of literary texts in our schools will either create or expand in our student-citizens feelings of both power and possibility, but as we saw earlier, it is precisely this belief that motivates and informs the efforts of the transactional teacher.

Therefore, to have brought the figure of the transactional teacher more sharply into focus is to have discovered the significant part this individual can play in facilitating the release of certain kinds of human potential. By facilitating the process of bringing texts and students together in a spirit of cooperative, self-critical inquiry, the transactional teacher can indeed become an effective agent of personal and social change. While neither minimizing the difficulties in maintaining a student-centered approach to learning nor downplaying the strength of resistance to it, this search for the transactional teacher has also uncovered important aspects of a particular vision for education in a democracy as a whole. The stakes are high; the transactional teacher understands this and is committed both to the frustration and exhilaration of accepting the challenge.

References

Beach, R. & J. Marshall. 1991. *Teaching literature in the secondary school.* New York: Harcourt Brace Jovanovich.

Bogdan, D. & S. B. Straw, eds. 1990. *Beyond communication: Reading comprehension and criticism.* Portsmouth, NH: Boynton/Cook.

Brubacher, M., R. Payne & K. Rickett, eds. 1990. *Perspectives on small group learning: Theory and practice.* Oakville, ON: Rubicon.

Cooper, C. R., ed. 1985. *Researching response to literature and the teaching of literature: Points of departure.* Norwood, NJ: Ablex.

Dewey, J. & A. F. Bentley. 1949. *Knowing and the known.* Boston: Beacon Press.

Dias, P. 1990. A literary response perspective on teaching reading comprehension. In *Beyond communication: Reading comprehension and criticism,* 283–99. See Bogdan & Straw 1990.

Dias, P. & M. Hayhoe. 1988. *Developing response to poetry.* Milton Keynes, GB: Open University Press.

Farrell, E. J. 1991. Instructional models for English language arts K–12. In *Handbook on research on teaching the English language arts,* ed. J. Flood, J. M. Jensen, D. Lapp & J. R. Squire, 63–84. New York: Macmillan.

Farrell, E. J. & J. R. Squire, eds. 1990. *Transactions with literature: A fifty-year perspective.* Urbana IL: National Council of Teachers of English.

Fenstermacher, G. 1986. Philosophy of research on teaching: Three aspects. In *Handbook of research on teaching,* ed. M. Wittrock, 37–49. New York: Macmillan.

Graham, R. J. 1990a. Literary theory and curriculum: Rethinking theory and practice in English studies. *English Quarterly* 22:20–29.

———. 1990b. Let's make a new deal: Louise Rosenblatt and the politics of literacy. *Teaching and Learning: The Journal of Natural Inquiry* 4:12–19.

Hynds, S. D. 1989. Bringing life to literature and literature to life: Social constructs and contexts of four adolescent readers. *Research in the Teaching of English* 23:30–61.

Jackson, P. W. 1986. *The practice of teaching.* New York: Teachers College Press.

Johnson, D. W. & R. T. Johnson. 1990. What is cooperative learning? In *Perspectives on small group learning: Theory and practice,* 69–80. See Brubacher, Payne & Rickett 1990.

McKeon, R. 1951. Philosophy and action. *Ethics* 62(2):79–100.

Norris, S. & L. Phillips, eds. 1990. *Foundations of literacy policy in Canada.* Calgary, AB: Detselig.

Paul, R. W. 1982. Teaching critical thinking in the 'strong' sense: A focus on self-deception, world-views, and a dialectical model of analysis. *Informal Logic Newsletter* 4(2):2–7.

Probst, R. E. 1988. *Response and analysis: Teaching literature in junior and senior high school.* Portsmouth, NH: Boynton/Cook.

———. 1991. Response to literature. In *Handbook on research on teaching the English language arts,* ed. J. Flood, J. M. Jensen, D. Lapp & J. R. Squire, 655–63. New York: Macmillan.

Roemer, M. G. 1987. Which reader's response? *College English* 49:911–21.

Rogers, C. R. 1951. Student-centered teaching. In *Client-centered therapy: Its current practice, implications, and theory,* 385–427. Boston: Houghton Mifflin.

———. 1969. *Freedom to learn.* Columbus, OH: Charles E. Merrill.

Rosenblatt, L. 1968. *Literature as exploration.* 2d ed. New York: Noble & Noble.

———. 1978. *The reader, the text, the poem.* Carbondale: Southern Illinois University Press.

———. 1990. Retrospect. In *Transactions with literature. A fifty-year perspective,* 97–107. See Farrell & Squire 1990.

Tom, A. R. 1984. *Teaching as a moral craft.* New York: Longman.

Tyler, R. W. 1949. *Basic principles of curriculum and instruction.* Chicago: University of Chicago Press.

Willinsky, J. 1990. *The new literacy: Redefining reading and writing in the schools.* New York: Routledge.

6

Exploring Reading: Mapping the Personal Text

Lorri Neilsen[1]

Because I believe, in literacy education and in life, that the unexamined text too often is ourselves, I approached the planning of a master's course in the foundations of reading and language instruction as a rich opportunity for exploring our own reading. Expeditions into understanding the act of reading in the last fifty years have given us reports on the mechanics of one second of reading, pictures of eye sweeps, accounts of prior knowledge (the reader's backpack, always carried separately), and, when computers became the dominant metaphor, megabytes of documentation on the human decoding software (see Hunt 1990; Samuels & Kamil 1984; Straw & Sadowy 1990; Venezky 1984).

As each explorer returns, triumphant with the news of having found a theory to explain what reading is—and thus, of course, how to teach it—publishing companies, teachers, curriculum supervisors, and the public have gathered to listen—and to pay, both financially and professionally. Millions of dollars have been spent to produce classroom materials based on theories developed largely outside classrooms. And millions of students have been taught by teachers who borrowed maps of a territory explored by someone else.

Recent forays away from definitions of the reading process into descriptions of it have caused us as educators to look beyond text to readers themselves. What happens as we read? What can we learn about what we do as we read so that we can help students as they begin the process? Our current explorations into understanding reading are marked by fundamental challenges: How do we map a dynamic process? How can we separate ourselves from the reading? How can we separate our reading processes from the social and educational practices that shape them? Trying to describe reading is like trying to describe a fish swimming out of water. As Klinkenborg (1990) writes:

96

A fish's colors fade rapidly when it's removed from water. You have one live instant in which to fix it with your gaze, to memorize the pattern and subtlety of its hues. In my experience, it cannot be done. (35)

And stopping to examine our own ways of reading, instead of getting on with teaching it, is time-consuming, challenging, and, for many teachers struggling with the demands of classroom life, impractical. How can navel gazing with a book help me teach students better? Why not simply use this "proven" approach—or that set of basal readers? I'm an adult reader; why should understanding my own processes help a beginning reader?

The answers are neither easy nor obvious but, as this account of teachers' examination of their reading shows, they are extremely important to our understanding of our roles as teachers of literacy and participants in a larger institutional and cultural text. When we understand what shapes us as readers, we are better able to see our part in shaping or reproducing the instructional context. Our theoretical beliefs, played out in our classroom behavior, are always individually forming in dialectical relation to the ideas of others and to the culturally reproduced texts in which our own schooling is written. Each of us approaches our own reading uniquely and in diverse ways.[2] And yet each of us has been "schooled" into literate behavior as a social practice that can privilege certain common patterns or beliefs. To paraphrase the playwright Arthur Miller, the fish and the water are in each other: readers are part of a larger societal text that they both read and are read by.

For more than two decades now, as educators have tried to approach the study of reading as more organic and less mechanistic in nature,[3] we have found ourselves in rich but messy territory. For what is "prior knowledge" after all except a social construction of reality, which is neither objective nor value free? What is a reader if not an individual composing the self in relation to others?

The journals of teachers who have examined their own reading show that those whose processes are violated rather than validated by the institutional narratives for school reading gain understanding that invites reconstruction not only of self but of their teaching practices as well. Understanding reading is understanding ourselves: we, as educators, are part of a larger text that we must constantly revise.

Exploring Reading: How We Started

For the last few years, several teachers in rural areas of Nova Scotia have enrolled in the master's program in reading and language instruction at our university. As "external" students, they meet off campus, often in school staff rooms or a borrowed college space. As practicing teachers willing to devote most of their nonschool time to professional growth, they typically come prepared to examine reading and writing with the endurance and enthusiasm of the experienced. As one of their instructors, I have learned from their classroom wisdom and have attempted to provide them with the support to continue to explore their teaching.

The first course in the program typically focuses on philosophical foundations of reading. Rather than assign a large reading list and require that everyone read and respond to the same articles or books, which is typically done, I see the course as an opportunity to fathom the depths of our own reading processes while we each read selectively from a variety of sources. My reasons for promoting this examination are both practical and pedagogical.

Practically, the teachers don't have ready access to a well-stocked library. And so weekly I must bring along a boxful of books and articles from which to choose and which the teachers supplement with resources they find from curriculum libraries, other teachers, or trips to a local campus. Pedagogically, I am committed to our plumbing the depths of our own understanding about reading to counteract the tendency in our profession, as I mentioned earlier, to use without question the maps of reading drawn by others. I know from my experience as a graduate student, for example, that as provocative as I found the work of Vygotsky or Rosenblatt or Iser, I had no basis from which to assess my reaction to their theories. My experience before taking a course in reading was simply the experience of reading, not the opportunity to reflect on my processes or to determine what my emerging theories might be. Further, the seminar-as-examination format typical of my graduate program presented fully baked theories on a plateful of course requirements: who was I to say that my experiences or beliefs about reading were not consonant with those oft-cited theorists? Now, as an instructor in a graduate program off campus, I see the need for a forum where teachers' ideas about reading—particularly the ideas voiced by women in the profession—are not silenced by deference to authorities and where anomalies teachers find in matching someone's theory with their own experience can be freely discussed.

This term I asked teachers to keep an extensive reading log, recording their attitudes, reactions, reading history and habits, concerns, quirks and questions, as they read anything and everything. Their reading included popular novels, professional materials such as journals and newsletters, and seminal works by theorists such as Rosenblatt, Vygotsky, Piaget, and Polanyi. Occasionally two or three would read the same book or article; but for the most part, they chose their own reading according to interest or recommendation by another teacher. Not being able to amass and read a common body of books and articles was fortunate, as it turned out. Selfishly, I knew this approach would feed my strong aversion to a canon (at whatever educational level); but more important, it provided the opportunity for each teacher—without fear of having to compete for the "right" interpretation—to read and present the ideas he or she found useful in the chosen readings and to offer his or her interpretation to others for discussion and for further reading. In other words, the teachers' journals and the reading selections they chose became their curriculum.

When the course ended three months later, no grand encompassing theory of reading had emerged from their individual travels or from the discussion as a group. But neither had we expected one to emerge. What did develop, however, had as much to do with professional renewal as it did with understanding reading. For the teachers, the most striking development was the rediscovery of the humanity of reading, its connection to who we are as people. In doing so, they began to recognize and accept diversity and anomaly in their and others' reading process and to express these insights using their own metaphors and in their own voices. And as one would expect, they began to translate these insights into changes in their understanding about learning and teaching. For many, it was a beginning step to freeing themselves from both curriculum and canon. And because most of the group were women (only two of twelve journals represented here are those of male teachers), the sense of relationship and connectedness the journals engendered among the group played a significant part not only in fathoming reading but also in gaining voice.

Reading Begins at Home but Real Reading Takes Place in School

Although many of the teachers were old enough to remember Tom and Betty and Dick and Jane, their earliest and most memorable reflections were not the white-picket-fence literacy of the early basal readers. Rather they were stories of beds, mothers, laps, books as treasures, and reading as a full-bodied experience. Janice M. wrote:

> Every weekend, Aunt Mary would read to me and my eight cousins and no matter how tired she got, she'd keep reading as long as one of us was still listening. I was always the one who stayed to listen the longest.

Janice G. recalled the day the encyclopedia was delivered to her home:

I remember gathering on my parents' bed to listen to my mother read from a huge book of Bible stories which mom had bought from the same salesman who sold her our shiny new set of encyclopedias. I remember him in our tiny living room, two huge briefcases full of samples. I thought he had written all the books himself, until he brought out the Bible. I knew God had written that so figured this guy must be important.

John C. recalled his mother "clipping out stories for her scrapbook—songs, news items, deaths, births, marriages, interesting events. This was before television. She often read the scrapbook to me. I don't remember my father reading or writing."

Carol R. remembered the family had "a maid named Wilhelmina who told us all sorts of stories, the most memorable being one about the Boogie Man. I remember playing The Three Little Pigs at about age three, so I must have heard all the basic children's stories."

The early memories of reading and being read to were for the most part connected to maternity and to nurture and were sensual: the softness of a lap, the feel of a shiny new Golden Book from the grocery store, the redness of an apple on a book cover, the warmth of a bed. These are associations that many capable readers share. They are associations of reading as a full-bodied, intimate experience: reading as connection with those around us, as though our egos had no margins, the words fusing with experience. But this denial of bodyreading,[4] as Grumet (1988) calls it, begins early in life. As she describes it:

Touch and the voice are the sensual passages between parent and child. Because these modes of contact are associated with the intimacy of familiar or erotic relations, they are barred from the classroom, where sensuality in any form is anathema. (141)

In North American society, the chants and songs of early reading instruction soon give way to the distancing that makes reading a private act in schools. Reading in a story circle gives way to reading at a desk. The tears and human connection a poem evokes give way to a study of iambic pentameter. Early reading for many is often associated with mother and with nurturing, and as Chodorow (1978) has reminded us, our ambivalence about that relationship in society causes us to vacillate and to feel guilty. Even now, as adults, we need an excuse to engage fully with text (and even then we resist it). Many, like Peter S., are apologetic about curling up with a book for pleasure:

On Monday, I was sick and took a day off school. I stretched out on my sofa, wrapped in a warm sleeping bag, and spent the day reading. *Owen Meany* is a 600 page book and I needed a day . . . the richer the story, the richer the world I become absorbed in. I slip away from the world I struggle with and become caught up in the book, until I finally give myself up to it, spending hours reading.

But "real" reading, as many teachers suggested in their journals, is not like this, not so full of passion, so embodied: "real" reading is disembodied, cerebral. Janice G.'s encyclopedia memory is a striking metaphor for the public (and patriarchal) text where we find real reading begins. And the place for that public text is in school.

Reading the School Text

Most teachers recalled the ritual and the linearity of reading instruction in their early years at school. They recounted anecdotes of reading groups with animal names, of waiting in their long rows to read aloud, and of, in anticipation, rehearsing the paragraph that would be theirs to read. Janet V. enjoyed the ordered nature of her schooling:

> My formal reading commenced with the old Ginn series, "My Little Red (Blue, Green, White) Story Book," and I recall taking great enjoyment and pride in reading them and progressing from one book to the next. . . . I always looked forward to reading time in school, for I could get caught up in the experiences, personalities and adventures of the characters. I liked the poems, deciphering their meaning, enjoying the lilting flow of words, and memorizing them by heart. The first week of school, I would complete the entire year's text, curled up under a blanket in the fall evenings, enjoying the private freedom to be selective in the order of which stories I read first.

Janet's enjoyment of the "private freedom" underscores her sense that by "curling up" and reading ahead, she was deviating from the institutional narrative that shapes our expectations of what reading is and how it is taught and learned. She returned, if only briefly, to the situatedness of home where her reading began. But in order to survive in school, readers must not only master each basal in turn, they must participate in the larger institutional narrative, or school text.[5] Dorothy Smith (1990) describes how such texts work:

> Our knowledge of contemporary society is to a large extent mediated to us by texts of various kinds. The result, an objectified world-in-common vested in texts, coordinates the acts, decisions, policies and plans of actual subjects. . . . The realities to which action and decision are oriented are virtual realities vested in texts and accomplished in distinctive practices of reading and writing. We create these virtual realities through objectifying discourse; they are our own doing. (61–62)

Many teachers described the "virtual reality" of reading instruction in their school history as linear and sequential, with accompanying routines, rules, and expectations. Everyone waited until all readers could progress to the next reader. No one was permitted to "read ahead." We all read the same books. Later, reading became the search

for the one "main idea" in a paragraph or "theme" in a novel. The
virtual reality of reading instruction, cast in basals in the early years
of school and in English courses in later years, is a reality that we sel-
dom challenge as students and that because of its canonical nature
becomes tied to virtue. Mike Rose (1989) claims that the model of
learning "implicit in the canonical orientation seems, at times, more
religious than cognitive or social" (237). In this way, both as students
and as teachers, we participate in ways with words that seem unim-
peachable. We dare not challenge the canon. We learn to read from
the first line to the last and to find the main idea. Such becomes the
school text of reading itself.

   Thus, response and connection, the vestiges of mother, are to be
cast aside in favor of what Kristeva (1980) has called the *father-
tongue,* the language of objectified knowledge, of rules and regula-
tions, of patriarchy. This patriarchal text, which wrote and shaped
the reading experiences of both boys and girls of twenty or more years
ago (and still does now, to a great degree), became the virtual reality
that has defined our conceptions as teachers of what learning is, what
knowing must be. Carol R., who is now a principal, described her first
inkling as a young girl that what she knew was not valid; that there
was, embodied outside her, a text she ought to learn, to appropriate:

> I don't know why this memory is so vivid. In response to a test question
> for our Brownie badges, "how does a Brownie brush her teeth?" I
> eagerly offered: "with a toothbrush and toothpaste." I was told no, that
> was wrong, that a Brownie brushes up and down. That moment initiated
> me into an understanding of how school worked. From then on, I lived
> from report card to report card.

   As Smith (1990) notes, institutions such as schools go a long way
toward eradicating the messiness of personal knowing. Pure knowing
is objective and must transcend the local, historical settings to which
the knower is necessarily bound. The pursuit of pure knowledge is
impeded by what Smith calls the social and personal "detritus" (62)
dragged in by the knower. And, of course, from the perspective of
women, whose knowing has been described by many as connected
knowing (e.g., Belenky, Clinchy, Goldberger, & Tarule 1986), marked
by responsiveness and fidelity to care, learning to live inside the institutional texts that value objective knowledge can be particularly
problematic. Learning to read then becomes learning to understand
not only the Ginn reader or the Shakespearean play, but also the
larger cultural text that mediates the reality of the student. For Janice G., this meant learning certain lessons, learning to read the rules:

My science teacher always encouraged us to read everything carefully and completely. I read through the first questions about stalagmites and stalactites on a test and figured I knew the difference, so I began writing the answers. When I got to the 25th question, the directions were not to put a mark on the paper. I was devastated. I now spend a lot of time going over questions first. [My English teacher] always filled his room with posters of illustrated quotes. Each year, he gave us a few minutes our first day in his class to read them all. Then we weren't supposed to focus on them in class time again. . . . In one university course, the mammoth reading assignments for each class were kept in large brown envelopes in the library and we could sign them out for two hours. For me, that meant photocopying each 30 to 40 page article, using student loan money that could be better spent. But if understanding the readings wasn't hard enough [the professor] added an element of anxiety. Each day one student on the hot seat had to paraphrase and explain the article for the rest of our relieved classmates. It was a nightmare. Sometimes this professor chose you two days in a row, just to keep you on your toes. I still feel anxious when someone asks me about something I have read.

Janice G. and Janice M. were among many who learned to live the institutional narrative. As they analyzed their own approach to reading as adults, they found they had so internalized ways of reading taught in school, they felt guilty doing otherwise. Both described their difficulties breaking away from reading as a linear, organized task; to deviate seemed to be a violation of "pure" reading. Janice M. talked about her reading of *Maclean's* magazine:

Last night, I tried starting at somewhere other than page one. *I couldn't do it.* I felt too guilty about skipping pages. This is a holdover from my school days when all textbooks and workbooks were done from page one and we *never* skipped a page. I'm an avid magazine reader and I always read in exactly the same way. Even the newspaper—I couldn't possibly read section B or C before section A. I've decided to commit myself to varying my reading order. I wonder if I can re-program myself to do it?

Rereading the School Text: Revising a Reader

As teachers compared notes about their reading experiences at school, discussed their personal histories and habits as readers, and read the work of theorists, they began to document their comparisons of their own reading process with others' and with their preconceived notions of themselves as readers. They began to broaden and deepen their understanding of reading, to chip away at perceptions of reading as a monolithic process. Diana G. realized her need to keep what she called a "goal-oriented" approach when she compared herself with a friend:

> This summer while my friend and I were picking blueberries and I glanced down at our two blueberry flats, I realized that those flats could tell quite a story about the two of us. The flats were in fact a representation of the way each of us approaches any task we have to do. My flat had full boxes. I concentrated on only one box at a time, topping it off before moving to the next. She was happily tossing handfuls of berries in the general direction of the flat and letting the berries land in whichever box they would. . . . When I read I generally use much the same approach. I read whole pieces of writing at a time. . . . My friend skips sections when she reads, endings here and chapters there.

John C. compared differences in readers to differences in choir members' approach to learning a new song:

> I know from my own experience that if I understand the message of the song, everything else appears easier. . . . I'd say that people who do not read a great deal or realize the power of the printed word have less difficulty singing what they do not understand. . . . I'm surprised at the number of people who leave everything to the choir director. This person often supplies meaning for the choir, as well as background and expression. It's as if some choir members are doing little more than sentence surfing.

After a discussion in which I described my own reading process as often one of "snacking" (a comparison, I realized later, that bespeaks a consumption metaphor that troubles me), Linda M. wrote about her approach to reading Cazden's (1988) work:

> As I began to read the book, I too found myself snacking. That is, I only had so much time to allot for reading so I tried to read the best first, to get a feel for the book. Usually, to warrant myself as a serious reader, I read a book from beginning to end. However, I have recently begun to make decisions as a reader based on my knowledge and understanding of reading

Elsa B. talked about variations in approach she noted as her colleagues read works by Halliday (1978) and LeFevre (1987). Recognizing variation gave her confidence:

> I'm amazed now at the panic I felt. Sharon said her ego wouldn't let her believe she was stupid. Judy and Susan laughed and said if they couldn't understand something they just read on and got the general idea. I couldn't do that then. But I'm now more confident. . . . Later, talking

with [a colleague] about Wilkinson's [1975] work, I was floored to hear
he found the reading difficult. I considered him to be super intelligent—
how could he find it difficult when I found it easy?

Carol R., who had been reading Vygotsky (1962, 1978), found
herself trying to solve a problem with the computer by talking herself
through the process. She found not variation, but a validation of her
process in Vygotsky's ideas.

> I suddenly realized I was in the act of egocentric speech to keep myself
> on task. . . . According to Vygotsky, the child's egocentric speech is the
> counterpart to inner speech, or verbal thought, before it has become
> entirely internal. The child produces such egocentric speech when he
> [*sic*] is planning or problem-solving. . . . As adults we probably revert to
> this externalized form of verbal thinking when we are having difficulty
> with a task. I had put Vygotsky away for awhile, but I am encouraged
> enough to go back.

Finding connections in Vygotsky's theory that described her reading behavior caused Carol to continue to pursue her reading of his
theories. Ann C.'s reading of Rosenblatt (1978) gave her an insight
into her memories of her schooling. The institutional text, she realized, denied her aesthetic response, and, by extension, denied her self:

> I found myself constantly reflecting on my in-school experience with lit-
> erature. I enjoyed reading, but the teacher was always seeking the one,
> right answer and I seldom constructed it. I relied solely on note-taking,
> a good memory and regurgitation of someone else's ideas. . . . [Rosen-
> blatt] has helped to focus on the reasons why I have such unpleasant
> memories and why learning environments like these stifled the develop-
> ment of my literary response. Did they also stifle the development of my
> personal voice?

Janice M. decided during the course to make it a personal goal to
break away from reading from beginning to end:

> I'm teaching myself that it's okay to stop reading something, to pick and
> choose. For the first 37 of my years I have read all of something because
> I felt it would be failure or admitting defeat if I didn't finish. I hope for
> the next 37 years, I can give myself some choice, and can feel less guilty.

Both Janice and Cathy commented that they are "learning to question what I read instead of accepting everything" just because it has
been published in a book.

Objectified knowledge stands as "a product of an institutional
order mediated by texts; what it knows can be known in no other
way" (Smith 1990, 80). Undertaking a critique of the school text—

what we have believed about reading and hence how we must read and teach reading—requires that we inquire into the actualities of our own experiences as participants in reproducing that text. By digging deeply into an understanding of ourselves as readers, we can expose the broader cultural practices that regulate reading and readers. Critical theorists, who typically view such introspection as narcissistic and politically irresponsible, fail to accept that a free act, as Maxine Greene (1988) has described it, is a particularized one: "it is undertaken from the standpoint of a particular, situated person trying to bring into existence something contingent on his/her hopes, expectations, and capacities" (70). Or, as the feminist slogan has it, the personal is political.[6]

By documenting their reading processes, by comparing what they do with the descriptions of theorists, and by being surrounded by diversity in idea and approach, these teachers found themselves rejecting the roles the school text had written for them, both as students and as teachers. In fathoming their own reading, they began to think of ways to rewrite themselves and the school settings in which they play a key role.

Revising the Reader: Revising the School Text

As Heilbrun (1988) notes, "power is the ability to take one's place in whatever discourse is essential to action and the right to have one's part matter" (18). Without question, the fact that these teachers were able to meet regularly as a group and discuss issues gave them a discourse community that offered both support and challenge for their ideas. Nonetheless, as their revisions of themselves as readers became apparent, their revisions of themselves as teachers were not far behind. Many described a new sense of, if not power, at least commitment to create different environments for students from those they had experienced.

Janice G. talked about her decision to weave into her Sunday school teaching what she realized had been important to her:

> My own warm memories of these [Bible] stories have made me somewhat of a radical. We follow a set curriculum but at the three- and four-year-old level it has few tie-ins with Jesus or the well-known stories. I decided to ditch the curriculum and focus on story. Hopefully, some of these children will remember these first book experiences as fondly as I have.

Linda M. rethought the "kind of reading experiences we offer the students in our classroom":

Often I felt guilty about not opening the basal reader and going through the guide—am I really teaching reading if I do not make use of this guide? Anyway, I have brought in my own books and books from the library and although students have read many, I realize I've never asked them to comment on them. On Monday, I'm going to talk about reading with them. Share my evaluation of a book, then ask them to do the same. Hey, maybe they could even share their comments with a friend, suggest a story to a friend.

Janice M. talked about giving students permission to abandon a book:

I've always given kids choice in what they read, but I have always expected them to finish the book. Perhaps if I give them the choice not to finish a book they don't like, they won't be so uptight and won't take so long to decide. Maybe they'll be more relaxed.

The marginalizing of self—the disembodiment of reading and of knowledge—is so pervasive in schools (and in university courses) that to return to an examination of our local and particular selves becomes, as it did for these teachers, a welcome relief. It becomes, finally, a validation. But it comes with difficulty. Sharon decided to write about her childhood, to begin to tell her stories and participate with her students, not as the teacher but as a writer. She was nervous, both about facing the students and facing herself:

The fact that memories that meant so much to me were languishing on the shelf begged the question: Why haven't you written this? Answers flooded back: I haven't the time. Who'd want to read it? . . . However, suppose that the writing helped me to deal with the past; to sort it and feel it and find the plot line. Maybe writing could help my life. . . . I wondered if my experience with the memoir was shared by students. Are they sometimes afraid of what they will find when they give voice to their story? Perhaps in sharing my experience I could help them, I thought. Then I realized that the writer who needed help was me.

As they came closer to valuing again the embodied process of reading—that is, not denying their connections, their bodyreading—and as they began to believe more fully in their own power to make decisions in the classroom, the teachers also questioned other texts that tacitly wielded authority. Karen K. realized that she

often felt that other educators knew all the answers and if I followed what they said I would be a good teacher. If it didn't work out, it was because of something I'd done. . . . But I now think it is all right for me to question whether a new teaching strategy is as good as they say it is. . . . We are all still searching for answers and we never really find them.

Carol R. was angry about an inservice on cooperative learning offered by the school board that was inconsistent with the board's stated holistic philosophy about learning:

> There was once a time when I would have wanted to find out which of these views was the truth. I now realize there is no objective truth. People become a reflection of the way they are treated. The Industrial Revolution, with its specialization of labour, and especially the production line, has created a "transmission of culture" model in education. We have to live with what that has produced while working to restructure institutions to work more holistically.

Carol expressed her concerns to the workshop leader, who called Carol's comments divisive. Carol claimed that promoting practices representing conflicting worldviews was "intellectual sloppiness." While there is no "truth," Carol argued, we can work toward coherence.

Janice M. reassessed the assumption of the societal text that claims literacy is for all:

> These kids who don't do as well in school shouldn't be made to feel that they have failed life because they have failed to meet our standards in reading and writing. . . . Literacy is not a solution to all the world's ills and we are failing our students by ignoring the fact that we discriminate against those not considered literate. One of the most caring, loving, best parents I know is my cousin who reads and writes poorly and who has little formal education. Unfortunately, she also has little self-esteem and little confidence in her parenting abilities. How sad that school failed her so miserably. Her three children are articulate, intelligent, considerate people like their mother. We have to re-think what we value.

Peter S.'s staff had met with a local Micmac Band Council recently and he later reflected on their day:

> We listened to some amazing people talk about the effect the school system had on them, about the importance of their language and how the school system stripped them of it, and of the deep spiritual nature of the Micmac culture. It was not hostile and it was incredibly instructive. They had very good reasons to fear white man's education.

He tied this experience with his reading of Iser's (1978) and Emig's (1983) work, and noted:

> [Teaching] is not the pretty pictures on the classroom wall or the plant by the window or the carefully constructed activities. . . . We need to be

constantly looking for ways to understand how others perceive the world, to tolerate differences.

By tracking their understanding of their own reading process and by uncovering the ways in which they, as readers, were shaped by the institutional narrative for teaching and learning reading, the teachers were able to rethink themselves as readers and teachers. Such revision, in many ways, enabled them to bridge the public and the private, the self and the social.

The teachers' journals show that reading began for them as an experience associated with feeling, imagination, and a celebration of the senses. As a school activity, reading became ritualized and disembodied, became the text "out there." For women, who are still heavily socialized to please, having to choose the school text meant denying the particularized and situated experience of their reading. While tracking their reading process, these teachers found others' maps helpful only to a point; what seemed more important was that they embark on the exploration themselves. Understanding reading requires both sense and reference, both what we know and how we live (Ricoeur 1976). I hear the call for such continued exploration in Maxine Greene's words (1988):

> The idea of freedom, so long linked to self-direction and a separation of the subject from the objective world, may be revised and remade to the degree we understand situatedness and knowing in connection with action and speech, knowing as an aspect of vocation, taking place in the midst of life. (76)

Notes

1. The author would like to thank the teachers of Pictou County and Annapolis Valley who participated in these courses and who so willingly shared their journal reflections and insights into their growth.

2. That our literacy is both a reflection and a creation of who we are in our individual and particular lives is illustrated at length in my ethnographic study of three adults, *Literacy and Living* (Neilsen 1989). I have described the individual's literate behavior as being inseparable from his or her worldview and experience and as being in constant revision through the dialectical relationship with social and cultural practice.

3. For a more extensive description of the differences between a mechanistic and an organic world approach to reading instruction, see Allan Neilsen's *Critical Thinking and Reading: Empowering Learners to Think and Act* (1989).

4. Madeleine Grumet (1988) uses the term "bodyreading" to describe reading as a way to "bring what we know to where we live, to bring reading home again" (129).

5. Some have referred to this institutional narrative (the story about how to "do" school, and the experience that such a narrative writes) as the hidden curriculum. I prefer not to use that term as it serves only to further validate separate and categorized knowing.

6. For a discussion of women teachers' struggle gaining voice in their situated experience, see my "Is Anyone Listening?" (Neilsen 1991). The discussion is a response to a colleague who referred to women teachers' discussions of the personal as failing to contribute to a larger social critique.

References

Belenky, M. F., B. M. Clinchy, N. R. Goldberger & J. M. Tarule. 1986. *Women's ways of knowing: The development of self, voice, and mind.* New York: Basic Books.

Cazden, C. B. 1988. *Classroom discourse: The language of teaching and learning.* Portsmouth, NH: Heinemann.

Chodorow, N. 1978. *The reproduction of mothering: Psychoanalysis and the sociology of gender.* Berkeley: University of California Press.

Emig, J. 1983. *The web of meaning.* Portsmouth, NH: Boynton/Cook.

Greene, M. 1988. *The dialectic of freedom.* New York: Teachers College Press.

Grumet, M. 1988. *Bitter milk.* Amherst: University of Massachusetts Press.

Halliday, M. A. K. 1978. *Language as a social semiotic.* Baltimore, MD: University Park Press.

Heilbrun, C. 1988. *Writing a woman's life.* New York: W. W. Norton.

Hunt, R. A. 1990. The parallel socialization of reading research and literary theory. In *Beyond communication: Reading comprehension and criticism,* ed. D. Bogdan & S. B. Straw, 91–105. Portsmouth, NH: Boynton/Cook.

Iser, W. 1978. *The act of reading: A theory of aesthetic response.* Baltimore, MD: Johns Hopkins University Press.

Klinkenborg, V. 1990. Come and gone. *Harper's Magazine,* June: 34–36.

Kristeva, J. [1977] 1980. *Desire in language.* Trans. L. S. Roudiez. New York: Columbia University Press.

LeFevre, K. B. 1987. *Invention as a social act.* Carbondale: Southern Illinois University Press.

Neilsen, A. 1989. *Critical thinking and reading: Empowering learners to think and act.* Urbana, IL: National Council of Teachers of English.

Neilsen, L. 1989. *Literacy and living.* Portsmouth, NH: Heinemann.

————. 1991. Is anyone listening? *The Reading Teacher* 44:494–96.

Ricoeur, P. 1976. *Interpretation theory: Discourse and the surplus of meaning.* Fort Worth: Texas Christian University Press.

Rose, M. 1989. *Lives on the boundary.* New York: Penguin.

Rosenblatt, L. M. 1978. *The reader, the text, the poem: The transactional theory of the literary work.* Carbondale: Southern Illinois University Press.

Samuels, S. J. & M. L. Kamil. 1984. Models of the reading process. In *Handbook of reading research,* ed. P. D. Pearson. New York: Longman.

Smith, D. 1990. *The conceptual practices of power.* Toronto: University of Toronto Press.

Straw, S. B. & P. Sadowy. 1990. Dynamics of communication: Transmission, translation, and interaction in reading comprehension. In *Beyond communication: Reading comprehension and criticism,* ed. D. Bogdan and S. B. Straw, 21–48. Portsmouth, NH: Boynton/Cook.

Venezky, R. L. 1984. The history of reading research. In *Handbook of reading research,* ed. P. D. Pearson. New York: Longman.

Vygotsky, L. S. 1978. *Mind in society: The development of higher psychological processes.* Cambridge, MA: Harvard University Press.

———. 1986. *Thought and language.* Cambridge, MA: MIT Press.

Books Available to the Teachers to Read

D. Bogdan & S. B. Straw, eds. 1990. *Beyond communication: Reading comprehension and criticism.* Portsmouth, NH: Boynton/Cook.

Cazden, C. B. 1988. *Classroom discourse: The language of teaching and learning.* Portsmouth, NH: Heinemann.

Emig, J. 1983. *The web of meaning.* Portsmouth, NH: Boynton/Cook.

Fish, S. 1980. *Is there a text in this class? The authority of interpretive communities.* Cambridge, MA: Harvard University Press.

Halliday, M. A. K. 1978. *Language as a social semiotic.* Baltimore, MD: University Park Press.

Iser, W. 1978. *The act of reading: A theory of aesthetic response.* Baltimore, MD: The Johns Hopkins University Press.

LeFevre, K. B. 1987. *Invention as a social act.* Carbondale: Southern Illinois University Press.

Pearson, P. D., ed. 1984. *Handbook of reading research.* New York: Longman.

Piaget, J. 1926. *The language and thought of the child.* London: Routledge & Keegan Paul.

———. 1970. *Psychology and epistemology.* New York: Viking.

Polanyi, M. 1958. *Personal knowledge.* Chicago: University of Chicago Press.

Rosenblatt, L. M. [1938] 1976. *Literature as exploration.* New York: Noble & Noble.

———. 1978. *The reader, the text, the poem: The transactional theory of the literary work.* Carbondale: Southern Illinois University Press.

Suleiman, S. R. & I. Crosman, eds. 1980. *The reader in the text: Essays on audience and interpretation.* Princeton, NJ: Princeton University Press.

Venezky, R. L. 1978. *Mind in society: The development of higher psychological processes.* Cambridge, MA: Harvard University Press.

Vygotsky, L. S. 1986. *Thought and language.* Cambridge, MA: MIT Press.

Wilkinson, A. 1975. *Language and education.* Oxford, UK: Oxford University Press.

7

Texts, Textoids, and Utterances: Writing and Reading for Meaning, In and Out of Classrooms

Russell A. Hunt

My teaching has changed a lot in the past few years, and it seems that I spend a lot of time trying to explain, to myself as well as to others, just what the changes amount to. The other day I heard myself saying that the most important difference was that I was trying to put meaning at the center of all the written language used in connection with my classes. The colleague I was talking to said that he didn't see anything unusual about that—what else, he asked, could possibly be at the center? I took a quick stab at answering the question, but I don't think I convinced him I knew what I was talking about. It was in trying to deal with that question for myself, later, that I discovered what's really happened: my notion of what meaning itself *is* has changed. I no longer think of it as something that's *in* texts or language: it seems to me far more powerful and useful to think of meaning as a social event.

Language as a Social Phenomenon

In recent years we've heard a lot about language as a social phenomenon. We've been hearing it from the lips (and reading it from the word processors) of people in an amazing variety of disciplines and areas of research. Those like Kenneth Kaye (Kaye 1982; Kaye & Charney 1980) and Jerome Bruner (1983), who are concerned with the earliest stirring of mental life in infants, have been telling us that Vygotsky (1978; see also Wertsch 1983; 1986) was right when he said, half a century or more ago, that intelligence itself was a social

phenomenon, intimately connected with that most social of phenom-
ena, oral language. Those like M. A. K. Halliday (1975; 1978), who are
concerned with the early stages of oral language development, have
been telling us that language is a social semiotic and not something
that grows in the isolation of an individual cognitive mechanism.
Those like Frank Smith (1982), Jerome Harste (Harste, Woodward &
Burke 1984) and Judith Newman (1985; 1986; 1991), who are concerned with the development of literacy in young children, have been
telling us that written language must be meaningful in order for it to
be something children want to and are able to learn—and that for
language to be meaningful it must be the vehicle for social transactions. Second language theorists like Stephen Krashen (1981) and
teachers like Anne Freadman (1988) have been telling us that the
best way to learn a language is to use it in real social contexts, for
genuine social purposes. In composition studies, indeed, "social process" has become the buzz term of the early nineties. Scholars like
Karen Burke LeFevre (1987) and Jim Reither (Reither 1985; 1990;
Reither & Vipond 1989) have made it clear that not only composition
and revision but invention itself is profoundly social. Even in literary
theory, the "new pragmatics" (Hassan 1987; Kamuf 1986; Mitchell
1986) and a dialogic view based on Bakhtin (1986; see also Bialostosky 1989 and Holquist 1991) have begun to look as though they are
about to shoulder aside deconstruction and reader-response theory.

And so at conferences we begin to make jokes about how often the
word "social" can be allowed to appear in the program. We struggle to
keep the term from becoming so general, so widely used, that it no
longer means anything, the way the dichotomy between "process and
product" did a few years ago or "current-traditional paradigm" did a
few years before that or "whole language" is doing today. And we race
to snatch the concept out from under the dusty tread of those who
want to appropriate the term for the snappy, colorful covers of grammar drill books, freshman comp handbooks, introductory English
readers, language arts texts, and literature anthologies—complete
with study questions and a handy section on writing about literature.

In the short time we have before the term vanishes into the dust
behind the wagon train of progress, I'd like to suggest some of the
powerful implications it might still possess for the way we teach reading and writing. These implications are easy to lose sight of; but I
think once we've lost them we're really not talking about treating
language as social any more.

Once we've accepted that language is a social process, our notion of
what meaning is must change radically. It has been clear for some
time, of course, that traditional definitions are inadequate. Michael
Reddy (1979), for example, pointed out the way using a "conduit"

metaphor for describing language leads us (wrongly) to think about language as a sluice down which chunks of meaning, like pulp logs, are channeled from sender to receiver, arriving essentially unchanged. The ERIC bibliography (Houston, 1987) used to offer "thought transfer" as a synonym for "communication." With reference to reading, Frank Smith (1985) has called this the "information-shunting" model. According to that model, meaning isn't particularly problematic: it is just information that is somehow contained in text. Our job as speakers and writers is to get the information into the conduit; as listeners and readers, to get it out. I don't mean to suggest that anyone has ever thought this was simple: a whole generation of reading researchers, linguists, and psychologists of language worked at trying to construct a model of just how that might work. But they didn't consider the question *problematic*; it was just *complicated*. For a long time it seemed as though it would be solvable in a purely mechanical way. In fact, many people still believe they're going to succeed in creating a computer program that will parse sentences into meaning and generate new sentences with "the same" meanings based on their "deep structures."

It's been apparent from the beginning, though, that in at least some cases the situation in which a particular syntactic structure was uttered could determine its meaning and do it without much help or interference from the kinds of internal structures that a computer program could apprehend. If you listen to any naturally occurring oral conversation for more than two or three minutes, you discover that the meanings of the overwhelming majority of oral utterances are determined not by their semantic properties and syntactic structures but—much more powerfully—by a sort of unspoken, continuously renegotiated social contract between the participants in the conversation.

"That's just great," you might say.

"Tell me about it," I might reply.

In an appropriate situation—say we've just been informed that there's going to be no overhead projector available for our conference presentation in ten minutes, the one that depends on forty transparencies of statistical data and charts—we both know that you certainly don't mean that it's just great and that I'm not asking you to tell me anything at all. How do those sentences come to have those meanings?

Although we might not all talk the same way about what those sentences mean, it's clear that we would all share a sociolinguistic competence that allows us to make the right sense out of them most of the time. But they may not seem normal or typical sentences. For one thing, they're rhetorical figures of some kind—the first is obviously irony, and probably Aristotle or Puttenham would have a name for the second. Thus, it might be argued, they're not really "standard language," not something we have to account for if we want to explain how language works. Serious language, we might argue, the kind we want to understand, works more directly than that, isn't so situation dependent, is more susceptible to analysis, and carries more information. "Tell me about it" doesn't actually convey information, does it? Wouldn't a philosopher of language like Bertrand Russell analyze it right out of existence, showing that it's really not properly language at all?

Yes, he probably would. But there are two problems with that sort of position. First, the kind of language we're considering is far from unusual. Virtually all naturally occurring oral language is like that. And if you want to account for—and understand—how language works, you can't very well argue that seventy or ninety percent of what you hear people saying isn't really language at all and therefore doesn't have to be accounted for. Second, it's becoming increasingly clear that both developmentally and logically, the information-conveying aspect of language is built on the foundation of these kinds of context-dependent, social-context–driven, linguistic transactions (see, for example, Halliday 1975). Most oral and much written language works that way, rather than according to any syntactic-structural model of pure information transfer. When information transfer occurs it's based on a preexisting foundation of that kind of transaction.

A Conversational Model of Reading and Writing

Against the background of this rather elaborate argument, let me see if I can now say what I've come to mean by "meaning." (It should be obvious that I'm not going to say that it has a lot to do with information.) I think it has a good deal to do with what sociolinguistics has taught us to think of as "point." Most relevant here is the work of Labov (1972) and Polanyi (1979; 1985) on the way conversational stories allow tellers and listeners to share "points." To state the insight I draw from their work as simply as possible: when I recount an incident in a conversation, if you attend to what I say as though it were a series of factual assertions to be remembered, you generally lose the "point" utterly. My colleague Doug Vipond and I have based much of our theory of literary reading on this study of what happens when people tell stories in conversation (Hunt & Vipond 1986).

Over the past several years, we have been tinkering with a conceptual model of the literary reading process (Hunt & Vipond 1985; 1992). I think this model yields a useful tool for thinking about almost any language event (perhaps especially one involving written language). What we suggest is that the nature of the reading process is influenced by a range of variables that can be grouped into three categories: the *reader,* the *text,* and the *situation.* Just as altering the text will affect the nature of the process that occurs and thus the kind of point or meaning that may be constructed, so changing the reader or the situation in which the reading occurs will equally affect that process and its outcome.

The most obvious example, because it has been the most regularly explored, is the *text.* A grocery list, for example, affords (but doesn't guarantee) an information-centered reading, whereas a letter of apology for an inadvertent insult would tend to promote (but again, of course, doesn't guarantee) a socially engaged, point-driven reading.

Altering the *reader* might make just as much difference. A shopper might read the grocery list for information; you might read it as a sign of the writer's mood or status; someone else might read it as a coded message; or I might recognize it, on the counter next to the door, as an indirect reminder that I'd forgotten to stop at the store on the way home. You might be the recipient of the letter of apology and read it one way, but someone else, years later, might read it as an example of the author's late-middle style or of how capital letters were used during the time period, or as evidence in some irrelevant court case.

Equally important—and much less often considered—is the *situation* in which the reading occurs. I might encounter the grocery list in a book of found or concrete poems, or the letter of apology as a text in a reading comprehension test. Students might read the grocery list in the book of poems as part of their cramming for a final exam in an English course. A friend might hand me the text of the letter found in a reading test and say, "That's exactly the way I feel." Each of these situations would, clearly, produce very different readings of the same text by the same reader.

The distinction I am making is one that depends on seeing a written language event as either having or not having the pragmatic potential to establish, maintain, and deepen the social relations between people, which are what make up a culture. I have called the kinds of fragmentary, inane, artificial, committee-constructed pieces of written language one finds in textbooks and reading tests "textoids" (Hunt 1989); Chris Anson (1986) has expanded the idea to suggest that readers and situations may render texts otherwise whole and natural into textoids, devoid of human purpose and "stripped of their human richness and complexity" (21).

Another way to phrase this is to use the distinction Bakhtin draws between "text" and "utterance." (This is, by the way, a quite different use of the word "utterance" from that posited by David Olson [1977; see also Luke, De Castell & Luke 1983].) Bakhtin, in an essay probably written in 1952–53 (Holquist 1986, xv), contrasts the set of words and syntactic structures used by someone in a given situation (the *text*) with what the people in the situation actually *use* the text for (the *utterance*). In the case of the example I used earlier, the four words "Tell me about it" constitute the text: the utterance is quite different in the situation I presented from what it is when the same string of signifiers is used as an example in this paragraph, and would be quite different again when the four words occured in a new situation. Combining my term and Bakhtin's distinction, it's possible to say that the texts that *resist* being made into utterances—whether because of the situation, the users, or the string of signifiers themselves—are textoids. Circumstances in which no one is using the text as an utterance, as a vehicle for what Bakhtin calls dialogue, create textoids.

Language transactions that occur in such circumstances are, I suggest, essentially without the kind of social meaning I have been describing. One thing that is clearly important about such lack of meaning is that, as I have argued elsewhere (Hunt 1987; 1989), it makes it much more difficult for us to use to their full potential our powerful language-learning abilities and propensities. But whether one accepts that argument or not, it is easy to agree that such transactions are in some sense peculiar. What is not so easy to agree about, I think, is that if we are looking for examples of language transactions that are of that peculiar, sterile, meaningless kind, the best possible place to find them is in school and university. I would contend, in fact, that the written language events that occur in educational contexts are virtually *all* like that.

I should make clear here that I'm not beating the dead horse of drill-and-practice sheets, fill-in-the-blanks grammar exercises, basal readers, and comprehension questions. (That horse, although it's dead, is not gone—it's still out there roaming classrooms like a malignant zombie.) What specifically concerns me here are (1) my own (presumably enlightened) practices as a teacher of English over the past twenty-five years and (2) what seem to me to represent some of the best and most imaginative and thoughtful strategies among my professional colleagues. When we examine those assignments and those strategies in the light of this notion of meaning as social event, we discover some challenging truths; further, some facts about student reading and writing that we've all known and accepted with a good deal of equanimity for years take on a new urgency.

Teaching Without Meaning

Let me offer an example from my own teaching. A few years ago I asked an introductory literature class to read Hemingway's "Hills

Like White Elephants" and write their own responses to it. This was late in the course, so they'd had time to learn, if they were ever going to, that this was not a test and that individual and peculiar responses would be valued—or at least would not be "marked down." Covertly, I was hoping to find out how many students knew, before we discussed the story in class, that the "operation" that's the implicit subject of the whole conversation between the two Americans waiting at a railway station in Spain is an abortion. More overtly, I was trying to help the students use their writing to explore and extend their own understanding of the story before we discussed it in class.

The writing they handed in to me was of course appalling (not more appalling than usual, naturally, but still of a kind that you would only ever expect to see in a freshman literature class). What I saw at the time were the disastrous handwriting, the incomplete and ungrammatical sentences, the complete lack of transitions, the absence of any sense of direction (or, indeed, of the existence of a reader out there beyond the page), and the highly skilled evasion of the story's central issue. Based on those papers—virtually all of which amounted to highly general summaries of the discussion between the two characters and elaborately phrased and entirely abstract value judgments about the artistic merit of the text—I absolutely could not tell whether any of them had constructed a point for the story that was even remotely related to mine. My own had to do with the impact of the sudden discovery of pregnancy on this carefree, adolescent, Hemingway-style relationship. (In research since then I've discovered, based on samples of similar students, that it is extremely unlikely that in that situation more than one or two of them realized that the story was about an abortion.)

I can no longer find that set of papers among my souvenirs, but virtually all English teachers will be able to supply comparable sets from their own experience (the classic description of this experience, of course, is Mina Shaughnessy's [1977] account of the influx of basic writers into her teaching). My conclusion then, and the conclusion most of my colleagues have drawn from similar stacks of papers, was that the students couldn't write, and, in fact, that when you came right down to it they couldn't read either.

It should not come as a surprise that I now think rather differently about that situation. I now think the problem wasn't a matter of the students' capabilities at all but something quite different. The situation in which the students were acting virtually guaranteed that both their reading and their writing would be of the kind I have been describing as meaningless—that is, completely disconnected from any real social occasion or motive.

First, the reading. The students were reading as part of an assignment. Whatever I might say about the assignment (and at the time I didn't say much), they knew that their job with school assignments was to read, decode, store, and remember. Most of the texts they had encountered in school, from basal readers to history and science textbooks, were of course really textoids. They were not manufactured and created because someone had a point to make to a real audience. They were created because certain pieces of information had to be encoded in a language whose rhetorical choices and limitations were determined not by readers and writers but by readability formulas and the intense scrutiny of banks of editors, consultants, censors, and curriculum committees. But it's also true that even when "real" texts are encountered in school—poems written by poets, stories written by Hemingways, even (very rarely) expositions written by John McPhees or Stephen Jay Goulds—they are normally encountered in situations where it's extremely difficult to treat them as anything other than textoids. The possibility that the author, like the person across the table telling a story, might be engaged in sharing values and inviting the reader to make points is obliterated by the fact that the story is in reality the possession of, and is being offered to the student by, the textbook and the teacher—by the educational institution. It is not being offered by its speaker or author. And it's being offered not as an utterance but—as noted by Anne Freadman (1988)—as *an example* of something, a pretext for a test.

Even more powerfully, the students knew (however cleverly I thought I'd concealed it) that they were being tested. Everyone was, after all, reading the same story—obviously some would understand it "better" than others. Whatever I might say about differences being okay had been said to them by many teachers before me—just as sincerely and just as deceptively. They knew there was a "right answer," and furthermore, they knew that as always the teacher was the person who had it. My illusion that I could change a dozen years' worth of hard-learned lessons with a few weeks' exhortations was not only ill founded, it was also, in an important way, dishonest: there *was* a right answer, and I *did* have it. It involved abortion.

In the terms of the model of reading I described earlier, what we have is a case where the text, for the right reader and in the right situation, clearly would have afforded an engaged, pragmatic, dialogic, "real" reading for meaning. But the situation and the reader powerfully pulled for an empty, asocial search for isolated chunks of information. If I were to try to characterize the process of reading as it occurs in such a situation, I might contrast it with what happens in a conversation or in a strongly meaning-oriented reading. If the speaker says something incomprehensible, you hold on to it and look (wait actively) for explanation, on the assumption that the speaker is intending something—you impute coherent pragmatic intentions to the speaker. In a situation involving what you see as a textoid, however, you make no such assumption and so when something incomprehensible is encountered you simply pass over it—or, at best, you try to memorize it for the test.

My first point about that assignment, then, is that—primarily because of the situation—the reading the students did was virtually guaranteed not to have meaning at its center. It would be a rare student who could read the story in such a situation as though the story might have some purchase on him or her, as though it were being told to him or her by someone who had a reason for telling it and to whom it was possible to impute normal human intentions. Such students would have a highly developed ability to ignore the real situation in favor of a fictional one, would have what I've come to call a powerful pragmatic imagination. Another way to describe such students is to say they are already readers. Still another thing one might say is that they don't need much help from a teacher.

Now, writing. A second concern has to do with the potential role meaning might play in the writing the students did on the basis of this reading. What was it possible for them to mean in what they wrote? With whom could they have been trying to make contact, and what values, structures of knowledge, judgments of importance, and patterns of expectation could they have been trying to share? From their point of view, they could hardly expect to have anything to say about the story. Having something to say is not easily distinguishable from having someone to say it to, and in the view of those students—even after a few months' evidence of ignorance and incompetence on my part—I already knew everything there was to know about stories. I was the teacher, after all.

I could tell them—I probably did tell them—to write not to me but to a general reader; I might even have specified a general reader who had already read the story (to avoid long, pointless summaries). But the ability to engage such a mythical rhetorical reader in the active process of composition is rare. It requires the writer to use that imaginary figure to decide in specific instances—moments where language is being shaped at the point of utterance (Britton, Burgess, Martin, McLeod & Rosen 1975)—precisely how much reference to the events of the story is necessary for that reader, what inferences that reader can be called upon to make, which ideas can be backgrounded as "given," and which ideas need to be foregrounded as "new." It requires the kind of powerful pragmatic imagination that a very few students—the readers and the writers—have managed miraculously to retain. Very few of my students—then or now—have it. It's hard to imagine where they might have acquired it, other than in the sort of uncommon home where—as Gordon Wells (1986a;

1986b; 1987) has demonstrated so clearly—attitudes toward books and language create writers and readers.

A resource skilled writers often turn to in such a situation is the knowledge of how writing of the kind they are trying to produce sounds. Rather than using the real situation to generate purposes and readers, the writer uses the kinds of audiences that have been "invoked" (in Ede and Lunsford's [1984] useful term) by other, similar texts as a model. But my students had never in their lives read anything like what I was asking them to write—like, that is, the sort of thing teachers had increasingly been asking them to write throughout their school careers. No wonder they didn't produce such great texts—and no wonder they didn't learn very much that was of use to them from the exercise. Everything about the situation promoted treating the text they were reading as a textoid and producing textoids in response to my assignment. Meaning in the sense of social engagement or the sharing of structures of evaluation and understanding or "point" was just about entirely absent from the situation. They didn't read for meaning or write to convey it. Nor, not at all incidentally, did I read what they wrote for its meaning: I read it to find out what they knew—a completely different matter—and to assess their ability to write.

The absence of meaning, motive, and social context from this sort of literacy event is made more dramatic if we contrast it with the kinds of events described by Lee Odell and others who have been studying writing in the workplace in recent years (Odell 1985; Odell & Goswami 1982). When Odell asked insurance executives to explain the rhetorical choices they'd made in business letters and memos, he discovered an astonishing (astonishing to many of us academics, anyway) metarhetorical awareness and an equally surprising ability to articulate reasons for subtle choices. Why? It seems clear to me: because there were real motives and real readers and real consequences. Just as Vygotsky's (1978) infant learns what a gesture means by having it taken as a gesture, so (I infer) Odell's businessmen had learned the impact of certain kinds of phrases and organizational patterns because they had seen them have that impact. They were accustomed to dealing with written texts as though—in the terms I've been using here—they were written and read for meaning.

If it is true that there are profound and fundamental differences between the processes of reading and writing when conducted as empty exercises and when conducted for meaning (as I am defining it), then it seems to me that most of the adventurous and exciting theoretical and practical work that has been done in recent years in composition and in the teaching of literature may be pretty much beside the point. Separated from what I'm calling meaning, language itself becomes an empty, pointless exercise.

In the absence of preexisting intention and audience, planning tends to become the sort of perfunctory outlining we've all come to recognize ("Teacher tells us we have to have an outline, so I always do one after I've written the essay"), and invention a kind of meandering ooze of wordage ("prewriting"). In the absence of authentic situation, purpose, and reader, revision tends to become an aimless and pointless alteration, a sort of syntactic Brownian motion. In the absence of pragmatic context and intention, reading tends to become a passive act of decoding and storage, and interpretation and response tend to wander into an endless maze of free association and unfettered fantasy. "Analysis of poems" in English classes is often this sort of exercise.

Unless the making of social meaning is at the center, none of these activities are likely to provide much opportunity for learning how to handle language when it *is* at the center. Even more serious, I think, the predominance of these kinds of activities in educational institutions tends to inculcate one lesson very powerfully: written language, especially in academic settings (which should, I think, be seen as the peculiar case, rather than Odell's writing in *non*academic settings), does not have meaning at its center.

Alternatives

The obvious question to be raised at this point is whether there are any genuine, practical alternatives to the present situation. Are there ways, within the limits set by the institutional contexts in which teachers work, to create situations in which student reading and writing is meaningful in these terms? If there are no alternatives, what I'm arguing might be a theoretically interesting viewpoint but would in practice amount to little more than a depressing and self-indulgent orgy of woe crying and nay saying.

Having said all that, I don't imagine you will be surprised to discover that I believe there are alternatives. The ones I know most about are the ones occurring among some of my colleagues at St. Thomas University, and I would like to describe a couple of specific examples of alternative ways of structuring learning, ways that hold, I think, real promise for addressing some of the problems I have been describing.[1]

The basic strategy is something we've begun calling "collaborative investigation." In general, it entails creating a situation in which the class members organize themselves into a team to investigate cooperatively some specific topic, using writing as the fundamental tool for that organizing, that investigating, and that cooperation. Here is one example of how that works in practice. I'm going to describe it as concretely as I can and hope you can see some of the ways in which the reading and writing is done in a situation that makes them rather different from more conventional models.

I usually require my introductory literature class to attend a number of plays on campus or at the local professional theatre during the year. One year (after we'd conducted, for our own information, a couple of collaborative investigations of productions we were going to see), I suggested that we prepare what we wound up calling a Playgoer's Guide to an upcoming professional production of Lillian Hellman's *The Little Foxes*. We began by getting hold of a copy of the play and reading it. We didn't order twenty-nine copies; we shared library copies. We even shared the reading—by having groups read and present different parts of the play. We then generated questions about the play, Hellman, and the production. In this case, everyone wrote down as many questions as they could in fifteen or twenty minutes; the class then formed into groups to read one another's questions and select a few to write on the board. Then we edited and selected among those, and set up *ad hoc* groups to go to the library (I went as well) and find out what they could about particular questions—regarding, for instance, Lillian Hellman's life, the composition of the play, its historical background, its previous productions, and so forth. Each group prepared a short, concrete report. Sometimes these took the form of a set of separate, individual reports; in other cases they were researched and written in collaboration. Each of these reports was photocopied, and in class the next week each of a new set of groups received a sheaf of documents that included a copy of each of those first reports. They read and discussed them and generated a new set of questions. Again these were written on the board, edited and discussed, and assigned to groups, which took the relevant reports, with their lists of references, and went back to the library to prepare additional or elaborative reports.

The second round of reports were also photocopied. We spent part of a class session arriving at a consensus as to what should go in the final handbook and set up groups to combine various reports into sections of the handbook. These sections were finally edited by other groups, and then given to a secretary (me, as it happened) to be typed into a computer file, typeset, laid out, and printed. The final handbooks were distributed in multiple copies to the class and class members left them around the university a day or so before the play opened. They were snatched up more rapidly than I could photocopy them, and many of my students reported instances of being thanked for their work by people they hardly knew who'd picked up copies somewhere.

In the final part of the process, everyone in class wrote a review of some aspect of the play. The reviews were read by everyone else in class, formed the basis of a discussion, and were then jointly edited by five groups into separate consensus reviews, which we photocopied and sent to the publicity director of the theatre company.

It may be important to point out that I was not the first or only or final reader of any piece of writing produced in this process; I did not mark, comment on, or edit any piece of writing (except that because I was secretary I ran a spell check on the final copy). There were no essays on or interpretations of or analyses of the play. And it is certainly important to make clear that the document that was finally produced is far from wonderful—it's scrappy, sometimes superficial, and in at least one case erroneous. But—like the texts produced on the way to it—it is clearly an authentically functional piece of written text. And it was obvious to everyone involved that without the social interaction structured by all those intermediate texts, it would have been impossible to accomplish the final task or learn what we learned about Hellman and her play. Perhaps more important, in every case rhetorical decisions were made, at the point of utterance, in the light of obvious, real demands: the writers knew who would be reading this, and how much they knew—and even, to some extent, how they felt about it.

There are a variety of other ways in which the reading and writing that students do in connection with their learning can be made more obviously and practically functional, more clearly something written and read for meaning rather than in order to demonstrate competence or exercise rhetorical skills. This is simply one fairly recent example; the classes of some of my colleagues at St. Thomas would offer a wealth of others. Many whole language classes that are engaged in what Frank Smith (1988)—and John Dixon and Leslie Stratta (1984) before him—call "enterprises" offer still more. What is most important is that such strategies are not difficult to come up with once one has embraced the basic notion—that the way to create a context in which students are writing and reading for meaning is to put the writing and reading into situations where they serve purposes the students can see as real and can adopt as their own. The danger, of course, is that once you've embraced that notion, there isn't any going back: the changes and the discoveries acquire their own momentum. You get hooked.

I didn't tell that to my colleague who wanted to know what I was trying to say about putting meaning at the center of my teaching. But

now at least I've finally figured out for myself what it was I was trying to say. Whether I can hook him remains to be seen.

Notes

1. I'm using an instance from work I've done in my own classes, but I should
make clear that it represents a great deal of shameless plagiarism from the ideas
of my colleagues—especially Thom Parkhill in Religious Studies, Doug Vipond in
Psychology, and Jim Reither in English (see Parkhill 1988 and Reither & Vipond
1989). And many aspects of these ideas are derived from work originally done by
whole language teachers with younger children, much of it by my wife, Anne
Hunt, whose work over the last four or five years on a research project involving
the writing of first and second graders has led her to develop many of these strategies for making writing and reading meaningful (see Hunt, Cameron & Linton
1989).

References

Anson, C. M. 1986. Reading, writing, and intention. *Reader* 16:20-35.

Bakhtin, M. M. 1986. *Speech genres and other late essays.* Trans. V. W. McGee &
ed. C. Emerson & M. Holquist. Austin: University of Texas Press.

Bialostosky, D. 1989. Dialogic criticism. In *Contemporary literary theory,* ed. G. D.
Atkins & Laura Morrow, 214-28. Amherst: University of Massachusetts
Press.

Britton, J., T. Burgess, N. Martin, A. McLeod, & H. Rosen. 1975. *The development of writing abilities* (11-18). London: Macmillan Education.

Bruner, J. C. 1983. *Child's talk.* New York: Norton.

Dixon, J. & L. Stratta. 1984. *Student enterprises with personal and social value.*
Series B: Writing 14 to 18. Discussion Booklet 3. ERIC Document ED 268
522.

Ede, L. & A. Lunsford. 1984. Audience addressed/audience invoked: The role of
audience in composition theory and pedagogy. *College Composition and
Communication* 35:155-71.

Freadman, A. 1988. "Genre" and the reading class. *Typereader: The Journal of the
Center for Studies in Literary Education* 1:1-7.

Halliday, M. A. K. 1975. *Learning how to mean: Explorations in the development
of language.* London: Elsevier North-Holland.

———. 1978. *Language as social semiotic: The social interpretation of language
and meaning.* Baltimore, MD: University Park Press.

Harste, J. C., V. A. Woodward & C. L. Burke. 1984. *Language stories and literacy
lessons.* Portsmouth, NH: Heinemann.

Hassan, I. 1987. Making sense: The trials of postmodern discourse. *New Literary
History* 18:437-59.

Holquist, M. 1986. Introduction. In *Speech genres and other late essays,* ed. C. Emerson & M. Holquist & trans. V. W. McGee, ix–xxiii). Austin: University of Texas Press.

———. 1991. *Dialogism: Bakhtin and his world.* New York: Routledge.

Houston, J. E., ed. & lex. 1987. *Thesaurus of ERIC descriptions.* 11th ed. Phoenix, AZ: Oryx Press.

Hunt, A. K., C. A. Cameron & M. J. Linton. 1989. *Writing workshop modules.* Fredericton: University of New Brunswick. Typescript.

Hunt, R. A. 1987. "Could you put in lots of holes?" Modes of response to writing. *Language Arts* 64(2):229–32.

———. 1989. A horse named Hans, a boy named Shawn: The Herr von Osten theory of response to writing. In *Writing and response: Theory, practice, and research,* ed. Chris Anson. Urbana, IL: National Council of Teachers of English.

Hunt, R. A. & D. Vipond. 1985. Crash-testing a transactional model of literary reading. *Reader* 14:23–39.

———. 1986. Evaluations in literary reading. *TEXT* 6:53–71.

———. 1992. First, catch the rabbit: The methodological imperative and the dramatization of dialogic reading. In *Multidisciplinary perspectives on literacy research,* ed. R. Beach, J. Green, M. Kamil & T. Shanahan, 69–90. Urbana, IL: National Conference on Research in English.

Kamuf, P. 1986. Floating authorship. *Diacritics* 16:3–13.

Kaye, K. 1982. *The mental and social life of babies: How parents create persons.* Chicago: University of Chicago Press.

Kaye, K. & R. Charney. 1980. How mothers maintain "dialogue" with two-year-olds. In *The social foundations of language and thought: Essays in honor of Jerome S. Bruner,* ed. D. R. Olson, 211–30. New York: Norton.

Krashen, S. D. 1981. *Second language acquisition and second language learning.* Oxford: Pergamon.

Labov, W. 1972. *Language in the inner city: Studies in the Black English vernacular.* Philadelphia: University of Pennsylvania Press.

LeFevre, K. B. 1987. *Invention as a social act.* Carbondale: Southern Illinois University Press.

Luke, C., S. De Castell & A. Luke. 1983. Beyond criticism: The authority of the school text. *Curriculum Inquiry* 13:111–27.

Mitchell, W. J. T., ed. 1986. *Against theory: Literary studies and the new pragmatism.* Chicago: University of Chicago Press.

Newman, J. M. 1986. *The craft of children's writing.* Portsmouth, NH: Heinemann.

———. 1991. *Interwoven conversations: Teaching and learning through critical reflection.* Toronto: OISE Press.

———, ed. 1985. *Whole language: Theory in use.* Portsmouth, NH: Heinemann.

Odell, L. 1985. Beyond the text: Relations between writing and the social context. In *Writing in nonacademic settings,* ed. L. Odell & D. Goswami. New York: Guilford.

Odell, L. & D. Goswami. 1982. Writing in a non-academic setting. *Research in the Teaching of English* 16:201–24.

Olson, D. R. 1977. From utterance to text: The bias of language in speech and writing. *Harvard Educational Review* 47:257–81.

Parkhill, T. 1988. Inkshedding in religion studies: Underwriting collaboration. *Inkshed* 7(4):1–4.

Polanyi, L. 1979. So what's the point? *Semiotica* 25:207–41.

———. 1985. *Telling the American story: A structural and cultural analysis of conversational storytelling.* Norwood, NJ: Ablex.

Reddy, M. J. 1979. The conduit metaphor: A case of frame conflict in our language about language. In *Metaphor and Thought,* ed. A. Ortony, 284–324. Cambridge, UK: Cambridge University Press.

Reither, J. A. 1985. Writing and knowing: Toward redefining the writing process. *College English* 47:620–28.

———. 1990. The writing *student* as researcher: Learning from our students. In *The writing teacher as researcher: Essays in the theory and practice of class-based research,* ed. D. A. Daiker & M. Morenberg, 247–55. Portsmouth, NH: Boynton/Cook.

Reither, J. A. & D. Vipond. 1989. Writing as collaboration. *College English* 51:855–67.

Shaughnessy, M. P. 1977. *Errors and expectations: A guide for the teacher of basic writing.* New York: Oxford University Press.

Smith, F. 1982. *Understanding reading: A psycholinguistic analysis of reading and learning to read.* 3d. ed. New York: Holt, Rinehart & Winston.

———. 1985. A metaphor for literacy: Creating worlds or shunting information? In *Literacy, language, and learning: The nature and consequences of reading and writing,* ed. D. R. Olson, N. Torrance & A. Hildyard, 195–213. Cambridge, UK: Cambridge University Press.

———. 1988. *Joining the literacy club: Further essays into education.* Portsmouth, NH: Heinemann.

Vygotsky, L. S. 1978. *Mind in society: The development of higher psychological processes.* Ed. M. Cole, V. John-Steiner, S. Scribner & E. Souberman. Cambridge, MA: Harvard University Press.

Wells, G. 1986a. The language experience of five-year-old children at home and at school. In *The social construction of literacy,* ed. J. Cook-Gumperz, 69–93. Cambridge, UK: Cambridge University Press.

———. 1986b. *The meaning makers: Children learning language and using language to learn.* Portsmouth, NH: Heinemann.

———. 1987. Apprenticeship in literacy. *Interchange* 1(1/2):109–23.

Wertsch, J. V. 1983. The role of semiosis in L. S. Vygotsky's theory of human cognition. In *Sociogenesis of language and human conduct,* ed. B. Bain, 17–31. New York: Plenum.

———. 1986. *Vygotsky and the social formation of mind.* Cambridge, MA: Harvard University Press.

8

Helping Students Control Texts: Contemporary Literary Theory into Classroom Practice

Jack Thomson

My aim as an English teacher is to help my students to construct themselves as choice-making human beings as well as literate ones. They will be highly literate people but conscious of their literacy and of the purposes for which they can use it, and able to make choices about how they will use it because they value some of those purposes and activities over others. Literacy, of course, is not something we have but—rather—is something we do. It is a practice, an activity, we engage in. Too often those we teach are seen as passive receivers of culture rather than as potentially active makers of it, as objects operated on by society rather than as operators in it, as readers not writers of the world. As teachers, I think we should see all learners as people who can be helped to write, or construct, their lives and their culture as well as to read and understand them.

My examples come largely from my work and research in reading and response to literature (Thomson 1987), but the principles these examples illustrate are more widely applicable to reading, writing, and responding to all kinds of texts and, more widely still, to all learning processes. By texts I don't just mean imaginative literature such as fiction and poetry, but all the sign systems and signifying practices of our culture from the poems of John Milton to the music of Elton John, from the films of Peter Weir to the portrayal of women in advertisements and the rhetorical techniques of *60 Minutes*. All our regular institutional and social practices, including our social rituals and ceremonies, are texts to be read and interpreted.

Here is a piece of writing by a seventeen-year-old secondary student whom I regard as a highly literate, thinking, choice-making human being.

Reply to Alexander Pope:
"The Characters of Women"

Poor Mr. Pope, how sadly sounds your jejune gibe
How little knowledge in your diatribe.
Pathetically it doth but prove
You are an outcast from the joys of love,
Which all great poets have inspired and amused
Leaves you silly, bitter and bemused.

Limited by a dated mind and a tedious sense of wit,
This diminutive bore (and nothing more),
A pack of lies hath writ.
In malicious words Pope seeks to explain
That which is above him. How foolish! How vain!
For women are superior, more complex and clever;
Pope could not grasp that if he tried forever.

Your rhymes have all the acid savours
Of one denied a lady's favours.
A cowardly boy and truant from the college
Of life's pursuit of pleasure and of knowledge —
Of how to capture women's interest and affection
You are condemned to ignorance and dejection;
Of which womankind presents the highest level
If only you could grasp it, poor old witless devil.

So let Pope write, complain and curse
For whatever our faults, men's are worse!

This student uses the structures of the poetry of Alexander Pope to argue against, to rebut, to reply to, what she sees to be his offensive, sexist ideology. The poem is not perfection, but there are some very effective couplets with the rougher ones. The writer knows how Pope achieves his effects, or how he works over his readers, because she has tried out his methods with some success.

How this girl and successful students like her learned to read and write so competently is the subject of the rest of this chapter. I want to speculate about her educational history, to outline and to give *some* examples of some of the range of activities in English that I believe need to constitute the curriculum because they develop students' literacy and give them power to control their whole learning—the kinds of things in reading and writing that happened in this girl's classrooms from kindergarten to grade eleven (where she is now) that helped her to develop this textual power.

Literary Theory: Assumptions for Practice

All of the activities I am going to outline are theoretically under-
pinned by the work in language and education of people like James
Britton, Douglas Barnes, John Dixon, Leslie Stratta, and Andrew
Wilkinson in England, James Moffett and Donald Graves in the
United States, and Garth Boomer (on negotiating the curriculum) in
Australia. They also emanate from my understanding of contemporary literary theories and my research with secondary school students on reading processes. Most English teachers will be very familiar with the theory and research on language as a tool of learning, and
probably with much of contemporary literary theory, some aspects of
which I eclectically dragooned to the service of my research. But I
want to say a few things about those aspects of it that were pertinent
in explaining the responses and attitudes of the eighth-grade (age
thirteen and fourteen) and tenth-grade (age fifteen and sixteen) students in that research. The main ideas I have derived from contemporary literary theories for practice in the classroom are these:

1. The meaning of a text is not in the words on the page. Meaning is
   made by readers in interaction with text. What readers bring to
   make sense of a text is their own personal experience, their cultural knowledge, including their sets of values and beliefs (ideology), and their experience of reading literature. We will all interpret a text in different ways because we bring different
   repertoires of experience, knowledge, belief, and understanding
   to our reading. For example, some readers might—even today—
   agree with Pope's eighteenth-century views on the place of
   women in society. The writer of the poem I began with doesn't!

2. Texts are constructs made by fallible human beings, and students
   can construct their own texts, using the rhetorics of authors they
   read, as the eleventh-grade girl did and as all students at all levels can. As students write literature of their own, they begin to
   read literature from a writer's viewpoint and write literature
   from a reader's viewpoint.

   In other arts subjects in the curriculum—art and music—
   students are required to perform and create as well as to appreciate the works of others. Only in English have we traditionally set
   up a portrait-gallery model of the curriculum as opposed to a
   workshop model. We have expected our students to walk through
   the gallery of great writers and admire what they see, but not to
   touch the works or to create any of their own. This emanates, I
   think, from a notion of the imaginative writer as divinely inspired,
   doing something beyond the capacities of ordinary mortals. I

think this is a Romantic myth; it turns literature into something to be approved of unquestioningly. To gain control over someone else's text you need to be able to write your own text, even if only as a response to the ideology of the one you have read when you disagree with its ideology, as the eleventh-grade girl did.

3. Writers and their texts, as well as readers, are shaped by their culture. Membership of different social and national groups, differences of class, race, gender, politics, religion, age, and so on, as well as their time and place in history, influence the way writers and readers write and read texts. This makes it important for readers to try to make explicit the underpinning ideology of texts they read—how they are being shaped by the values implicit in a text—as well as to work out their own ideologies as readers. A key question for readers to answer about their reading is, then, "What is it that I am bringing to the text that causes me to respond as I do?" (See the Appendix for an extract from the course outline of the first English unit for students training to be primary teachers at Charles Sturt University: Mitchell, in Bathurst, Australia. It shows the way literary theory is initially formulated for introduction to students who have just finished secondary education.)

    The ideology of a text is something that we need to help students to read and get control over, and it can be done from kindergarten through university.

4. As well as reading the ideologies of texts and self, readers should also make conscious to themselves their own constructive reading strategies. This reflexive understanding is very powerful knowledge, and it helps people control their own learning processes. If we know what we know, and if we know how we came to know it, we are powerful people. If we don't know what we know that is relevant to the task or problem at hand we can't use that knowledge to complete the task or solve the problem. As the students in my research became conscious of the constructive strategies they were using in their reading, they began to move toward higher levels of response and to gain greater control of what they were reading in doing so.

5. Because we all bring different repertoires of experience, cultural knowledge, literary understanding, and belief to the texts we read, it must be permissible in the classroom to dislike texts that other people like and be bored by texts that other people find exciting. The important point is that boredom and antagonism in response to a text should not be seen as the end of response, but rather the beginning of an exploration of these responses by

those who experience them. The questions to explore, then, are "What does boredom mean to me in relation to this text?" and "What is it that I am bringing to the text, and what is the text bringing to me, that causes me to be antagonized by it?"

All of the secondary students in my research saw their English teachers as custodians of the great texts of literature, custodians of this secular scripture (Scholes 1985), and believed that teachers required them to admire all the texts they asked them to read. Their schooling has conditioned them to believe that they are required to like all the texts in their course if they are to pass it. As an antidote to this, I tell first-semester students that I lost out to my colleagues in the selection of texts for their course and that I dislike most of the books on it. Students are invariably stunned at this. The idea of an English teacher actually disliking a published text on an English course is a shock. I tell them I hope they'll like at least some of the texts but that liking is not the most important issue, that when they don't like a text they can still derive a great deal of value from it—and succeed in the course—by exploring themselves and the text concerned in order to find out what it is about them and the text that causes them to dislike it. They find this permissibility to dislike texts liberating.

Reading literature can help people think about significant issues in their world, but it doesn't help people think at all if they believe they are expected to regurgitate someone else's more authoritative interpretations and judgements.

6. Teachers have a responsibility to make explicit to students what their purposes and intentions are in asking them to engage in all the activities they devise for them. Teachers need to pass on the secrets of the curriculum. Students need to know why they are being asked to read this particular text and to engage in these specific activities related to it. Students also need to be trained to ask "why" questions about the curriculum: "Why are we doing this? What's the point of it? How does it further the basic aims of our course?" Also, at the completion of each unit of work in English, students should be required to reflect on what they have learned and to make explicit to themselves how they learned it, so they have conscious understanding—and therefore control— of their own knowledge and learning processes (including, of course, their own reading and writing processes). It all depends, of course, on what the teacher's purposes are. If you want your students to become conscious learners and independent, choice-making human beings, these are the kinds of approaches you will

use. If you want them to be ciphers for the industrial and commercial machine, you will do something else. However, if we don't help our students to control their reading, writing, and learning processes and to become decision-making human beings, if we persist in socializing them into compliance with the prevailing modes of thought in our society, English, like the rest of the humanities, risks a future of being merely an aesthetic frill in the curriculum or, worse, an instrument of manipulation for the technical training of clerical ciphers.

Reading, Interpretation, and Criticism

A very useful set of strategies for helping students to gain control over textual processes in reading and writing is offered by Robert Scholes (1985) in his outline of teaching the progressive skills of "reading," "interpretation," and "criticism" (18–73). I will illustrate Scholes' approach very briefly by using it to explore the significations of a minor character in Conrad's *Heart of Darkness*. I did this in one of my own classes because several students asked about this character, "Why are we not supposed to like the Russian? What has Conrad got against him?" and other students had replied, rather impatiently, by saying things like, "Because he's so obviously stupid," "ridiculous," "ignorant," "weak," "clueless," "a babe in the woods," and so on. To pursue these questions and replies takes us from reading, through interpretation, to criticism. The students who asked the questions in the first place were actually at the stage of Scholes' "interpretation," but they saw their problems here as faults in their reading, not entertaining it as a possibility that there might be incoherences or contradictions in the text. The students who replied in a way that suggests they saw the answer as simple and obvious were reading in what Catherine Belsey (1980) calls an *expressive-realist* way, assuming that language is a transparent window on reality, that there is a direct connection between word and thing, and ignoring the constructedness of character. They were not aware that the language used constructs the objects and characters described. They certainly needed to be helped to progress beyond Scholes' "reading" stage. Scholes' "reading" is a "submission to the power of the text," a giving of oneself to the text uncritically, a largely unconscious activity, which requires some tacit knowledge of the conventions of narrative and very little conscious skill. The knowledge required to "construct characters, situations, and a world out of words" is of the "codes" or conventions "that were operative in the composition of the text and the historical situation in which it was composed" (21). "Interpretation" involves moving from a summary of textual events to a consideration of their significance; and "criticism" is "a critique of the themes developed in a text, or a critique of the codes out of which a text has been constructed" (23); that is, the reader criticizes the text by exerting his or her own power against the text to resist its representation of the world and/or the ideology underpinning it. Too often our students see literary criticism as the practice of subordinating their human, ethical, and political reactions to some ideal of literary value. I think we have a responsibility to help them unravel and evaluate the themes and ideologies of texts they read rather than see them as some kind of divine or secular authority. As Scholes puts it,

> In working through the stages of reading, interpretation, and criticism, we move from a submission to textual authority in reading, through a sharing of textual power in interpretation, toward an assertion of power through opposition in criticism. (39)

As teachers, Scholes says, "our job is not to intimidate students with our own superior textual production, it is to show them the codes upon which all textual production depends, and to encourage their own textual practice" (24–25).

Reading

Coming to understand our own "reading" involves being able to answer questions like "What makes a story a story?" and "How does a writer construct a character?" To help students make explicit (so that they become fully conscious of) how they construct a character, Scholes invites them to list and discuss the adjectives and adverbs applying to the protagonist (in this case the young Russian) and to his oppositional character (in this case Marlow) in the scenes in which they appear together. Here are some brief extracts from Marlow's narrative of scenes between these characters so that you can do for yourself what my students did. The narrator is Marlow.

> His aspect reminded me of something I had seen—something funny I had seen somewhere. As I manoeuvred to get alongside, I was asking myself, "What does this fellow look like?" Suddenly I got it. He looked like a harlequin. His clothes had been made of some stuff that was brown holland probably, but it was covered with patches all over; with bright patches, blue, red, and yellow—patches on the back, patches on the front, patches on elbows, on knees; coloured binding around his jacket, scarlet edging at the bottom of his trousers. . . . A beardless, boyish face, very fair, no features to speak of, nose peeling, little blue eyes,

smiles and frowns chasing each other over that open countenance like sunshine and shadow on a wind-swept plain. . . .

I looked at him, lost in astonishment. There he was before me, in motley, as though he had absconded from a troupe of mimes, enthusiastic, fabulous. His very existence was improbable, inexplicable, and altogether bewildering. He was an insoluble problem. It was inconceivable how he had existed, how he had succeeded in getting so far, how he had managed to remain—why did he not instantly disappear. (Conrad 1986, 90,93)

After a discussion of the descriptions and the impressions formed from them, the next reading steps were intended to get students to characterize both the young Russian "harlequin" and Marlow (as he appears in these scenes) in their own words, to describe Marlow as the Russian might have described him, and then to describe the Russian again, as they, as readers, saw him. In this way, not only is the constructedness of character made visible to the students, but so is the opposition between the two characters upon which meaning will depend. Students will recognize, in the difference between their impression of Marlow and the impression they hypothesize the Russian might form of him, the way interpretations are created out of different points of view. (Meaning depends on who is telling the story to whom, where, and when.)

Interpretation

Interpretation depends on understanding the cultural codes "implicated" in any text. How do we get our students to make the move from "It's about this young Russian in Africa and his meeting with an Englishman" to "It's about experience and inexperience, age and youth, worldly wisdom and ignorance"—from characters and events to generalized themes and values? We can use the structuralist insights into repetitions and oppositions, similarities and differences, parallels and contrasts, and consider what they represent. This is a matter of "making connections between a particular verbal text and its larger cultural text" (Scholes 1985, 33). In discussion emanating from the "reading" activities, the oppositions between Marlow and the Russian were formulated. Also, this discussion produced relevant information about the cultural coding of the story, its location in politics and history. That is, most of the students knew enough about European imperialism in Africa in the nineteenth century and the exploitation involved to "place" the novel. In cooperative group discussion, various students produced insights about the differences between the historical accounts of imperialism they had read at school in different history

texts, about Russian industrial backwardness at the time (the "slum-
bering Russian bear" one student said she read in a history book), and
the way an Englishman, like Marlow, would feel that while it was
appropriate for an Englishman like him to be in Africa as a representative of a progressive, colonizing, and civilizing nation, a Russian
would not only be an unexpected visitor but an out-of-place one as well.
(Sometimes, students may need to be sent to the library to get the
cultural and historical information they need to understand these
codes of a text so they can use them to make meanings.) From this
pooled information, patterns of understanding—or interpretation—
emerged. Students began to see that in the context of both the historical setting of the novel and the cultural context in which it was
produced and consumed, Marlow and the young Russian might represent not only an age/youth opposition but an English/Russian opposition as well, with attendant oppositions like advanced/backward,
enlightened/unenlightened, and so on. To interpret and to criticize a
text it is essential to get outside its own boundaries. Where the New
Critics would describe the cultural codes that enable us to go beyond
submission to the text as "non-literary" or "extra-literary" considerations, using them to respond is absolutely essential if readers are to
exercise textual power.

Criticism

"How can we honestly encourage our students to be critical—to produce texts against text?" asks Scholes (1985, 35). In the case we are
looking at here, this was not difficult. The students connected the binary oppositions they had located and the cultural codes relating the
text to the world with their recognition that the point of view of Marlow, the narrator, is fully endorsed by the implied author: they both
have the same notions of British superiority. We never really see the
Russian youth "as he is" because Marlow constructs our perception
for us, and this perception is warmly endorsed by Conrad. In pointing
out the pleasure Marlow takes in mocking the young Russian as a
figure of fun, some of the students asked questions about his and Conrad's motives and speculated that it might be Conrad's cover for his
own bitterness at finding the whole imperialist enterprise wasn't living up to his ideal of civilization. Not all the students took up the same
position of resistance to the text: they didn't all end up agreeing that
the Russian "harlequin" is a cartoon figure produced out of notions of
British superiority, one who commits the cardinal sin of being young
and not in the know. However, those who rejected this meaning did not
merely submit docilely to the superior authority of the text but argued
from evidence to support their own "criticism," knowing not only
what they believed and valued, but also why. Everyone did end up

questioning the authority (and ideology) of the text and recognized that it was not necessary to see the Russian as deficient in some way and Marlow as the arbiter of wisdom and right values.

One way of helping students to move from "interpretation" to "criticism" is to ask them where their sympathies are in a text and where they think the author's sympathies are. If their sympathies as readers are the same as what they see to be the sympathies of the implied author, they can be further asked whether they think it is possible that they are being manipulated by the text. This produces really penetrating discussion and enlightenment.

Finally, another useful teaching idea for helping students to criticize texts and unpack their concealed ideologies is transposing their elements (Hollindale 1988). For example, if parts of the text were rewritten by students so that Marlow were to become Malinkov, a Russian; Kurtz to become Curtis, an English trader; and the "harlequin" to become Windsor, a young Englishman just down from Oxford, the ideology implicit in the original text becomes a little more apparent in the reversals. Changes of gender, race, nationality, class, and age like this can be both entertaining and revealing. Imagine Miss Marlow, for example, as black, African, working-class, female, and young! Further, change the setting and have the Company headquarters in London rather than Brussels and the "great river" in the United States, not Africa. Further still, modernize the details: for example, have the "big river" as the Mekong in Vietnam in 1960 rather than the Congo in the nineteenth century and turn Marlow into an educated, middle-class black American senator on a fact-finding mission. Textual silences and contradictions start to open up for students when they are engaged in this kind of deconstructive re-creation.

Classroom Activities

Students Monitoring Their Own Reading Process

One of the most productive and unanticipated findings of my research workshops is that students can be taught to become conscious of their own constructive reading strategies whatever their stage of reading development. Here is an example. After reading the opening paragraph of a short story or novel to a group of nonreaders, I asked them two questions:

1. What happened in your head while you were listening?

2. What do you think might happen in the story?

All of these students were surprised at the notion that they should be doing anything mentally active. They thought that text operated on readers rather than that readers operated on texts; that the minds of

good readers automatically processed print into understanding; and
the fact that their minds didn't seem to do this too well indicated that
they were "bad" readers because they were unintelligent. The act of
asking students what questions they were asking of the text read to
them led them to ask productive questions, and the enabling security
of the workshop situation led them to think aloud while doing so.

Here is one boy, a fourteen-year-old nonreader in a remedial class
responding to the opening sections of Betsy Byars' novel *The Cartoonist*. At the beginning of this novel, the central character, Alfie,
rejects his mother's request to come downstairs to watch television
with her. He prefers to stay in his room drawing a cartoon. Following
my reading of this bit to him, the student said, "I would really like to
know what his comic strip shows and why it is so important to him."
Here is the description of the cartoon being drawn by Alfie:

> In the first square a man was scattering birdseed from a bag labelled
> "Little Bird Seed." In the next square little birds were gobbling up the
> seeds.
>   In the third square the man was scattering birdseed from a bag
> labelled "Big Bird Seed." In the next square big birds were gobbling up
> the seeds.
>   In the fifth square the man was scattering huge lumps from a bag
> labelled "Giant Bird Seed." In the last square a giant bird was gobbling
> up the little man. (Byars 1981, 5–6)

The listener's response to this was a surprised laugh and the following unprompted comment:

> I expected the giant birds to eat up the giant food instead of the man, and
> I thought it would go on to have super giant seeds for a Super Bird to eat.
> But that's great. I really like that, the way you expect one thing and it gets
> turned round on you. It gives you a surprise and it's very funny. I really
> like jokes like that. Are there lots more like that in the book?

Later on, he speculated that since Alfie would rather draw cartoons in
his room than watch television with his mother, "he might be a boy
who does things on his own and mightn't get on with other kids."
This student has taken the first step to becoming an active reader. As
with all the other nonreaders and reluctant readers, his developing
consciousness of his own reading strategies is turning him into a real
reader. Almost all the nonreading students said at the end of the
workshops things like "I didn't know so much happened in my mind
when I read" and "I've never been any good at reading but I know
some of the ways to make it more interesting now." In the workshops
the students became conscious of the productive strategies that the
questions led them to use. The workshop situation did for students'

reading what Donald Graves' (1983) "conferencing" approach does for their writing. It was not that these students were intellectually incapable of reading with enjoyment and understanding but rather that they had not been placed before in situations in which they could learn how to go about it successfully. They possessed the capacity for reading productively but seemed not to have experienced situations that called on them to use that capacity.

Here are some extracts from the transcript of a discussion with a more successful fourteen-year-old Bathurst boy about his reading of Robert Cormier's novel *I Am the Cheese*. They illustrate that paradoxical combination of emotional involvement and cool detachment that characterizes the reflective and evaluative processes of the good reader.

> In *I Am the Cheese* you feel really sympathetic with Adam and you like him, but you only realize at the end that the journey was a dream world, his imagination. I found the ending terrifying, not because it was hard to understand but because it became so clear. . . . Adam was a total victim. He is treated as a threatening thing, not as a boy or a person. He had no chance. If he knew anything they'd kill him. If he didn't they'd have to keep him permanently drugged in case he remembered something. It's not until the last section that you completely understand his problem and it's a bit of a shock.

> Sitting back reading, you don't have the same feelings as the character himself has because you are not in his position but judging. A character might misjudge his predicament but you as reader don't because you're not in the situation creating fear, panic, or happiness or whatever it is. It's like looking at a football match from the stand where you can see the mistakes and the tactics that go wrong, but the person playing is doing his best under pressure and he can't see the patterns you can. I have no wish to be a backseat driver. Some kids like to be backseat drivers in reading, but they might think the novel is life when it's only a picture of life. It's not actually happening. It shows you what the writer thinks life is like . . . and you're trying to learn what his view of life is like. . . .

> You judge where the character might misjudge because of his emotions. You know more than they do. Even in *I Am the Cheese,* where you don't know more than Adam until the last bit, you are not him, but you know the author will let you know even if Adam doesn't find out. So you will understand something about life and something about him that he mightn't understand himself.

This boy sees the events as the character he empathizes with sees them, but he understands them as the author does. He has that meta-cognitive understanding of his own productive reading strategies that

makes him a powerful reader and learner. It is in getting students to
first articulate their honest responses and then reflect on the knowledge implicit in these responses that this powerful reflexive understanding can be developed.

Another fourteen-year-old boy said that one of his productive
reading strategies was to compare the endings of novels with their
beginnings to see the significant changes:

> At the beginning I like to think what's going to happen towards the end,
> what changes might take place, and what things are going to be the
> same. You want to know if the characters will solve their problems, if
> they will continue to make the same mistakes, or if they will learn from
> them, and what all this shows about them. At the end, I like to compare
> events with the beginning and think about what's changed and why.

Students Writing Reading Journals

One effective way of developing this reflexive understanding is
through the keeping of reading journals. In the reading journal,
because of its first-draft, instant-response, thinking-aloud-on-paper
kind of informality, students make discoveries in the act of writing.
The personal and exploratory style helps to generate interpretive
abstractions. Writing really does become an instrument of learning.

Here is a sixteen-year-old Bathurst boy's comments in his reading journal about his difficulty in becoming the implied reader of Jane
Austen's novel *Northanger Abbey*:

> Perhaps I cannot relate to such experiences that Catherine endures
> because I'm NOT a female in the eighteenth century in Bath, and I also
> haven't been accustomed to going to balls enduring the pleasure of
> meeting ODD people and discussing PETTY things such as clothing
> and hats. I just don't have any sympathy with wealthy people who never
> work and have unlimited time to gossip.

His teacher's written question/comment in response shows the way
in which knowledgeable teachers can help teenage readers to understand and control both the conventions of literature and their own
reactions to texts. This student was an enthusiastic reader of science
fiction, so his teacher wrote:

> Would you react in a similar fashion to a science fiction novel peopled by
> weird aliens and set far into the future on another planet? Try to explain
> your reactions to this question. What are you learning about literature,
> yourself, and your own reactions to texts from this?

Here the student came to recognize that he objected to nineteenth-century literary conventions in a Jane Austen novel but that he was perfectly happy to accept contemporary literary conventions in science fiction, and that he did this because he was used to accepting the conventions of science fiction. He learned about his own cultural assumptions. From comments like these, students become more conscious of the constructedness of texts and of the ways they read them, and so develop greater textual power as readers and writers.

In their reading journals my students have to "tell the story of their reading of texts," which Aidan Chambers (1985, 132) says is precisely what literary criticism is. For example, after reading Robert Lowell's poem "Skunk Hour," jotting down their first responses, and then sharing these with one another in small groups, students were asked to spend some time reading over their first-response statements and to make another written statement about what they had found out about their own reading strategies and cultural assumptions. Here is eighteen-year-old Eliza's reflexive commentary on her first response:

> I look through for statements in the text that interest me or that I can relate to easily. Things that I find hard to comprehend or that don't interest me I tend to leave and try to connect later to what I have more easily understood from the text. I think my own personal experiences are important as a way into a poem, because things you can relate to make more sense as you know about them already, at least a bit. If a poem seems to go against my values and I feel uncomfortable I ask myself why.
>
> Actually, at first I got fed up with [the] poet's pessimism and melancholy. This was because I felt he was being too melodramatic and didn't see his own life or the lives of his neighbours in proportion. A lot of people around me have been like this lately so I immediately picked up on this tone. [Here the student shows she recognises that the text is framed by recent experience and the attitudes that come from that experience.]
>
> I must admit that it took me a while to recognise that the skunks could represent some hope to the poet because of their endurance and natural courage. I was too prone to see the WHOLE poem as morbid not only because of my own recent experience with over-melodramatic people who want to mope all the time instead of doing something about their problem, but also because of my more optimistic Christian view of the world. I think there is some good and some value in everyone. The parable of the talents is real truth for me. Feelings need to be examined or a text can take hold of you and close your mind. I seem to be very able to resist the values of texts I disagree with, but I am so concerned to

avoid being manipulated that sometimes—such as with this poem—I don't give myself up to it enough and condemn before I understand. I think I need to adopt a more sympathetic stance initially and not be so suspicious, and after I think I've seen things from the author's viewpoint to stand back then and be more skeptical of the ideology.

As this student's response shows, becoming conscious of one's own reading processes increases interpretive options. Once readers realize how and why they have read a text in a particular way, they can then choose to read it in alternative ways. They can also control the texts they read rather than being controlled by them. They are starting to learn to read not only to discover "what the text means" but also to look at how it and their responses to it are influenced by larger cultural forces.

Before the final submission of the journal for assessment, students have to read over all they have written in their journals and draw conclusions about literature, the way it works, themselves, their own reading processes, their own beliefs or ideologies, and how these ideologies have been more strongly confirmed or modified or changed in any way during the course. Here is a brief extract from a student teacher's final summary comments at the end of his first semester:

When I read a text I try to go into it with an open mind knowing all the time that that is impossible because like everyone else I am part prisoner of the perceptions of my culture. But knowing that it is impossible to be objective makes me less a victim of my society than those who don't know this. . . .

The exploration in class of Salman Rushdie's and Gunter Grass's idea that fiction is lies that tell the truth has made me more aware of the writer's craft in the various ways they construct their characters, events and meanings to influence the reader. By understanding this I can build upon my beliefs and argue with books instead of being led by the will of the author, unconsciously submissive like a dog. . . .

I could write a story about a student who discovered—let's be honest—stumbled upon the hidden curriculum in a class. I could manipulate the reader to believe the student was going to get a distinction, when all along the teacher was manipulating the student into thinking he knew the ideology of the course and was really going to fail him! When suddenly . . . Got you again! One for the road.

By the way, if you thought it was the real date at the top of this entry I've got you again. Pull camera out to midshot of Jack hunching over Gilbert's journal a broken man. Theme music rises, credits roll. Picture fades to black. Film fades, music fades. Child gets out of seat and asks mother is this the end of the movie or just the beginning. Mother breaks

frame and yells at author to stop writing this journal and leave me and my
child alone. Author stops. Child and mother no longer exist. Wasn't she
sorry she opened her mouth! Pull camera out to midshot of Gilbert
hunched over journal, a broken man, no longer knowing who is in control.

These are powerful reflexive statements. This student understands the constructedness of literature and is gaining mastery of the
rhetorics of texts like *If on a Winter's Night a Traveller* by Italo
Calvino, and *The Name of the Rose* by Umberto Eco. He has also
mastered the ideology of the texts of the course and gained control
over these texts and over his own learning processes.

Students Learning Textual Constructedness

The constructedness of literature is often neglected in our teaching,
and it is of considerable importance that students see texts as constructs rather than as divine truths or secular scriptures. In her
research examining the literary theory and learning theory underpinning twelfth-grade English lessons in Adelaide, South Australia,
Peggy Mares (1986) concludes that "readers who learn that what
teachers and examiners value is the ability to submerge themselves in
texts and take the characters as 'real' make the perfect audience for
soap operas like *Dynasty* and *Dallas*" (17). So, students who leave
school believing that texts are uncontestable scriptures written by
divinely inspired individuals, Peggy Mares says, "are unlikely to have
the skills to distance themselves from the manipulative power of
advertisements and political manifestos" (17).

My next example is of a student grappling with the problem of the
constructedness of literature in writing in his reading journal in response to the ending of Aidan Chambers' novel "for new adults,"
Breaktime. He is reflecting on his own reading process to gain control
of this important new understanding about it. *Breaktime* is very in-
sistent on drawing readers' attention to its own artifice and helping
them to see it—and all literature—as a construct. One of its major
themes is an exploration of the nature of fiction, a motif that begins
when one of the characters, a sixth-form student called Morgan, writes
out a list of "charges against fiction" that he challenges his more literary friend, Ditto, to answer. One of Morgan's charges is that literature is a lie and a pretence, not convincing as a representation of
reality. Ditto answers Morgan's challenge by purporting to arrange an
adventure for himself—including his meeting for amorous purposes
with a girl called Helen—and writing whatever happens as his fiction,
to see whether Morgan finds it contrived, too neat, and false (uncon-
vincing) or entertaining, realistic, and true (convincing). Most of the

rest of the novel is Ditto's "fiction," and, like Morgan at the end, readers are tempted to accept the truth of its obvious fictitiousness.

Students often argue about whether Ditto's account of his weekend with Helen "really happened" or if he "made it all up." Here is a student's comment on Chambers' joke about the nature of fiction. It comes from his reading journal:

> I am so used to believing there is a final authority for a book—either in the text as the author, or outside it as a critic—and one correct interpretation, that even after our class discussion I still found myself really wanting to know whether Ditto had made up his story of the weekend with Helen or whether it "really" happened. Every time the question came into my mind I got really angry with myself because I know that it was all made up by Aidan Chambers. It's hard to get rid of old habits though! I wasn't going to tell you this next bit and if I had gone on to do what I thought of doing I wouldn't be putting it in this journal. I actually thought of writing to Aidan Chambers to ask him. (You said you'd met him, and you might remember I asked you one day in class where he lived and you named some town in Gloucester, so I thought I could easily get his address.) Well, when I started to write, feeling pretty embarrassed, I had to work out what I was going to say so he wouldn't think I was a complete idiot and laugh at me and not reply, so I started to try to present a good image of myself. Then I realised that what I was writing wasn't either the truth or a lie about me, so much as a fiction, something I'd made up for myself. That was what made me finally realise what fiction meant, and that Aidan Chambers couldn't have said anything in reply to my letter that wasn't another fiction. If he was kind and patient and sympathetic to my stupid question he would have had to give me some explanation of the nature of fiction like the one I've just given here for myself. If he wanted to humour me and tell me what he thought I wanted to hear and said, "Yes, it really happened. I based it on something that really happened to me, so it's true," that would have been another fiction, and if he'd said, "No, it couldn't have really happened because it's only part of a novel that I made up anyway," that would have been an embellishment to his original fiction, a bit more to add to the novel. This might sound like a lot of going on about the obvious, but it takes a while for me to see things for myself and really understand them.

This student has not only come to understand for himself the processes of textual constructedness in Chambers' novel, but in articulating his own progress from expressive-realist mystification to the understanding demonstrated above, he has gained control of these processes in a way that telling him about them certainly would not have achieved.

Students Reading Resistantly

Once students see the constructed nature of literature, they can easily be taught to gain control over textual ideology, and I believe that
this can happen from preschool on. Let me elaborate on and illustrate
this assertion.

A key proposition from contemporary literary theory is that the
meaning of a story changes according to who is telling it to whom,
when, and where. I mean that meaning depends not only on what the
teller/writer intends but what function the story actually serves for
all the participants in the conversational situation, and all the participants (writers and readers) bring different "repertoires" of experience, of cultural and literary knowledge, and of beliefs (or ideology) to
this situation. The same book read by four different children will be
four different books. The different reception of Salman Rushdie's
recent novel *The Satanic Verses* in different communities illustrates
this proposition.

Here is an example from the classroom. The hilariously irrever-
ent description of his grandfather by the Australian author and international television personality Clive James in his "autobiography,"
Unreliable Memoirs, produced uncontrollable laughter from most of
my students, but it left three black aboriginal students absolutely
smoldering. One of them said, "I hate him. I hate him. If he was a son
of mine I'd belt him so he'd never forget." And she went on to elaborate: "In our family we all learnt to respect the elders." The description Margaret had objected to is on page thirteen of a book of one
hundred and seventy-four pages. Initially, when she read that bit she
stopped reading the rest of the book. To her, literature was not only a
foggy mystery, but offensive as well. She really believed that rejecting
the values underpinning James' description of his grandfather would
lead her to fail the course, that to pass a course in literature you had
to come up with "right" answers, the approved authoritative interpretations. The rest of that two-hour class session was spent trying to
help all the students to demystify literature so that they would see
that not only are there no "correct" or "natural" responses to literature, but that it is impossible for readers with different cultural repertoires and experiences to read the same book the same way. After
this, Margaret was quite happy to read the remaining 161 pages of
Unreliable Memoirs without being dominated by it but, rather, arguing with and against its ideologies. Other members of the class began
to read the text for its multiple and contradictory meanings, some of
the girls being pretty revolted by its exultant sexism, but now not
feeling shy of resisting the dominant male reading. Many of the students mentioned in their journals that this class session liberated

them from their previously restrictive notions about appropriate ways to respond to literature—and to all other "authoritative" texts in their society. Again, they began to get some feeling of control over texts instead of being controlled by them.

Ideology is an inevitable factor in the transaction between text and student, and as Peter Hollindale (1988) says, "Our priority in the world of children's books should not be to promote ideology but to help children to understand it ... so that to the limits of each child's capacity that child will not be at the mercy of what she reads" (10). I believe there is a real point in inviting students to investigate textual ideologies as a way of becoming more conscious of their own values and of how they are being shaped by others. I also believe that we can help students to understand ideology at all levels from kindergarten through twelfth grade. Here are some examples:

1. A kindergarten child of my acquaintance found himself odd man out with his peers and teacher when he criticized the film of *Snow White and the Seven Dwarfs* after the class had been to see it. He complained that Snow White betrayed the loyalty and devotion of the dwarfs when she left them for the first rich guy who came along, a prince on a shining white horse. Now we might argue with his understanding of the conventions of fairy tales and what princes represent, but we would have to recognize the logic of his point of view and admit that from it there is an ideological contradiction in the text.

2. Children in a primary school class in Bathurst were discussing the BBC's televised version of *The Wind in the Willows*. In this version the characters we are positioned to empathize with—Mole, Badger, Rat, and Toad—speak in highly educated upper-class accents, and the characters we are bidden to disapprove of—the stoats and weasels—speak in lower-working-class accents. One boy said about the unsympathetic characters, "You can tell they're supposed to be bad because they look ugly and they speak different." He is reading the underpinning classist ideology of the production and, in so doing, is exercising textual power to control the text rather than being controlled by it.

3. Here is an extract from the reading journal of an eighteen-year-old student writing about *Heart of Darkness*. His response shows that he is coming to realize that as all texts contain contradictions and can, therefore, support a multiplicity of readings, he can choose his own reading, that is as long as he explains the reasons for constructing his preferred meaning. In this extract he is also working out how the text and his responses to it are themselves constructed by larger cultural forces.

There are contradictions in the novel. Conrad criticizes the evils of imperialism but seems to believe in the possibility of "good" white people improving the natives, which is very patronising, but he shows all the whites except Marlow as greedy and corrupt but doesn't show their behaviour as being part of their job. How could you be charitable and Christian while your work required you to rip off the natives all the time? Conrad can't blame the white workers as individuals when they are only doing what they are being paid to do by the Company that sent them, and the European governments stand by and let all the robbery and murder go on. The only reason these guys are in Africa is to make profits from ivory. This whole bit about civilising the locals is just hypocrisy.

Am I missing the subtle stuff in this book or is Conrad making contradictions? Perhaps because imperialism is better understood now than it was in Conrad's day and what is obvious to us wasn't so obvious to him. Wasn't the survival of the fittest an idea that was around then influencing international politics after Darwin's theory of evolution? Anyone who did any Modern History at school would see things that Conrad doesn't seem to me to be able to see. It shows that what we see in what we read has a lot to do with our education and upbringing. It's scary to think how we are brain-washed. Still it happened not all that long ago in Vietnam and it was us that was involved with the Americans. We repeated what had happened in the nineteenth century between Europe and the Third World. The closer you are to things the less you see your prejudices.

As a conclusion to classroom activities involving resistant readings of texts, students should always be invited to reflect on what they have learned and how they have learned it. For example, in the work on the televised version of *The Wind in the Willows* with the primary school class, children were invited to analyze the processes of value transmission in the production and draw some conclusions about them. They identified the associations the program tempts them to make as follows: middle-class people are good, honest, reliable, and trustworthy; and working-class people are bad, dishonest, unreliable, and untrustworthy. They then went on to explain how many viewers would take these associations to be natural or true, rather than constructs of the production emanating from a conscious decision on the part of the program producers.

Similarly, the students working on Conrad's novel *Heart of Darkness* explored the processes of character construction in the whole text. They reached the conclusion that character is not natural but constructed of words that carry the assumptions of the society that produced them, and they then went on to construct resistant readings of the female and native characters in what many of them now saw as a text with strong sexist and racist elements. Where the text positions the reader to see Marlow's aunt as a stupid woman living in a world of illusions and uttering the racist clichés of the white man's burden "to wean those ignorant millions from their wicked ways" (39), one student constructed her as a shrewd power broker going along with her socially imposed role of ignorant-but-amusing middle-aged woman with influential acquaintances, accepting the stereotype but deliberately exploiting it to have her fancies indulged and her wishes granted as a way of achieving some control in a phallocentric society. ("Cynthia's bags of fun, you know, always a good sport, and a jolly good sort, too, old boy!") Finally, at any level of the school system, students can and should be asked to formulate the theory that underpins the work they have done and to evaluate the worth of doing it. In examining the binary oppositions underpinning sexism, racism, and nationalism in *Heart of Darkness* (male/female, white/black, them/us, English/other European), the secondary students went on to draw important conclusions about the ways in which our language constructs rather than portrays the social reality we experience.

Students Writing Literature: Imitation and Parody

Finally, here are some examples of students writing literature themselves, imitating and parodying the works of professional writers as a way of making their own comments on the world and, in the process of making these comments, gaining some real mastery of different literary structures, rhetorics, and styles.

The first was written by an eleven-year-old primary school boy during some work on aboriginal legends organized by two student teachers. The student teachers had read and discussed some legends with the class, and they asked the children to write some of their own legends. Here is one of the stories.

How the Apes Turned into Man

Way off in the Dreamtime when man looked like monkeys and apes, an ape had a tremendous fight with a kangaroo. The kangaroo went hopping half over the country with the ape close at this heels. Soon, nearly all the apes and monkeys were in pursuit of the kangaroo. When evening came they were sitting around making plans among themselves.

The kangaroo, meanwhile, was getting tired of the chase so he made up nasty plans to get rid of his enemies. Excited by his plans, he led his enemies to a giant hole with trees growing on the sides. The kangaroo took one big leap across the hole, while the apes in pursuit were unable to stop and piled into the hole. By instinct, the apes and monkeys tried to grasp the trees as they fell, but the apes, being too heavy, broke the branches and rolled further on down. As they rolled, sharp rocks tore at their hair, leaving tips only on the top of their heads. The monkeys, being lighter, were able to hold on to the branches without breaking them. That's why monkeys today remain the same, and only a few apes live with hair, as the rest have turned into man.

You will recognize how different these sentences are from the everyday language of eleven-year-olds. These very literary structures are the internalized after-effects of the boy's reading of aboriginal legends. I doubt whether the invitation to write a discursive analysis of the style of the original aboriginal legends he read would have resulted in such linguistic knowledge and control as he demonstrates in his imaginative piece.

The second is a tenth-grade girl's imitation of William Blake's "The Tiger." Imitations and parodies are ways of getting students to become conscious of the rhetorics of texts they read and to gain some mastery of them to use for their own purposes. Doing this gives students inside knowledge of how texts are constructed and enables them to reconstruct them in their own ways.

In Response to "The Tiger"

Tiger, Tiger burning bright
In the forests of the night,
Slinking low, a snake of gold,
Treasure rare yet heart of cold.

A mind of terror, blackness, fear
I wonder what your business here.
From the fiery eye you fell?
Or cast out from the depths of hell?
What your maker? Was it He
Who plucked you from the light that be?
What your root, from whence you came?
Perhaps the black of ash we blame.

Coat of flame, the glory, power,
Is fashioned from the heaven flower,
Heart of serpent, eye of fire
Tell the devil is thy sire.

Who else has a heart of stone?
Who else dare defy your throne?
Of light and darkness you are King,
Alone you crouch, alone you spring.

In imitating other voices, in trying them on for herself, as it were, Michelle is on the way to finding her own voice.

The third is a version of "The Lord's Prayer" written by a fifteen-year-old ninth-grade student in "hippie" idiom:

Hey Old Man, way up there in the Big "H,"
Your name in lights,
Make this joint your scene
Like it is in the blue beyond.
Spare me a crust for I am hungry,
Forgive the mistakes we make,
As I forgive the burk next door for being noisy.
Don't give us any crazy notion, and get us out
Of trouble if we leave this straight and narrow,
After all, You run this circus,
You've got top billing.
The writing on the posters won't ever fade.
Stay cool!

To handle this kind of parody effectively, students must understand the concepts inherent in the original text and sharpen their understanding of different language registers.

When parodies and imitations are particularly compelling in their own right, it may be difficult for others to know which is the better of the two, the original or the parody. Then the Romantic notion of a supremely gifted, creative talent or divinely inspired artifact we are bidden to admire in the portrait-gallery model of literature teaching becomes nonsense and is seen through by students themselves. If you can write like a media personality or like a supremely gifted, divinely inspired instrument of God's will, then you are in the same league as a media personality or a supremely gifted, divinely inspired instrument of God's will. The binary opposition between them and us, between writers and readers, is broken, and students are using the rhetorics of the masters to impose themselves on their world for their own purposes. They have achieved textual power.

Appendix
Your Approach to the Course and Its Texts

• The English class is not a neutral site for your interaction with texts. Your personal response is inevitably affected by your knowledge that the texts have been selected—and thus authorized—by your teachers, cast in the role of custodians of what you have been socialized into seeing as the sacred scriptures of "Literature" conceived of as great works about eternal truths. However, you are entitled to dislike, be bored by, and/or get angry with any or all of the texts chosen for you, and the right to plan part of the course by suggesting and selecting additional texts.

• Literary texts are not divinely inspired artifacts dropped from the skies for our edification. Nor are they what Robert Scholes calls "secular scripture," works that embody the accepted moral precepts and agreed wisdom of the community that values them. They are constructed/manufactured by fallible human beings who are, like the texts and their readers, constructed, inscribed, or shaped by their language, history, and culture.

- Your responsibility is not to read texts as transmissions of divine truth or as cultural wisdom to be absorbed unquestioningly. Neither is it to beg, borrow, or steal the authorized, definitive interpretations of course texts from those prestigious readers called literary critics, or even from teachers of English in this department. Your job is to ask yourself: *What is it that I am bringing to the text that causes me to respond as I do?*

- There is no such thing as a non-ideological text or reader. You must argue with and/or against the text's ideology quite consciously as a way of finding out, clarifying, and testing your own values and beliefs; of finding out what your own ideology is (as most ideologies are held unconsciously); and as a way of avoiding indoctrination.

- So, the questions we are primarily concerned to answer in this course are:

  - Not "What is the meaning of the text?" as this reifies the text and makes readers passive consumers and ciphers;
  - Not just "What is my personal interpretation of the text?" as this reifies readers and leaves no room for growth and change, restricting them to what they already know and believe;
  - But "What do I bring to the text that causes me to respond as I do?" which helps readers to become conscious of themselves and the factors influencing their response;
  - And "How am I influenced by language and society to respond as I do?" and "How am I being positioned by the author and by my culture to read this text? and "What is the author's ideology?" and "Can I relate to it/ refute it with my own?" which help readers to become conscious of the processes of their own cultural shaping and their need to resist manipulation.

References

Belsey, C. 1990. *Critical practice.* London: Methuen.

Byars, B. 1981. *The cartoonist.* Harmondsworth, UK: Penguin Puffin.

Chambers, A. 1985. *Booktalk: Occasional writing on literature and children.* London: Bodley Head.

————. 1978. *Breaktime.* London: The Bodley Head.

Conrad, J. [1902] 1986. *Heart of darkness.* Penguin Classics. Harmondsworth, UK: Penguin.

Cormier, R. 1977. *I am the cheese.* London: Victor Gollancz.

Graves, D. H. 1983. *Writing: Teachers and children at work.* Portsmouth, NH: Heinemann.

Hollindale, P. 1988. Ideology and the children's book. *Signal* 55:3–22.

James, C. 1981. *Unreliable memoirs.* London: Picador Pan.

Mares, P. 1986. 'Personal growth' as a frame for the teaching of literature. In *Shifting frames: English/literature/writing,* ed. K. Hart. Typereader Publications No. 2. Geelong, AU: Deakin University Press.

Scholes, R. 1985. *Textual power: Literary theory and the teaching of English.* New Haven, CT: Yale University Press.

Thomson, J. 1987. *Understanding teenagers' reading: Reading processes and the teaching of literature.* Croom Helm: Methuen Australia. (Reprinted by the Australian Association for the Teaching of English, 1990.)

9

Looking Through Critical Lenses: Teaching Literary Theory to Secondary Students

Deborah Appleman[*]

> Suddenly, the way I read everything has changed. I think I'm just reading, without really thinking about it, and then I realize I was looking through critical lenses without ever remembering putting them on.
>
> Tom, grade eleven

When the above comment was offered in the final class discussion of a semester-long high school literature course, the classroom teacher and I exchanged barely suppressed glances of glee. "Critical lenses" was our collective term for four literary theories we had introduced to the students in a college preparatory modern novel course. We had approached our pedagogical experiment with skepticism shared by college English professors, literary theorists, and adolescent psychologists who believed that the multiplicity of perspectives required to sustain and create several literary readings of a single text was perhaps too cognitively sophisticated for secondary students. With a few isolated exceptions, teaching literary theory is rarely attempted with secondary students. Then, when students are finally introduced to the formal study of literary theory in college after at least six years of reading and studying literary texts in school, it is no wonder they often struggle with what seems to be an exotic and difficult subject.

* The author wishes to thank Martha Cosgrove for her skilled teaching and the Modern Literature students of Henry Sibley Senior High School, Mendota Heights, Minnesota, for their enthusiastic reading.

The purpose of our study was to challenge the current theoretical and pedagogical paradigms of the teaching of literature in the secondary schools by including the teaching of literary theory in a semester-long literature course. The theories on which we decided to focus included reader-response, structuralist, Marxist, and feminist literary theory. The guiding assumption of the study was that the direct teaching of literary theory in secondary English classes would significantly enhance traditional methods of teaching literature and better prepare adolescent readers to respond reflectively and analytically to literary texts.

Theoretical Background

Literary theory has clearly informed and in many ways shaped pedagogical practice, but in a monolithic, almost corrective way. That is, a single theoretical vision tends to dominate the teaching of literature until it is replaced by another. For example, literary study in the high schools was initially dominated by Matthew Arnold's view of literary studies as "cultural transmissiveness," a view in which texts are presented to young readers as "cultural artifacts which exist as repositories of knowledge about ourselves and the world around us" (Corcoran & Evans 1987, 8–9).

I. A. Richard's new critical perspective took hold of the secondary English classroom in the thirties, and its influence is still felt today. The teacher became the primary explicator of the meaning of the text, correcting wrong or ill-conceived responses. This model gave rise to the primacy of the text in the literature classroom to the exclusion of the reader. In *Practical Criticism,* Richards demonstrated how he trained his students to uncover a single predetermined meaning for a literary text. Teaching literature to students involved removing the blinders from students' eyes that had previously rendered them incapable of seeing such meaning (Withbroe 1990). As Richards (1929) said:

> Inability to construe may have countless causes. Distractions, preconceptions, inhibitions of all kinds have their part, and putting our finger on them is always largely guesswork. (40)

New Criticism, popularized by such works as *Understanding Poetry* by Brooks and Warren (1938) created a generation of teachers who viewed themselves as the gatekeepers to the "true" meaning of the text, viewed literary works as cultural treasures, and who viewed students as passive literary neophytes. Nelms (1988) describes the effect of this positioning in the following way:

I learned to think of the literary text as an edifice. Almost as a temple. Complete, autonomous, organically whole, sacrosanct. We approached it with reverence. We might make temple rubbings and we were encouraged to speculate on the organic relationship between its form and function. But it was an edifice and we were spectators before its splendors. (1)

The New Critical methods of teaching the aesthetic appreciation of the intricacies of literature that Nelms describes has not translated into practice very well, despite its prevalence as a predominant mode of literary instruction. New Criticism appears to encourage external and, in some respects, artificial responses to texts and discourage internal original responses. In *Exploration in the Teaching of English,* Tchudi and Mitchell (1989) address the inadequacies of the traditional New Critical method:

> The schools have aimed at producing people who love literature, who can read it and respond to it skillfully, who know the great ideas and values of civilization. Yet too many of the students who leave our schools are book haters and functional illiterates . . . and the reading of literature seems to have had no impact on our nation's values. (111)

Bretz and Persin (1987) point out that twenty years after the proliferation of many post-New Critical theories, many teachers still employ a New Critical method in their classrooms. As Withbroe (1990) argues:

> The teacher seeks to bestow meaning mysteriously encoded in highly esteemed literary texts upon students, in order to acquaint them with the values and literary artifacts of their culture. The teacher possesses the wisdom, the true meaning of the text, and trains students to explicate those meanings in a systematic fashion. While many schoolwise readers may become adept at using this method, they often feel removed from it, viewing literature as a school subject whose content is to be mastered and memorized, perhaps appreciating its cultural and aesthetic significance but unable to relate it to their own lives. (1)

Over the last two decades or so, reader response has made its way into the secondary classroom, with many teachers rejecting the New Critical notion that literary interpretation should yield "correct" interpretations of a text. Teachers of literature have increasingly granted the power and potential of the notion of reading literature as a transaction between reader and text, a dialectic.

As Mailloux (1990) succinctly states it, "the goal of reader-response criticism is to talk more about readers than about authors or texts" (38). Rosenblatt (1968), whose theory of reading is perhaps

the most frequently favored by secondary teachers who adopt a
reader-response approach, explains:

> What, then, happens in the readings of a literary work? Through the
> medium of words, the text brings into the reader's consciousness certain
> concepts, certain sensuous experiences, certain images of things, peo-
> ple, actions, scenes. The special meanings and more particularly, the
> submerged associations that these words and images have for the indi-
> vidual reader will largely determine what it communicates to *him*. The
> reader brings to the work personality traits, memories of past events,
> present needs and preoccupations, a particular mood of the moment
> and a particular physical condition. These and many other elements in a
> never-to-be-duplicated combination determine his response to the
> peculiar contribution of the text. (30–31)

Ideally, according to Bretz and Persin (1987), in the reader-response
classroom when students are "freed from the need to 'explain' the
correct meaning . . . the classroom becomes a place of discovery, of
dialogue, and of cooperative reading." (166)

Yet reader-response theory has not proved to be a panacea for all
the pedagogical ills created by the New Critical method. In an article
aptly titled "Which Reader's Response?" Roemer (1987) questions
whether teachers actually respect and privilege all student responses
to literature. She claims that teachers and critics, as part of the dominant structure that governs society, overlook the ideological and cultural dynamics that are present in all classrooms. Many teachers may
espouse a reader-response approach, but the reality is reminiscent of
Animal Farm: all readers' responses are created equal but some are
more equal than others. Roemer argues for a broadening of Fish's
notion of "interpretive communities" by incorporating the diverse
social and cultural perspectives that shape each reader's responses to
literature. Many teachers still fail even within a reader-response
framework to take into account the social, ethnic, economic, and cultural realities that shape their responses.

McCormick (1985) also raises some problems with adopting a
reader-response approach exclusively. Like a good number of critics,
she worries about the absence of textual boundaries in a reader-
response approach, at least as it is often practiced in the classroom.
While New Critics may privilege the text exclusively, McCormick
points out the danger of privileging individual readers' self-
awareness at the expense of illuminating the text. Reader-response
discussions can become indulgent exercises in self examination, with
students diving off into autobiography with little regard for the text.
McCormick pleas for a middle ground, where readers' responses are
bounded by the text itself, with personal and cultural backgrounds,

historical information, and standard close reading techniques combining into a comfortable yet workable method for the teaching of literature.

In many high school classrooms, reader response has become the current orthodoxy of English education (Marshall 1991). Although the emphasis of this approach does focus on the reader rather than teacher or text as the source of literary meaning, the problem of a single theoretical perspective remains. Students may be able to derive a plurality of interpretations using the reader-response approach, but they are still not taught multiple critical approaches.

The Case for Teaching Literary Theory

Robert Scholes (1985) argues that there are three basic textual skills: reading, interpretation, and criticism. Although there are many teachers skilled in all three, all too often they relegate the reading to their students, while they predetermine the appropriate critical approach for the literary text in question and either provide a single reified interpretation for the students or allow students to create interpretations within the context of that singular critical approach.

There have been few systematic attempts to provide students with a plurality of critical approaches to reading literature. A recent publication of the National Council of Teachers of English devoted to the teaching of literature endorses the notion of providing students with alternative interpretive tools but does not present any concrete evidence of instructional practice that reflects that perspective (Nelms 1988). Similarly, in *Readers, Texts and Teachers* (Corcoran & Evans 1987), teachers are urged to employ some deconstructive strategies in addition to reader response, but no plea is made for the explicit teaching of reader-response theory and deconstruction to students.

Broadly stated, teachers either present literary texts as cultural artifacts and literary masterpieces whose authoritative meaning is to be mastered by neophyte students or they employ a reader-response approach relying heavily on students' personal experience. Although the influence of literary theory can clearly be seen in secondary literature teaching, rarely have several theoretical models been considered simultaneously by teachers in their instructional approach. And even more rarely, if at all, has the actual teaching of different critical approaches to reading literature been attempted.

In *Literary Theory and English Teaching,* Griffith (1987) argues for the importance of teaching a multiplicity of perspectives. He describes the tension between presenting literature as cultural artifacts or as vehicles for transmitting ideology, and the aim of many educators, especially those who favor a progressive approach to education, to use literature as a vehicle for self-exploration and expression. Griffith describes the dilemma of the teacher who "on the one hand clings to a largely conservative belief in the beneficial effects of reading good books, and on the other sustains a broadly progressive faith in the interconnectedness of individual personal development and social change" (4). Griffith points out that the teaching of literary theory to secondary students can facilitate the study of literature:

> Certain applications of literary theory can lay bare what the text does not say and cannot say, as well as what it does and, as part of the same process, to make certain aspects of the context in which the reading takes place visible as well. . . . To be able to offer pupils this sense of power over their environment seems a desirable goal, especially if the sense of power is more than a delusion and can lead in some way to an effect on the pupil's environment. (86)

While it is not widely reflected in the practice of secondary teachers, the notion that literary theory can be useful for classroom teachers has gained greater voice in the field of English education. Emig (1990), in a conference talk as president-elect of NCTE, makes an eloquent plea for the case of the teaching of theory in literature courses:

> Theory then becomes a vivid matter of setting out the beliefs that we hold against the beliefs of others, an occasion for making more coherent to others, and quite as important to ourselves, just what it is we believe, and why. (93)

Emig also echoes Scholes's argument for allowing students to develop their own interpretive and critical skills. All too frequently the literature teacher assumes too much interpretive responsibility, thus reducing the students' opportunities for independent meaning making. Even if we superimpose a more "reader friendly" construct such as reader response, we are still limiting our students' abilities to be truly constructive in creating not only original readings of texts but in choosing the constructs in which those readings take place:

> Our students come to us with constructs about reading and writing. Through their private and their school encounters with text, their creation, comprehension, and interpretation, our students have built constructs about what reading and writing are and about what roles these processes serve, or do not serve, in their lives. Where theory contemplation begins, then, is with our attempting as instructors to elicit *our students'* constructs—not ours; not a noted theorist's about the nature of literacy. Because our students' constructs are probably tacit, we must devise and enact methods for eliciting their set of values and beliefs. (Emig 1990, 92)

Method

We set out, then, to create a high school literature course that would enable students to choose from a variety of theoretical constructs as they responded to literary texts. We began with the notion, perhaps offensive to critical purists, that the theories themselves weren't the focal point or purpose of the course, that the theories would provide students with multiple perspectives. We began simply enough. We introduced the idea of viewing a single text from several perspectives by using Russell Baker's (1981) "Little Miss Muffet," which retells the familiar story of a tuffet-sitting girl and an intrusive spider from the perspectives of a sociologist, a militarist, a book reviewer, an editorial writer, a psychiatrist, a student demonstrator, and a child. The students then wrote their own versions of familiar tales from at least two perspectives of their own choosing from among those of parent, child, talk-show host, school counselor, or policeman. The following is an example of how one student retold *The Three Little Pigs* from two perspectives, that of a policeman and that of a father.

Three Little Pigs and the Big, Bad Wolf
Police Report 1/22/90 18:22 Hrs.

Squad 2232 arrived on the scene at 16:15 hrs. He found two destroyed houses, one constructed of straw, the other of wood. Upon entering the third structure, a brick structure, the officer found three distraught pigs.

Alan Pig, of 3233 Ren Way and owner of the straw hut, stated that he fled from his residence upon its destruction by what Mr. Pig described as a wolf. Mr. Pig then entered his brother's house, Robert Pig, 3234 Ren Way.

Robert Pig said that the same event happened and both pigs then proceeded to their other brother's house, Don Pig. This structure of brick construction was able to withstand the wind force of the suspect wolf.

The suspect is described as a male, 6 ft, brown wolf. He is described as having a deep voice, and long winded. He is unarmed and considered dangerous.

Father of Three Pigs Who Were Involved with a Bad Wolf

I am very, very upset at you three boys, frankly though, I'm glad you are all right. You three boys have to learn that you cannot go off and build houses by yourself.

However, on the other hand, you did the right thing by going to Robert's house. For that, I'm grateful.

We then moved to an Updike story, "Separating," told from the male protagonist's point of view and asked students to rewrite sections of the story from the perspective of several of the other characters, including the wife and child of the main character (who is contemplating leaving his family but hasn't yet told them). Next, we read several texts of noted ambiguity, including Theodore Roethke's "My Papa's Waltz" and Sylvia Plath's "Mushrooms," noting the diversity of the students' responses and refusing, to the students' initial frustrations, to privilege one over the other. They demanded to know which of their responses had come closest to the "right answer." Nearly all of the students had received their pervious literary training in the context of a traditional canonical American literature program (*The Scarlet Letter, The Red Badge of Courage, Death of a Salesman,* and the works of Whitman, Emerson, Thoreau, etc.) in which their teachers, armed with teacher study guides and college notes, had led the students time and again to "see" and then rehearse single predetermined interpretations of the text.

Up to this point, no mention of literary theory had been made. We introduced students to the notion of "critical lenses," that is, the existence of literary theories that help us view texts differently, by reading Lynn's (1990) "A Passage into Critical Theory," an extremely useful essay that examines a piece by Brendan Gill from several theoretical perspectives—New Critical, structuralist, deconstructive, psychological, and feminist. We discovered that although we had two classes of college-bound high school juniors and seniors, they had never heard of any of the literary theories described in Lynn's essay.

We had chosen a variety of texts both traditional and contemporary. Texts included *Of Mice and Men, Ordinary People, The Great Gatsby, Native Son,* Anne Tyler's *Dinner at the Homesick Restaurant,* and a reader's choice novel whose only restriction, since the course was called Modern Literature, was that it be considered a "modern" novel (written since 1930). We decided to teach the theories inductively, to introduce them gradually according to the qualities of each text, rather than force all of them on every text we read. Throughout the course, we supplemented the novel reading with a variety of poems and short stories to give students as many interpretive opportunities as possible.

We began with *Of Mice and Men,* discussing plot, character, setting, theme, using the traditional tools of literary analysis. When we refused to accept students' texts as they tried to return them after their test, they woke from the complacency of the familiar. Sitting in a circle, we proceeded with what appeared to be a non sequitur discussion with them about the "key ideas of Marx." Phrases such as "oppression of the working class," "evils of capitalism," "the ruling elite," "alienation of workers," "the bourgeoisie," "class struggle," "powerlessness," and "disenfranchisement" filled the room and the blackboard. We then asked students to think about Lenny and George and Crooks and Candy and Slim and Curley and Curley's wife in terms of those phrases, and we heard: "Curley represents the ruling class." "This is a struggle between the haves and have nots." "Crooks and Candy and Lenny and George are the downtrodden workers." "The dream of the rabbit ranch is a dream to be in control of one's own destiny, to be one's own boss, to not have to work for anyone except themselves." "This is a struggle between classes." "Steinbeck feels sympathy for the workers."

Only after the frenzied offerings of such comments had died down did we offer a few modest comments about the existence of something called Marxist literary theory, about a different way of seeing that it could offer us as well as the role of the author as part of a cultural dialectic. The first critical lens had been introduced.

Because we didn't want to establish the notion that there was always a one-to-one relationship between a particular literary text and a critical theory that seemed to fit exceptionally well, as was the case with Marxist literary theory and *Of Mice and Men,* we decided to introduce structuralism as another way of viewing *Of Mice and Men.* Using a lesson devised by Quick (1988) based on Barthes's structuralist activity, we asked students to do a close rereading of the last chapter of the novel, grouping words and phrases according to action codes, enigma codes, word codes, communication codes, and culture codes. Powerful passages previously skimmed (e.g., the snake being eaten by the heron and other animal imagery) took on heightened importance as we moved from a macrodiscussion of Marxism to a microscopic examination of the words and phrases that made up the novel. More important, as Quick points out, the five codes that make up the structuralist activity provide students with a "structure, a heuristic method, a probe to accomplish this critical process of questioning, sharing tentative answers, arriving at conclusions about literature" (146) without relying on teacher-initiated questions.

Our next novel, *Ordinary People,* seemed especially appropriate to introduce a reader-response approach. The suburban setting, adolescent protagonist, realistic language, and the contemporary issues of troubled families and adolescent suicide make the text particularly accessible and evocative for teenage readers. Although, as discussed above, reader response has found its way into many secondary classrooms, all too often only the teacher is aware of the theoretical context of the responses. While reader response clearly privileges students' responses more than the New Critical approach that dominated most high school literature teaching until recently, if teachers do not share the critical framework in which student responses occur, whether reader response or New Critical, they are withholding an important part of the act of reading from their students.

Before reading *Ordinary People,* the students responded to several poems and short stories that were selected for their ambiguity and openness to a wide variety of interpretations. As a prelude to each whole-class discussion, students wrote brief response papers on each literary work before any teacher or whole-class explication occurred. Students then shared their response papers and were encouraged to listen not for the most plausible or seemingly "correct" interpretation but for the diversity represented in their peers' responses. We then discussed some of the general factors that can influence an individual reader's response to a literary text as well as the specific factors that were at play in their own responses. Students were then introduced to the basic tenets of Rosenblatt's (1978) transactional theory of reading and were asked to list both the textual and reader characteristics that had influenced their response to the literary texts they had been discussing.

After the students began reading *Ordinary People,* they were given a diagram that represented Rosenblatt's (1978) transactional theory of literary response and were asked to list both reader and textual characteristics that might influence their response to the novel. The reader characteristics the students listed ranged from difficulty with parents, sibling rivalry, death in the family, parental conflicts, depression and firsthand experience with suicide attempts, thoughts of suicide, or friends and family who had attempted or committed suicide. The students listed such relevant textual characteristics as the contemporary realistic setting, the use of everyday language (including profanity), the proximity of the protagonist's age to their own, the flashbacks, the changing point of view , and the relevance of the issues presented: difficulty with parents, peer pressure, sibling competition, and suicide.

Mindful of Rosenblatt's (1978) assertion that literary meaning arises from the unique transaction between an individual reader and a text, we asked students to write several statements of meaning that arose from their transaction with *Ordinary People.* The statements ranged from personal insights to general comments about families and society. The following are representative:

1. Everyone has problems, even "ordinary people." The only difference is in the way people deal with their problems.
2. Families that look perfect on the outside are not always perfect on the inside.

3. Most answers to problems lie within yourself.

4. Life isn't fair, right or nice, it just is.

Through this exercise the students saw more clearly that as individuals, they brought salient personal qualities that were not irrelevant or unimportant but crucial to the act of reading. They also learned that the self-knowledge they might be gaining from the text was not incidental but central to the literary experience (Appleman, in press).

We next read *The Great Gatsby,* and as we had hoped, a Marxist reading seemed to emerge naturally in the discussion as well as in the students' response journals. Students responded strongly to the material indulgences of the main characters, the apparent shallowness of their lives, the corruptive qualities of excessive wealth. After reading the passage about hundreds of orange rinds having been squeezed by someone's thumb in preparation for one of Gatsby's extravaganzas, one student exclaimed, "But what about the guy whose thumb it was? What about him? Who does Gatsby think he is?"

We thought it appropriate at this point to introduce our fourth "critical lens," feminist literary theory. We approached it in a manner similar to how we had introduced Marxism, with a circle discussion about feminism and feminist literary theory. We revisited Lynn's (1990) example of feminist criticism from his article "A Passage into Critical Theory" and then circled back to Curley's wife in *Of Mice and Men,* Beth in *Ordinary People,* and Daisy in *The Great Gatsby.* We asked students to make "traditional" descriptions of these female characters and then make a different sort of statement in light of our discussion of feminist theory.

The resulting statements showed how easily students' interpretive vision adapted to the lens of feminism. Here are a few representative examples:

Curley's Wife

Traditional statement: She was a bad girl, a tease and a flirt.

Feminist statement: She has just been treated poorly by her horrible, selfish, chauvinistic husband. She is not bad.

Beth

Traditional statement: She's the great American bitch.

Feminist statement: She's a repressed woman who is trapped by society's expectations of what a mother should be.

Daisy

Traditional statement: She was a poor little fool who depended on her husband to take care of her.

Feminist statement: Her husband took control of her and wouldn't like her to think for herself. She was doing her best within the limits of women's role in society.

As the above statements indicate, the students had little trouble recasting their original assessments of the female characters they had encountered in the light of the critical lens of feminism. Their reinterpretations, however, did remain somewhat superficial and predictable, and it remained to be seen whether students would invoke the lens naturally and independently.

We felt it time, having introduced all four lenses in class, to see what students would construct if left to their own interpretive devices. So we offered a reader's choice unit, where in groups of three or four, students would read a novel through at least two of the critical lenses we had discussed. Both the novels and critical lenses could be freely chosen, although we did make some suggestions, such as *Black Boy, 1984, The Hobbit, Dandelion Wine,* and *The Chosen.* Some groups availed themselves of these choices; others chose works as diverse as *Lord of the Flies* and *Fear and Loathing in Las Vegas* in addition to one or two Stephen King selections. Our role in all of this, as the classroom teacher bluntly put it, was to "keep my mitts out of it. I roamed from group to group, helped when needed, but pretty much listened to some great discussions from the students."

The resulting presentations, which we videotaped, were thoughtfully and competently done. Students were less enamored with the reader-response approach than recent teaching practices would have led us to believe. They understood it, they liked it, but they were more likely to invoke the other lenses. Few students tackled structuralism; feminism and Marxism prevailed. Some interpretations seemed a bit forced and strained, while others were startlingly fresh.

What was perhaps more important than the presentations was the kind of learning that went on outside the classroom. That is, the product was important only in terms of the kinds of learning processes it helped facilitate.

Here are some excerpts from the classroom teacher's journal:

The first day a couple of groups came to me to ask for advice—someone in the group was not keeping up with the reading—what to do (!) After a few days a couple of kids reading the Hobbit came in with an alarming report—they were ahead (!) and a few days later the same kid came in

announcing he did not get his math analysis done, because he was reading!! This is Tony Denardo—for whom hockey is his life.

Kids talked about the profound discussions about literature they had
late into the night—and without a teacher!!! Some kids observed they
didn't think they could figure out symbols, etc. without a teacher, and
found out they could. Parent conferences came during this unit. I was
thrilled by how many parents came to find out "what was going on in
that class." Several parents echoed that their child was talking about
books and never had before, or was talking about books in a way they
never had before.

For the remainder of the semester-long course, in addition to
more poetry and short stories, we read *Dinner at the Homesick Restaurant* and *Native Son*. In students' reading journals, dialogue journals, and class discussions, they independently invoked the "critical
lenses," focusing primarily on reader response and feminism in their
responses to *Homesick,* and Marxism and reader response in their
reading of *Native Son*.

As a culminating activity to the course, we asked students to discuss three of the texts we had read as a whole class through at least two
of the critical theories we had discussed. As with the student presentations, most of the students demonstrated a remarkable ability to
shift perspectives on a text, twisting and turning their interpretations
through the prism of critical theory. Students discussed the oppression of Bigger Thomas and the workers on Curley's ranch through the
Marxist lens; the cultural limitations and unique struggles of women
ranging from Curley's wife to Daisy to Beth to the voice of the female
author in *Dinner at the Homesick Restaurant* through a feminist lens;
the revelations of a close textual reading of the language in *Of Mice
and Men, The Great Gatsby,* and *Native Son* through their somewhat
obscured structuralist lens; and the degree to which their own personal experience had shaped and enriched their readings of nearly all
the novels through their reader-response lens.

In addition to their specific textual explications, many students
also commented metacognitively on how their reading had changed:

Before I came to this class I would read a book and only listen to the
story it told. Now I know that stories can be interpreted in many different ways using many different critical lenses.

With critical lenses, you can uncover new meaning in these books.
Sometimes a different lens can totally reverse the ideas you used when
reading the book.

These literary theories, or critical lenses, will likely change the meaning of a text to the reader. What is seen through the lenses depends on the reader. Thus, this is how I have seen these works through the Marxist and feminist lenses.

Looking at a piece of literature from a different angle allows us to see a new side of the story, and our knowledge of the work grows deeper.

Conclusion

Our goal for teaching the critical theories to our secondary students was not to make them, as we surely are not, experts in four schools of literary criticism but, as Lynn (1990) says, to get them to inhabit the theories comfortably enough to construct their own readings:

> I am assuming that plurality is better than unity, that the relative is better than the absolute (or even a quest for the absolute). . . . Plurality offers us a richer universe, allowing us to take greater advantage of the strategies our culture makes available—strategies that do not approach a text, but rather make it what we perceive. Our students therefore should learn how to inhabit the theories mentioned here—and a good many others. (112)

On the whole, we were encouraged by the students' understanding of the theoretical perspectives to which they had been introduced and the degree to which they applied them in their reading. We were also impressed with the students' ability to generate critical readings of texts as they read independently. We were pleased to see how students gradually deemphasized the teacher's primary role in literary interpretation and took responsibility for their own meaning making. Finally, the student response to the course, based on their written evaluations, was overwhelmingly positive. They recognized that "there was something different about how we learned in this class," and they liked it. They reported enjoying their reading more, thought the critical lenses were "interesting and helpful," and felt more free to participate in class discussions.

The classroom teacher came to realize that when she changed her students' mode of learning, she had dramatically changed her way of teaching. When she relinquished her position of privilege in this course, she discovered that all her classes became less teacher-centered and more exploratory.

Our attempt to teach literary theory to secondary students was not, however, an unqualified success. Students' understanding of the theories remained somewhat superficial and simplistic and often lacked layers of complexity. They remained baffled by structuralism.

In retrospect, we realize we could have provided more background and perhaps supplementary readings for the literary theories. Several students saw the approach to reading as no more than a different wrinkle in the please-the-teacher game; we may not have been "keepers of the key of meaning," but they knew that was exactly what we wanted them to tell us. Did they really entertain different interpretations of the texts, or did they parrot us, offering teacher-pleasing responses? Had we, too, replaced one pedagogical ideology with another, forcing students to play our hand? The ubiquity of student references to critical lenses made us wonder if we hadn't overdone it. The sincerity and the integrity of the students' responses surely demand close scrutiny as does the degree to which students were actually cognitively capable of creating and sustaining different and genuine readings of an individual text.

Griffith (1987) writes that "literary theory is about more than just literature. . . . To feel that you are able to say something about the effects and workings of a nineteenth century novel, a pop lyric, a Jacobean play, a Clint Eastwood film, a Great War poem and a soap opera is a good experience; to be able to demonstrate this feeling in terms of actual practice is even better" (87). We believe that the power of multiple perspectives enabled our students to turn texts against the prism of theory to see the different colors cast. It also allowed them to believe that they had something truly unique to say about texts and that there wasn't a single monolithic truth that could be applied easily to texts or perhaps anything else. We, and our students, came to see that having a plurality of theoretical constructs from which we as readers could choose was the beginning of true textual power.

The students also recognized that the plurality of theoretical constructs or literary theories reflected different interpretive communities with varying literary and political perspectives. Acknowledging the influence of interpretive communities on the construction of literary readings enabled the students to examine their own membership in a community of readers. This examination enhanced their understanding of their own readings, as well as their understanding of the content and effects of the literary theories we explored.

We found that introducing literary theory to students helped our classroom become a place of constructive and transactive activity where students approached texts with curiosity and initiative, not with trepidation or reverence or deference to the teacher. We believe that our teaching began to meet the important challenge that Emig (1990) offered to literature teachers:

> We must not merely permit, we must actively sponsor those textual and classroom encounters that will allow our students to begin their own odysseys toward their own theoretical maturity. (94)

One student in her final journal entry wrote:

> A book is not just black ink on paper—it's creation, feelings and images
> that you as the reader, reading through the lenses of Marxism, Feminism,
> structuralism, and reader-response as well as others I don't know yet,
> make them out to be. I used to read books just for the story, but there is
> so much more there now. I find myself thinking as I read in a way I never
> did before. Reading was never my favorite pastime but slowly it is now
> taking up much of my time.

This student also offered the idea that we should rename the course
"Through the Eyes of the Beholder." That suggestion indicated to us
that for this student, and for many of her classmates, her "odyssey
toward theoretical maturity" had begun. Her position as a reader in
a literature classroom had changed from the receiver to the construc-
tor, from the mirror that reflects a teacher's literary vision to a
"beholder" of literary texts with multiple visions of her own.

References

Appleman, D. 1992. I understood the grief: Reader-response and *Ordinary People.* In *Generating reader's responses to literature,* ed. N. Karolides, 92–101.
New York: Longman.

Baker, R. 1981. *Poor Russell's almanac.* New York: London and Lattles. Distributed by St. Martin's Press.

Bretz, M. L. & M. Persin. 1987. The application of critical theory to literature at
the introductory level: A working model for teacher preparation. *Modern
Language Journal* 71:165–70.

Brooks, C. & R. P. Warren. 1938. *Understanding poetry: An anthology for college
students.* New York: Holt.

Corcoran, B. & E. Evans, eds. 1987. *Readers, texts, teachers.* Portsmouth, NH:
Boynton/Cook.

Emig, J. 1990. Our missing theory. In *Conversations: Contemporary critical theory
and the teaching of literature,* ed. C. Moran & E. F. Penfield, 87–96. Urbana,
IL: National Council of Teachers of English.

Griffith, P. 1987. *Literary theory and English teaching.* Philadelphia: Open University Press.

Lynn, S. 1990. A passage into critical theory. In *Conversations: Contemporary critical theory and the teaching of literature,* ed. C. Moran & E. F. Penfield, 99–
113. Urbana, IL: National Council of Teachers of English.

McCormick, K. 1985. Theory in the reader: Bleich, Holland, and beyond. *College
English* 47:836–50.

Mailloux, S. 1990. The turns of reader-response criticism. In *Conversations: Contemporary critical theory and the teaching of literature,* ed. C. Moran & E. F.
Penfield, 38–54. Urbana, IL: National Council of Teachers of English.

Marshall, J. 1991. Writing and reasoning about literature. In *Developing discourse practices in adolescence and adulthood,* ed. R. Beach & S. Hynds. Norwood, NJ: Ablex.

Nelms, B. F. 1988. Sowing the dragon's teeth: An introduction in the first person. In *Literature in the classroom: Readers, texts, and contexts,* ed. B. F. Nelms, 1–16. Urbana, IL: National Council of Teachers of English.

Quick, D. M. 1988. Ninth graders making meaning: A structuralist activity with *Of Mice and Men.* In *Literature in the classroom: Readers, texts, and contexts,* ed. B. F. Nelms, 129–37. Urbana, IL: National Council of Teachers of English.

Richards, I. A. 1929. *Practical criticism.* New York: Harcourt, Brace & World.

Roemer, M. G. 1987. Which reader's response? *College English* 49(8):911–21.

Rosenblatt, L. M. 1968. *Literature as exploration.* 3d ed. New York: Noble & Noble.

————. 1978. *The reader, the text, the poem: The transactional theory of the literary work.* Carbondale: Southern Illinois University Press.

Scholes, R. 1985. *Textual power: Literary theory and the teaching of English.* New Haven, CT: Yale University Press.

Tchudi, S. & D. Mitchell. 1989. *Explorations in the teaching of English.* 3d ed. New York: Harper & Row.

Withbroe, N. 1990. *A comparison of new criticism and reader-response theory.* Carleton College, Northfield, MN. Typescript.

10

Literature and Social Change: A Feminist Approach to Gordimer's "The Catch"

Mary Beth Hines

There were many times when I felt inadequate as a high school teacher, moments when I was catapulted into the private lives of my students, inexorably challenged to deal with racism, child abuse, suicide attempts— markers of difference, some visible, some not. When these intensely private and painful experiences surfaced in our public discussions of literature, I moved between the parameters of "appropriate" and "inappropriate" subject matter, my personal and professional selves at odds as I struggled to discuss "the meaning" of the text while skirting "the meaning" of students' lives. When our dialogues strayed too far from the textual hearth, I commandeered the discussion back, waffling between those ostensibly competing impulses of being a "good" teacher and a socially responsible human being. During those years, I struggled— and failed—to envision a classroom where "reading" burgeoned into critiques not only of literature but of students and culture, where real life was not co-opted by textual representations of it. I was unable to tap my students' quickening sensibilities about social inequities, inept at harnessing their energies, experiences, and analyses into viable modes for discussing literature and working for social change.

Yet, despite my own inabilities—or perhaps more accurately because of them—I recently completed a study of successful teachers who encouraged students to assess their lives and their worlds as well as their texts. Among them was a literature instructor, Lillian, who crafted an approach to literature based on feminist principles. Because a variety of feminist theories exist, it is important to note that she endorsed a version of feminist theory embracing race and class as well as gender issues, inviting learners to explore issues of social justice that permeated not only their texts, but also their lives. I spent a semester in her required undergraduate literature course for non-English majors, and this chapter will highlight the ways of talking, thinking, and writing that Lillian and her students practiced as they assessed race and class oppression in the culture and in the literature they read. I hope to convince teachers that while feminist theories can be adapted to literature classrooms in powerful and productive ways, we must reconcile the tensions between our approaches to texts and our approaches to students as we formulate new classroom practices. The issues that stem from widening our "ways of knowing" literature became evident as Lillian and her students studied Nadine Gordimer's (1983) "The Catch." Before examining the dynamics of that classroom, let's look at the principles of feminist and educational theories that informed Lillian's student-centered pedagogy. In so doing, I hope to highlight the interplay between educational theory and literary theory that became manifest in Lillian's classroom.

A Teacher's Perspectives

Lillian explains why she links analysis of social issues to discussions of texts. Although she readily depicts herself as a feminist in our conversations, she never uses that label with her class because "it's really alienating to the students—it's like a red flag." She recounts her concerns this way:

> Quite simply we're born into this world as loving human beings without a sense of differences that separate us. Then we are taught a hierarchy of values based on what sex we are, what class we are, what race we are, what religion we are, and what our abilities are—both physical and mental. And in that process of learning those things, we're hurt; it's a very painful process. And those pains continue to surface in our lives and keep us from being the whole beings we can be. Since we learn those behaviors—ways of separating ourselves from others, ways of seeing— we can unlearn them.

Lillian's eloquent words commit her to engaging with injustices that affect her students and the world, those located inside and outside texts. As a feminist, she seeks to dislocate that "hierarchy of value," as she says, that oppresses those marked by difference. Her priorities on "learning" and "unlearning" behaviors and attitudes that cause others to suffer resonate with critiques of "normal"—that is, white, male, middle-class—values and practices articulated by feminists. For instance, Linda Brodkey (1989) explains,

We're talking about the limits of universality, about the need to recognize that the negating value of difference—*not* white, not middle class—is socially constructed and can therefore be socially reconstructed and positively valued. (598)

Lillian, echoing Brodkey, argues for moving beyond the mere acknowledgment of linguistic, experiential, racial, and cultural features to the validation of them. Both Lillian and Brodkey speak of the proliferation of ideas and behaviors that empower the majority at the expense of the marginal members of society, those we view as "different." Lillian recognizes that learners can sensitize people to apprehending "difference" as an asset, a cultural resource, rather than as an index of deficit. Lillian, like Brodkey, points to the transformative power of the classroom, for there students can "learn and unlearn" prejudice, discovering ways to participate in making the world a better place.

When such inquiry enters Lillian's classroom, she struggles to create a forum where students feel comfortable. She offers a cautionary note on the teacher's role:

When you are talking about race and class and gender in a classroom, you're inevitably tapping that pain and anger and hurt that are wrapped up in our learning about those things. So it's dangerous. You have to be very careful because you never know what pains and hurts students bring into the classroom with them.

Lillian emphasizes the importance of recognizing not only the words but the emotions underpinning students' experiences of discrimination. She argues that the classroom must offer what feminist Paula Rothenberg (1985) calls a "safe space" (124), a forum for students to talk confidentially without fear or censure. Consequently, she maintains that a listening mode rather than an interpretative or valuative stance provides the best response to intimate or controversial subject matter.

Initially we may imagine Lillian's classroom as an encounter group or a political rally rather than a literature class. But Lillian's instructional priorities indicate otherwise:

I think more than anything else I'm trying to get my students not so much to develop "tastes" or "preferences," or even necessarily to like the literature that we read, but much more to develop critical thinking skills—to be able to represent their ideas both verbally and in writing with clarity and originality, developing their own voices.

She focuses on analytical reading and writing skills, critical thinking. These goals reflect not only her personal commitments but the institutional priorities established for the course.

Her attention to critical analysis suggests the workings of a more traditional pedagogy, one perhaps based on New Criticism. However, she claims that students cultivate their reading and writing skills as they discover their responsibilities for social justice. Through a focus on the constructed nature of texts and society, she pursues these goals in tandem:

> I want them to end up seeing fiction and poetry as constructions, rather than assuming that's just the way the text is. Everything is a representation; and gender, race, and class are the big categories of otherness that we use in this culture to both reward and to penalize people.

Lillian links consciousness of textual patterns to social patterns, for in both cases the categories that cause inequality to proliferate are not "natural" but created.

And, for Lillian and her students, that awareness of textual and cultural order is nurtured through critical inquiry. She describes how reading becomes the focal point of the educational enterprise:

> Ideally what you want them to be is readers, not necessarily of books, but of the world . . . active readers.

For Lillian, effective teaching and working for social justice crystallize in the interpretative act: "reading" requires interpreting not only texts but the world. (See Freire [1989] or Freire & Macedo [1987] for accounts of other political pedagogies that discuss this view of reading.) Consequently, she emphasizes the "active" dimension of the process. She elaborates:

> I want them to have a sense that literature is what we make it. They too can decide—it's just not that there are these powers who decide what literature is.

Here Lillian joins forces with feminists who challenge the authority of those "powers who decide what literature is." (See Anzaldua 1990; Fetterly 1978; Gates 1990; or Showalter 1985 for a fuller discussion of these debates.) She insists that her students understand that "literature" is a contested term, open to debate by all, not just those who possess academic credentials.

Lillian, however, draws her classroom priorities not only from feminist theories but also from educational ones. She focuses primarily on enacting student-centered discussions:

> I'm the facilitator whose goal is to make myself expendable. I feel the best about teaching when they are talking. I know the class is working when they are talking to each other, not to me.

Just as Lillian promotes the student's taking the role of the "active" reader, so too does she endorse the student's becoming an engaged participant in discussion. She explains:

> I'm trying to come up with ways in which they can become more involved–so that they can be the directors of the discussion.

By purporting to become "expendable," Lillian delegates responsibility for education to the learners. As "directors of discussion" it is their agenda, not hers, that shapes the inquiry. It is with these goals that Lillian aligns herself with educational theorists subscribing to student-centered learning. (See, for instance, Britton 1970; Elbow 1990; or Lloyd-Jones & Lunsford 1989.)

We can see how feminist principles buttressed this student-centered framework in the first session. In a round robin, students gave their names and then collaboratively created a story. When students completed the narrative, Lillian asked them to identify any stereotypes or assumptions they had relied on. Students cited the equation of athlete with dumb jock, blonde woman with frivolity and irresponsibility. Lillian then explained that literature was replete with assumptions about life and culture and that the class would assess those beliefs and norms as they discussed texts. She pointed out that just as the group had assembled their story to produce reactions (e.g., laughter), writers construct texts to produce certain effects on readers. However, because readers bring prior knowledge and experience to the text, their responses to those textual designs vary.

Lillian's dual emphasis on multiplicity and awareness of textual construction serves several purposes. First, by acknowledging pluralism, students recognize that diversity among readers results in multiple responses, a first step toward respecting difference. Second, she lays the groundwork for ideological critique when she asks students to examine the assumptions informing their collaborative text. If students can locate the stereotypes and suppositions that they use, that they "automatically" and "naturally" insert, then they can begin to recognize them in other texts and in society, she hopes. Finally, Lillian suggests a particular orientation to literary works, cuing her students to what and how they might discuss texts in future sessions.

But topics and approaches to literature are also contingent upon the particular works chosen for study, Lillian emphasizes. Her choices are governed by the options offered by her department; among those, she selects texts in which social inequities— particularly those of gender, race, and class—are "embedded," as she says, in the literary works.

We can see how the twin goals of analyzing texts and working for social change entwine as students assess Nadine Gordimer's "The

Catch." In the story, set in South Africa, a wealthy white couple on vacation befriends an Indian, a factory worker also on vacation, who spends his time fishing. When the Indian catches a huge salmon, he heads for a restaurant a mile away, laden with the unwieldy fish. Meanwhile the couple learn that another couple—white, upper-class and from the city—are in the vicinity, and the two couples arrange an evening of entertainment in nearby Durban. On the way, they recognize the Indian, stopped on the roadside, burdened with the cumbersome fish. When the driver offers the Indian a ride, his wife and the other couple protest, unhappy that they are going to be inconvenienced by the Indian and his fish, even momentarily. They insist that the driver drop the Indian off, for further assistance will make the group late for dinner. As they drive away, they titter at the Indian's predicament and their own involvement. Lillian asked students to write entries about the story prior to the discussion, and we can examine excerpts from students' work to understand how students wrote and thought about literature in Lillian's class.

Written Responses

Although Lillian did not assign journal topics, most of the responses focus on one issue, the white couple's "abandonment," as more than one student says, of the Indian fisherman. Through student excerpts, the multiple "ways of knowing" that are endorsed in this class become evident. For example, Rose comments:

> I felt bad for the Indian when the girl stereotyped him. The girl seemed to think manual labor was normal for Indians. She said, "A mile, they're strong, and they're used to it." She left the area without a second thought about his carrying the fish a mile.

This excerpt from Rose's reading log demonstrates an incipient transaction of text and reader, one oriented toward racism. Rose expresses her feelings and quotes the text to support her view of an event in the story in which stereotyping of the Indian occurs. She blends personal response with textual analysis to identify a racism she sees suggested by the story.

Andrea also takes a perspective on the text that focuses on that racism, incorporating multiple elements in her response:

> As I read the story, I got the picture that the white people were looking down on the Indian. One passage read, "The fact that he was an Indian troubled them hardly at all." Another read, "He was 'their' Indian." This, and their attitude towards him, makes him seem like a play thing. . . . Throughout the whole story I felt sorry for the Indian. I felt

that he was used and just cast aside when something better came along, like a small fish thrown back in the water in the hopes of catching something bigger and better.

Here, too, Andrea shifts dialectically from her own feelings of pity for the Indian to the text, illustrating the racist assumptions propelling the characters' behaviors. When Andrea concludes that the whites objectify the Indian, befriending him for their own purposes and later rejecting him, she relies on textual evidence to support her position, that suggesting racist overtones in the characters' thoughts and behaviors.

With this particular selection, as with many of the others the class discussed during the semester, students incorporated history and culture into their responses. Dee's journal entry illustrates how students brought these elements together in informal writing. Here too the purpose is to discuss racism:

> The fact that the story took place, in essence, between whites and an Indian reminded me of the United States' abuse of the American Indian starting in the 1600s and reaching a climax in the 1800s. . . . Times arose when Indians were on land we wanted to develop. Paralleling the way in which the couple did not recognize the fisherman's identity, our country did not—and continues not to—recognize the identity of that race.

For Dee, the story triggers associations with American history, patterns of Native American "abuse," as she says, which persist today. She concludes by creating a comparison between the story and our country's treatment of Native Americans: in both cases whites act as oppressors.

Here analogy functions not only as a device for making comparisons; it enables the writer to enunciate prior knowledge that has enriched her reading experience. In this case, Dee's comparison of the story to domestic policy suggests that her reading is filtered through the history of oppression of Native Americans. She also believes that she as a reader is implicated:

> The reader is entertained for a while by a seemingly "harmless" plot, like a typical yuppie couple on vacation. At the end, the reader— particularly a Caucasian—is forced to look into the mirror and be faced with the truth that what is seen is not as beautiful as he or she may like to believe.

Dee assesses her own responsibility as an Anglo-American reader who may have been seduced initially by the "harmless" tale of a couple on vacation, who may have empathized with the affluent couple at the beginning of the story, only to resist that identification at the end when the whites reveal their priorities, leaving the Indian by the wayside so that they can enjoy a lavish dinner. Readers are "forced to look into the mirror," as Dee says, indicating a self-reflexiveness precipitated by the reading experience, a critique of one's own racial biases.

For other students the text triggers reflections on issues of social mobility and class position. Jerry tells of the struggles in his own life:

> The reason I have no respect for these people is because I look at my own situation. I've had many problems growing up, being from a broken family and being raised by my grandparents. I'm on my own now and going to college, working two jobs. . . . The lower economic level people dwell on negatives in life and don't fight to make the best of it. . . . They lack motivation—the key of success—and fear the world of work.

Jerry cannot accept what he calls the "lower economic level people" because he himself is managing to overcome the obstacles he has encountered. He identifies with the Indian's status as a lower-class minority member and suggests that the Indian, like himself, simply requires motivation and hard work to do well. However, what Jerry does not recognize here is the interlocking of race and class that characterizes the Indian's subordinate social position but does not describe his own. In the subsequent class discussion, however, Jerry is challenged to acknowledge not only the similarities but also the differences between his experiences and the Indian's—divergences due to race and culture as well as to class, his classmates argue. It is this tangled web of oppression that some feminists analyze in their work, and Jerry's comments provide the springboard for a discussion of those interacting forces.

Before turning to that class session, let's examine Lillian's written discourse, focusing on her response strategies; for she frequently corresponds with students via their journals. Her words reflect her dual goals of encouraging close reading and raising feminist concerns. For instance, Lillian's comments on journals demonstrate that textual analysis is a priority:

> What in the story gives you that impression?
> What has led you to believe this?
> Can you cite an example?
> Intriguing suggestion, but I'm not sure how you see it working in the story.

These questions and their variations suggest that Lillian invites students to loop back into the text to support generalizations, whether they focus on the work or on the world. Furthermore, she offers

positive comments when students embellish responses with lines
from the text. She becomes more explicit about this goal with a student who omits references to the story:

> Follow your intuition by looking for support in the story itself. Trust
> your own ideas, but back them up with evidence from the text. I'm very
> interested in what you think. I just need a clearer picture.

Lillian's remarks reveal a belief in a transactional approach to reading, an approach in which both reader and text contribute to the
shaping of meaning. However, it is through the text that Lillian
hopes to develop a "clearer picture" of the student's ideas.

Another tactic that Lillian employs in her written comments is to
use questioning strategies directed toward the investigation of
assumptions and behaviors we take to be "natural," the critique of
ideologies. Some feminists (e.g., Newton & Rosenfelt 1985) find such
inquiry vital, and Lillian counts herself among them. Lillian highlights response excerpts containing assumptions about the world that
might be questioned. The written exchange between Chris and Lillian demonstrates this. Consider Chris's excerpt:

> The story also tells of human nature. . . . It's amazing how people act
> differently depending on whose company they are in. Until Les helped
> the Indian, I had almost lost faith in him.

Lillian comments:

> Do you think it is natural for us to be so unkind? If not, how is it human
> nature?

As a feminist, Lillian seeks to expose those conventions and
norms we take for granted, uncovering the power relations that
might keep them in place. If students recognize them as social and
historical constructions rather than as timeless and universal concepts or behaviors, then they can locate sources of oppression that
might be changed. In this case, Lillian highlights Chris's conflation of
character behavior with human nature, challenging the notion that it
is "natural" for humans to mistreat one another.

Another student, Jesse, recognizes the workings of ideology in
the story. He writes:

> It's as if they unconsciously fell into habits because that is what they feel
> they should do when they are on vacation. After they drop the Indian off
> she then realizes that she has treated the Indian not as she wished to but
> as she thought her friends thought she should. I think realizing that she
> had been so misled by the force of habit, she was devastated with herself
> and couldn't believe that she had acted the way she did.

In her comments, Lillian accentuates this passage, which focuses on the unexamined assumptions motivating the characters. She says:

> You get at the central point of Gordimer's depiction of the white couple—the way we behave "by habit" and "social convention" without considering what such conventions mean. Nice work.

Lillian rewards Jesse for attending to the workings of ideology. Her words encourage the student to pay attention to those dimensions of the text.

The written responses of Lillian and her students reveal the complex interplay of text, reader, culture, and history as students forge their responses. To say that the elements and strategies manifest in these writings are subordinated to race issues would be reductive, for students write on a variety of themes, incorporating textual analysis, personal response, and cultural studies. Despite the multiplicity of topics and approaches, all of the entries in one way or another allude to or discuss the mistreatment of the Indian because of his skin color. In some cases, the references are means to an end—commenting on racism; in others, racism provides an impetus for discussion of other subjects, such as relationships or character traits. Furthermore, the journals of Dee, Rose, Jerry, Jesse, and Andrea reveal the possibilities for widening the range of thinking and writing afforded by a feminist approach. Drawing from personal opinion, experience, and history, students report associations and memories stimulated by the reading; but they also respond by performing the more traditional close reading of lines and passages. All of these provide insertions into the text for students, and all are considered legitimate and appropriate "ways of knowing" in this class.

But what probably is most significant in terms of a feminist orientation is how this broad spectrum of elements converges in inquiry about racism, both that inscribed in the text and that circumscribing students' lives and cultures. Lines are not cited for the pleasure of explicating them, as a formalist may do, or for the articulation of the reader's connection to them, as a reader-response theorist may urge. Rather, passages are cited to highlight the racist assumptions possessed by characters; history is recalled that recollects a national policy of racism; personal experience is detailed that enables the reader to identify through class position with the characters. The central issue is the analysis of the vacationing white couple's behavior toward the Indian fisherman. The pervasiveness of that theme, and its generative power in raising issues of racism, reinforces the importance of text selection in promoting social change, as Lillian emphasizes. Let's turn now to the oral discussions stimulated by "The Catch."

Classroom Discourse

Consistent with her emphasis on the text as construction, Lillian opens the discussion by calling attention to the author's choices. She says:

> I'm asking you to think about what you think the author thinks about the characters given what she tells us in the story. How do you think she wants us to feel about these characters? What's her attitude?

Lillian focuses on these questions not to discern authorial intention but to encourage students to become conscious that literary works have designs on readers, that textual elements are arranged and selected to produce certain effects, as Fetterley (1978) argues in *The Resisting Reader.*

Here, as in the written discourse, issues of social justice predominate as discussion topics. A student asks what motivates the white couple to ignore the Indian at the end of the story. This question proves to be a linchpin for debate, eliciting response as varied as the written work done in Lillian's class. In discussion, as in the journals, students attribute the couple's behavior to racist attitudes. Jessica, for example, says:

> I thought it was a racial thing because I noticed specifically in one part that they were talking as they were driving down the road, and the husband says, "I wish I had picked him up instead of making him carry that big fish," and the wife ways, "Oh, no, they're used to that kind of work." I was really annoyed with the couple because they didn't recognize the man's identity as a person. Then again I read that the fact that he was an Indian "troubled him hardly at all," and they had almost forgotten he was an Indian.

Here the student's comments demonstrate a close reliance on the text, as she shares her feelings of frustration over the white couple's behaviors, as she attempts to make the class aware of the racial dimensions of the story.

In the class discussions students frequently shift between the text and their lives:

Jesse: Aren't we in the same position, you and I? We see people walking down the streets all the time with cans in their hands.

Steve: But we don't talk to somebody on a daily basis and then ignore them when they're in some sort of trouble.

Andrea: Yeah, we don't even talk to them.

Jesse: Right, but I'm saying with this guy they can be friendly.

Jesse's question, "Aren't we in the same position, you and I?" challenges students to recognize the race and class biases that they might be guilty of, that their behaviors might reveal. Embedded in this exchange are several references to events in the text, such as Steve's comment about one person's ignoring another and Jesse's final line about the "friendly guy," the Indian.

But textual analysis is not the only response called for in this class. Consistent with a feminist emphasis on personal experience, Lillian shifts the discussion from the safe ground of the race and class prejudices suggested by the text to the more immediate—and more troubling—assessment of their own biases. She asks:

> If I were to ask all of us in this class who think of themselves as racist to raise their hands, how many of us would?

Here we see Lillian enacting her belief that reading is a political act, that she, as a feminist teacher, can link textual issues to social change. Following the teacher's lead, a student follows suit:

> Now I ask, who is classist?

It is important to understand these questions from a feminist perspective. In both instances, the questions are not asked with inflammatory tones, to indict or accuse, or to count heads. Rather, both questions are designed to promote what feminists call "self-subversive self-reflection" (Penley 1986, 142), the sort of inquiry feminists engage in not only to establish a position but also to critique the foundations for that opinion. Lillian's subsequent question, asking students who raise their hands to explain why, generates that sort of analysis.

These questions encourage students to take a stand and then to consider the basis for their opinions, whether or not the grounds for such claims are valid. Jack, for instance, reports why he characterizes himself as racist and classist:

> Think about watching TV. The bad guys tend to be the black guy. It's everywhere, so how could you not be shaped by that?

Jack describes the pervasive influence of the media not only on himself but on all viewers. He demonstrates self-reflexivity by recognizing the power of television and the destructive images it can perpetuate, on the one hand, and by acknowledging the effects of those images on him personally, on the other.

As students confess to being "shaped" by society—particularly television—others incite them to resist those forms of indoctrination. Jack explains:

But I think all of us are trying to fight what we have been shaped by too.
I know the United States isn't perfect in race relations, but we're becoming more aware. I know I have these biases that are subconscious, but I,
myself, try to fight against that. I try to push the other way.

Here the students are exploring, although not naming, the role of
ideology in the construction of individuals' conscious and unconscious behaviors and attitudes. It is through resistance to "biases
that are subconscious" that he can subvert media indoctrination and
work for social change, Jack says.

At other points in the discussion, the conversation centers exclusively on the lived experience of the students, how their behaviors
make explicit their attitudes toward race and class oppression. Sue
challenges her peers to account for their actions:

You can change racist attitudes. To this day it's really hard to go against
society and its principles. I mean, all of us say we have friends that are
black. We say, "Well I have friends that are black." But how many of you
will date or marry them? It's really hard to combine societies.

Sue expresses the tension that is admitted frequently during this session, that despite their best intentions, students fall prey to cultural
norms that discourage integration.

Aware that all the students are Anglo-Americans, that most students in the class admit to prejudices, Andy explains that he is presently dating an African American woman, that he has dated black
women for several years. He praises his high school and junior high
for promoting racial harmony, and he credits his parents with
encouraging antiracism. He adds that he is thinking about joining an
African American fraternity on campus, and that he will meet his
girlfriend's parents the following weekend. He states:

I've got a black girlfriend, and I've dated black girls over the last two
years. I think people can; I know a lot of interracial relationships. I don't
think they're unmanageable. Maybe everyone is racist or classist in a
subconscious way, but that doesn't make people bad. It just means it's a
fact; it's going to happen. It's not bad. It's just hard to deny it. It's never
going to be perfect.

What is most compelling about Andy's contributions is his compassion
for those struggling to purge existing traces of discriminatory
thoughts and behaviors. Despite his avowedly antiracist history, he is
sympathetic to the contradictions and conflicts his classmates
articulate and offers his own history as a testimonial to those struggling with these issues. He promotes tolerance because he sees "subconscious" racism and classism as an inevitable part of our culture,
what one of his classmates describes as "baggage." However, both his

words and his actions suggest that, despite the cultural conditioning students experience, they can combat racism too. Andy's willingness to divulge his experiences signals the existence of that "safe space" Lillian hopes to cultivate. In this exchange students shift from discussing the representation of fictitious events and characters in a distant, unfamiliar country at an unspecified time to assessing the actual, immediate, localized, and personalized forms of oppression they might perpetuate—or prevent—as members of society.

Tensions Between Approaches to Texts and Approaches to Learners

Dialogues that center on the personal opinions and experiences of students might be considered "divergences" in some classrooms. In Lillian's class, however, they become resources for enriching students' understanding of the story, their lives, and their society. Because Lillian's students bring their prior experience and knowledge to the text, their positions on social issues inform their readings. Lillian finds that when their views on social issues crystallize, students become more effective readers. Consequently, she advocates forays into topics and issues that intersect, even tangentially, with the text. She says:

> I want them to get a greater sense of clarity on their own positions about relationships between people of different classes. And once they have a greater sense of clarity, then they are able to look at what the writer is doing.

One of the students, Donna, describes it this way:

> It's vital to understand the writer's point of view and to understand the characters. You can't just accept literature. You can't just read it and say this is how it is.

Lillian suggests that a "clarity" about social and personal issues enables students to view their reading experience more critically, to assess "what the writer is doing" to produce effects on readers. For Donna, knowledge of social issues provides a context for assessing characters and work, a way of resisting "this is how it is," as she says.

But as students struggle to assess the text within the web of social forces affecting author, readers, and characters, Lillian encounters a difficulty. Students invoke their prior knowledge of history and culture, but as she attempts to extend the inquiry to explore the social context surrounding the characters in this story, the discussion founders. In the beginning of this episode, students attribute the oppression facing the Indian exclusively to racial bias, ignoring the story's setting near Johannesburg, South Africa. When one student suggests that class issues may be involved in the prejudice the Indian experiences, Lillian uses that comment as a scaffold for extending their analyses of oppression:

> What is the relationship between race and class in South Africa? What do you know about race and class, the relationship between them in South Africa?

Note that as a student-centered instructor, she begins by asking students to contribute information, their prior knowledge. Two students explain that blacks rank as the lowest class, that whites hold the primary position.

However, when Lillian inquires about the status of Indians in this hierarchy, no one can answer. One student summarizes the class's reaction: "I don't even think of Indians being in South Africa." In this case, Lillian's desire to enrich the discussion by considering the cultural context is stymied by her students, who simply do not know anything about South African Indians.

At that moment, Lillian finds herself in an uncomfortable position, her approach to texts at odds with her approach to students. When she discovers that students lack knowledge of the cultural context circumscribing the story, she is faced with two options: either redirect the conversation toward the topics students do know, thereby maintaining the consistency of a student-centered approach, or temporarily abandon these practices, resorting to the "transmission" mode (Barnes 1976, 140), in order to illuminate the complexities of a social order in which systematic race and class oppression have victimized not only fictional figures but actual human beings. Lillian opts for the latter, momentarily employing a lecture mode to explain the South African caste system and the Indian's place in it. Although this is an isolated incident, it does represent one of the longest turns taken by Lillian, and that fact magnifies its significance. But the silence following her explanation is worthy of consideration as well, for students are struggling with an emotional as well as intellectual comprehension of the injustices perpetuated by the South African government.

As teachers determined to preserve the interactive nature of our discussions yet hoping to widen the "ways of knowing" in our classrooms, we should consider the questions that this conjuncture raises. Is it possible to practice a cultural studies approach within a student-centered pedagogy? What are the consequences of undercutting those inquiries of "otherness," as Lillian says, when students express little knowledge of the social system and setting? And if we do make students responsible for providing this background, do we not merely disguise the lecture mode when a student "reports" the information?

I raise these issues here not to suggest that we shy away from new approaches to texts but to propose that we consider the implications of our choices. As we formulate new approaches to teaching and learning literature, we must assess the "ways of knowing" they require. Just as Lillian's attempts to maintain the dynamics of a student-centered classroom are held in tension with her desires to enrich literary studies, so too might we inevitably experience the competing impulses of our approaches to texts and our approaches to learners.

And we should remember that Lillian elegantly demonstrates that integration of feminist theory and student-centered learning throughout the semester. We can see her effective enactment, for instance, in a moment where she confronts an issue common to both educational and feminist circles, power relationships in student-teacher interactions. Feminist literary critic Nina Baym (1990) comments on the tensions surrounding the feminist literature teacher:

> One problem then is how to empower students in a situation where the ultimate power must remain with the teacher. A second problem is what comprises knowledge in the literature classroom. A possible solution to both problems, it seems to me, is for the feminist teacher to relinquish her interpretation. Or, at least, to hold it more lightly. (66)

Baym suggests that power and knowledge are linked in the classroom and that the teacher might subordinate her views in order to "empower" her students. In a pedagogy oriented to social justice, such a strategy seems most consistent. Lillian demonstrates that deferral on many occasions, affirming responses that compete with her own political agenda. Her restraint becomes evident in a moment when a feminist perspective could easily have been inserted. For instance, Dan says:

> If it had been somebody they knew, not an Indian, but a person they knew, they wouldn't have helped him. Those people were selfish, and it might have something to do with—or nothing to do with—his race or class. They're just selfish.

It is another student, not Lillian, who elaborates on this comment, who argues that the white couple's "vacation" signifies a freedom from social and ethical responsibilities, that their refusal to aid the Indian should be construed as selfishness, not as racism or classism.

In an interview, Lillian explains how she views the interpretation of the white couple's behavior as "selfish": "That's sort of the human level at which racism and classism work. A protection of yourself from what is different." While Lillian in this case recognizes that link between selfishness and oppression, her students do not.

And, despite her political commitments, she does not ask questions that might enable students to link race and class with selfishness. Furthermore, she declines to introduce gender issues with this story when her students do not. She "relinquishes her interpretation," as Baym says, to build on those ideas her students generate. We can look at that episode as a demonstration of feminist practice working in concert with student-centered learning. A teacher not only recognizes that a multiplicity of readings is possible, but that in working for social change, a multiplicity of political stances is available as well.

Donna describes Lillian's intervention from a student's perspective:

> She has certain points that she would like to bring up for discussion, but she does not impose her values on anyone. She wants to understand how we are feeling. She wants to discuss certain topics, but she doesn't want us to come to a uniform decision on anything.

Donna locates Lillian's role as a facilitator, introducing ideas but not controlling the discussion. As teachers interested in promoting social justice and equality, we are, like Lillian, most likely to select texts that highlight issues of gender, race, and class, raising questions about how we can instigate social change. However, as Lillian's example so effectively demonstrates, we can construct frameworks that cultivate equality and respect for difference inside our classrooms as we work together in promoting social justice beyond those classroom doors.

References

Anzaldua, G., ed. 1990. *Making face, making soul: Creative and critical perspectives by women of color.* San Francisco, CA: Aunt Lute Foundation Books.

Barnes, D. 1976. *From communication to curriculum.* New York: Viking Penguin.

Baym, N. 1990. The feminist teacher of literature: Feminist or teacher? In *Gender in the classroom: Power and pedagogy,* ed. S. L. Gabriel & I. Smithson, 60–77. Urbana: University of Illinois Press.

Britton, J. 1970. *Language and learning.* New York: Penguin.

Brodkey, L. 1989. Opinion: Transvaluing difference. *College English* 51:597–601.

Elbow, P. 1990. *What is English?* New York: Modern Language Association and the National Council of Teachers of English.

Fetterley, J. 1978. *The resisting reader: A feminist approach to American fiction.* Bloomington: Indiana University Press.

Freire, P. 1989. *Pedagogy of the oppressed.* Trans. M. Ramos. New York: Continuum.

Freire, P. & D. Macedo. 1987. *Literacy: Reading the word and the world.* South Hadley, MA: Bergin & Garvey.

Gates, H. L., ed. 1990. *Reading black, reading feminist: A critical anthology.* New York: Meridian/Penguin.

Gordimer, N. 1983. The catch. In *Selected stories,* 31–42. New York: Viking.

Lloyd-Jones, R. & A. Lunsford. eds. 1989. *The English coalition conference: Democracy through language.* Urbana, IL: National Council of Teachers of English.

Newton, J. & D. Rosenfelt, eds. 1985. *Feminist criticism and social change: Sex, class and race in literature and culture.* New York: Methuen.

Penley, C. 1986. Teaching in your sleep: Feminism and psychoanalysis. In *Theory in the classroom,* ed. C. Nelson, 129–148. Urbana: University of Illinois Press.

Rothenberg, P. 1985. Teaching about racism and sexism: A case history. *Journal of Thought* 20(5):122–136.

Showalter, E., ed. 1985. *The new feminist criticism: Essays on women, literature and theory.* New York: Pantheon.

11

Print and Televisual Literacies: Uneasy Companions

Judith Millen

Literacy teachers have a great deal with which to contend. We must teach certain skills to students who come to us with different backgrounds and hence different literacy potentials. In this chapter I would like to pursue a few possibilities for literacy teachers using television, popular culture, and the teaching of reading in combination. Indeed, I have found that teaching traditional reading skills can be improved upon if teachers gain a deeper understanding of the literacy that many students already have when they come to us—namely televisual literacy. This televisual strand is actually just one of the many ways that students, already literate in popular culture of all kinds, can be helped in print literacy.

Competing Literacies?

The history and social relations of teaching have regulated teachers into assuming that print is the only valuable literacy. We assume that competing literacies are detrimental to the effective development of print literacy in our students. I have begun to question the ways that the taken-for-granteds about competing literacies, embedded in class, gender, and race assumptions in general, affect us and our students.

Progressive educational theorists have turned my attention to considerations of the social and historical conditions of schooling. Sometimes, in the beauty of contradiction, it has also been other middle-class parents who, arriving at my door to complain about the lack of socially conscious approaches to literacy, have prodded me on. But these parents are relatively few in number and their smaller numbers are regularly drowned out by the mainstream. Even in the 1960s, the so-called heyday of liberal-left schooling, the majority of teachers continued to teach from the Platonic/Socratic philosophical position so dear to the hearts of conservative educators. The gap between the liberal policies of theoretical educators and the actual classroom practices of teachers remained, even through these so-called liberal times. As an English department head of some ten years, primarily through the 1970s and early 1980s, one of the tasks I was never able to accomplish was to talk the majority of teachers in my department into practicing progressive and "relevant" teaching strategies. Many of them expressed a real interest in new approaches, but they continued to repeat the habits formed by their traditional teacher training and by their own experiences as students. What I could not unravel was why there was such a disjuncture between their professed interest in change and what was being done in their classrooms.

I have found part of the answer in myself: my own assumptions about the superiority of print are deeply surrounded by middle-class assumptions about what constitutes good reading material and what constitutes bad reading material, and hence what constitutes proper, legitimate literacy. We must account in some way for how our middle-class assumptions organize education for all people (Rose 1985). It is the conservative intellectual interests of the white middle class that have had the primary influence in defining and regulating literary curriculums.

This part of the intellectual middle class may be said to have controlled the naming of the literary canon through the universities, boards of education, and the publishing houses that have aligned themselves with these educational sites. Even with the affiliations that can be seen between the intellectual middle class and the interests of capital, this has been a decisively narrow and self-interested form of control. This regulation of the canon, however, has translated itself into a general "truth" in the middle class even though some middle-class practices are not consistent with these "truths." Indeed, my experience with some middle-class parents is that they complain heatedly about the lack of the classics (especially Shakespeare) in the junior curriculum but do virtually no reading in their own home. They come to teacher/parent meetings to complain about a form of schooling that they believe is superior but that they do not practice. This ideological construction of good literacy has a long history not easily shaken.

My own teaching was intensely informed by these assumptions, shored up by my own learned pleasures and aesthetic responses to reading "great books." My teaching continued to be informed by these assumptions until I stepped back from the specific conditions of teaching a discipline to look at the larger social issues that were quietly regulating my actions. Knowing that we are all embedded in the

arbitrary circumstances of what the middle class does and believes
about literacy was a basic step in my coming to terms with the ways
that decisions are made about literacy. That is, I came to understand
that these "rules" about what constituted preferred literacy were not
absolute truths but were, and are, historically and socially contingent. I had first to acknowledge that my idea of great literature was
actually produced by the arbitrary choices of a few white men of the
middle class.

What I see now is that a piece of the answer lies in what it is we
choose to teach. If we are of the "print only" school, then we are
always trapped by considerations of literacy that ignore the rapid and
diverse technological changes taking place today. Teachers have pre-
cious little time to begin anew a study of the conditions and regula-
tions of their work. And so what happens? We fall into the already-in-
place actions of the people around us. Here's an example. We are
asked to set an examination for the eleventh-grade literature class.
There are three other teachers whose classes will take this exam. The
chances that all four of us will be looking for new and progressive
ways of setting and administering exams are impossibly small. We
compromise and end up setting an exam that looks remarkably like
the one we wrote when we were in the eleventh grade. Actually, our
mothers would also recognize this exam. Examples like this (and
there are many more) illustrate that if tests for literacy are institu-
tionally regulated in this fashion, most teaching strategies are
equally solidified. Allowances for differences among students are
erased in the standard structures of literacy teaching.

But, if we choose to change our focus, if we take up and legitimize
other forms of literacy as part of the basis for our teaching, then we
are already on the way to breaking with the past history and practices
of literacy teaching. If we choose our steps very carefully, we can
begin anew and change the conditions of our teaching to better suit
the history and cultures of students in classes that we teach. That is,
if we change our focus to the literacies that students bring to school,
then we begin to dislodge the primacy of print as the only literacy of
value, and we begin to dislodge ourselves (white, middle class) as the
authority. If we say to students: "Teach me what you already know
and then maybe we can draw some connections between that and
what I can teach you," then we put ourselves in touch with the
knowledge that students have when they approach schools. We automatically, if our request of them is sincere, put ourselves in a position
to learn about race, class, gender, ability, age, and the seemingly endless variety of socialness that constitutes our students. But our question must be sincere. If we are using that proposal as a ruse to direct
students to what is really important (namely print and great books)

they will catch us at it. A long time ago I used Bob Dylan songs as examples of poetry. The students were angry. I believe they were angry not, as is the common wisdom, because I was ruining "their turf," but because I was insincere. They could see that I didn't really think Bob Dylan was as good a poet as Dylan Thomas, and that was what caught me. Today, I look to television and a new connection to popular culture to stir up and transform the conditions of my teaching. My snobbery and my unquestioning dependence on hierarchical ordering to define what is (and what is not) worthwhile can be seriously shaken up with this approach.

There are no English teachers who would claim that we can teach English without training in the canon, but there are many who freely make (negative) judgments about a medium like television with which they have very little contact and about which they have little understanding. One of the barriers that exists for our making pedagogical use of the viewing of students is our ignorance of the medium on the one hand, and our valuing of the elite forms of the literature canon over the "lower" forms of popular culture students use on the other. We need to see the complexity, diversity, and positive value of television.

A close look at excerpts from the analyses of television and popular culture undertaken by critics such as John Fiske (1987) and Giroux and Simon (1989) shows us that we are gaining some understanding about how television and popular culture operate in the lives of some students and that these operations can be very relevant to the teaching of literacy. Surely one of the traditional aims of the teacher of literature is to open students' sensitivities to a particular type of meaning making through their reading of literary texts. This specialized form of meaning making is what many of us mean by the category of "theme" in literature. Fiske (1982) tells us that in a somewhat similar struggle to make meaning in the interaction with cultural products, students "use" television to begin to understand cultural categories and their own socially constituted lives. They use it "to think through their experience . . . from their own position, to make a kind of sense . . . that suit[s] their social interests. . . . " (69). Such a use of text has echoes of the traditional understanding of how a literary text would operate on its readers. But there are some significant differences.

This use of television is more striking in that it suggests a way that students might be "allowed" a social position of their own. The viewer of television is understood to be someone who can use a text for social understanding that comes out of that viewer's subject position. This viewer is no couch potato: indeed, the interaction with popular culture provides, for some theorists, the very ground upon which to develop democratic relationships between teachers and students. These democratic relationships take place when the knowledge of the student is highlighted. Student literacies become as important as anything else in the curriculum. We are thus brought back to a version of student-centeredness. This time, however, we teachers must change. We have to begin to privilege all forms of literacy in addition to the content of mainstream curriculums and print.

Finally, it is important to emphasize that such student "use" of television, most often narrative, is just one of the means whereby they formulate worldviews and take action in their world. Nevertheless, these uses (as singular and falsely isolated as they are here) can be, as we shall see, instructive for a literature classroom.

What's Happening in the TV Room?

Looking at some specific examples of how students "use" television might be helpful at this point. In particular, it is vital to note the ways television is used to delineate relationships to power. Some white middle-class boys, for instance, will move from more diverse and multiple preadolescent viewing (which can include soap operas, normally considered as female viewing) to relatively exclusive sports viewing. This can be seen as one of their ways of "becoming masculine." These boys quickly come to "know" that "real" forms of masculinity are expressed in such things as sports. Such masculinity is partially expressed through the sports narrative of dominance, submission, and "mastery." This viewing choice may not, however, preclude some form of print literacy. Among these boys, reading skills may get practiced through newspapers and magazines. These print adjuncts to the sports narrative are important to them because a display of sports knowledge is part of the essential narrative of mastery. Reading sports statistics and articles is vital as sources of information.

Other boys, however, may not take up the sports narrative but will rather choose action and adventure of the "lone male hero" sort where masculinity is regularly represented as a form of expressed or tacit violence, misogyny, and withdrawal from emotional interaction. These choices for gendered viewing are found most often now in television movies featuring the machismo of Rocky, Rambo, James Bond, the Terminator, or Clint Eastwood's characters. Network series such as *MacGyver, Hunter, Jake and the Fat Man,* and *Nightheat* are slowly being replaced by ones such as *Beverly Hills 90210.*

Still other boys' choices illustrate how class, as well as gender, does some of the work in enabling these boys' use of television viewing. One fifteen-year-old, for instance, whose father is a lawyer,

watches *LA Law* regularly and is already beginning to define his
future in terms of the practice of a profession that may or may not be
the law but that does include maintaining or "improving" his social
status. Nevertheless, the desires of this boy for his future are not
simplistic. That is, he is often ambivalent and contradictory in these
desires. At times he will say he wants to help others, at times he
wants to own a very expensive car. Still, the material desires do have,
in spite of the contradictions, a strong hold on his design for his
future. Boys learn, variously, to admire dominance in sports, in and
through action, not only on the screen but also in the professions,
where male mastery is part of the structure. This is how dominant
narratives become part of real lives.

There is a complexity through which students make meaning out
of popular culture. The viewing strategies of the young begin to form
in multiple ways. The choice of action/adventure can indicate a state
of disempowerment rather than privilege for a certain type of male
viewer (Walkerdine 1990). His watching of "male hero" television
narratives may point to his sense of hopelessness—and acceptance—
or anger or resistance regarding the world. We must be aware of the
subtleties in how viewing practices are located. Viewing choices can
be compliant with dominance either as a statement of social potential
or of resignation. What, for instance, is happening for girls who
choose action/adventure (*Thelma and Louise*)—or for boys who
choose less macho models than that of the male hero?

Choices might also be oppositional or a complex mixture of these
two poles. Many viewing choices do not fall in line with the dominant
meanings of inclusion and exclusion that would be consistent with a
teenager's gender, race, and class. Viewing choices are never indicative of strict binary opposition. In Fiske's terms, these viewing practices run across a continuum. Oppositional viewing choices range
along the spectrum from partial rejection of dominant ideologies to a
full-scale rejection of dominant structures. For instance, a white,
middle-class, female student might watch soap operas in the face of
clear-cut disapproval of this viewing within her family and school. At
the same time she might maintain a standard of literacy in print that
does not jeopardize her status as a "good" student. On the one hand,
she opposes a general class rejection of the soap opera form; on the
other, she continues to fashion her life in a way that values the construction of a middle-class girl's literacy. She has expressed some
opposition to middle-class standards for literacy, but at the same time
she has not. Indeed, a closer look at any soap opera illustrates that
soap operas can actually be helpful in creating the accommodation of
capitalism and traditional gender roles that keep girls "in the fold" in

ways more numerous than these popular or cultural forms ask her to violate. She may reject the high-culture condemnation of melodrama, but she remains ideologically and materially accommodating of the race, class, and gender interests that describe her privilege.

In another instance, a black working-class teenage girl might take up the narratives of, for instance, *The Cosby Show,* by seeing it as an instance of the oppressive predominance of class struggle over race struggle. In the *Cosby* narratives, the pride in African American heritage is deeply infused with the conditions of capitalism and the middle class. Many teenagers are aware of these discrepancies and see them as a false promise to the majority of black North Americans. They do not see opportunity for black North Americans in a narrative that presents two working professionals (she a lawyer, he a doctor) as the norm for African American access to education and privilege. Some students call the Huxtables "Oreos," black on the outside, white on the inside, a term that ironically indicates their awareness of class as much as race discrepancies. Such students also see the promise of a "traditional" family (mother and father and five children) as blatantly opposed to their experience. They think of the Huxtables as caricatures. Consequently many black teens watch *The Cosby Show* with derision or anger, as a form of resistance not of accommodation or acceptance. Miller (1988) has pointed to the fact that the largely white audience for *The Cosby Show* is indicative that middle-class whites are relieved to see a representation of a black family that is clearly organized by capital and therefore poses no threat to the security of capital. The sign at the door reads, "Rich African Americans Welcome." The mixture of race and class in this instance is contradictory.

Other examples of negotiated and/or oppositional viewing can be observed in some viewers of the numerous family-oriented shows (*Who's the Boss, thirtysomething, Growing Pains,* and so on), who also watch (in 1991–92) a cartoon like *The Simpsons* or the sitcoms *Roseanne* and *Married with Children.* These latter renditions of family seem to satisfy a need to acknowledge more openly the flaws in the middle-class family. One student expressed relief at being able to laugh at the things she recognized as part of her experience, an experience she does not see represented in *Growing Pains* or *Cosby.* These shows can be negotiated as the antithesis of the well-regulated middle-class capitalist family and thus become forms of resistant texts and viewings.

If, as teachers, we ignore these texts or see them as crass, vulgar, or "dangerous," we have not listened. We forego the opportunity to engage and legitimate the actual knowledge, competence, and literacies of our students through their uses of other media.

What's Happening in the Classroom?

Mainstream opinion quickly identifies oppositional televisual texts as having a strong influence on teenagers. The narratives of many rock videos, for example, are described as negative influences in the lives of many youths (as are the narratives of *The Simpsons* and *Married . . . with Children*), especially when these narratives are oppositional to middle-class senses of order and hierarchy. But when similar textual "effects" are suggested about the literary canon (Morgan 1987; Rose 1985) and the inculcation of dominance within the canon, there is an eerie silence. The texts that are understood to be "good" texts are those that conceptualize social structures (the sort of thing we call "literary themes") and with these themes normalize ideals of hierarchy and superiority. This is where the work must be done.

Many of us use narrative in an effort to teach reading. We assume that a "good" story will guarantee student attention for the time necessary also to teach literacy skills. But we are still left with the question of what exactly constitutes a "good" narrative. In many cases stories are seen as the neutral vehicles for adventure or suspense (Poe, Conan Doyle, London). In other instances a good story is the carrier of historical and timeless (universal) understandings about the world (Shakespeare, Shaw, Hemingway, Robertson Davies). In the best of instances, a good story is exemplified both by its ability to hold interest through adventure or suspense and to be the carrier of absolute truths about the world.

If we assume that print narrative is the only legitimate avenue to literacy, then we are doubly removed from an investigation into the social and historical operations of literacy discourse. As a result, there are few efforts made to uncover how stories operate on extraliterary levels even as we are actually making them extraliterary in the name of thematic studies. But, when "good" stories are analyzed in the same light as those of television narratives, they can no longer be seen as neutral vehicles of universal wisdom. Narratives from "great literature" are as much mythologies (Barthes 1973; Fiske 1982) as any text. "Culture is seen as the sphere in which class, gender, race and other inequities are naturalized and represented in forms which sever (as far as possible) the connection between these and economic and political inequalities" (O'Sullivan, Hartley, Saunders & Fiske 1983, 60). Cultural studies, (de Lauretis 1987; Kaplan 1982), feminist studies, (Fetterley 1981; Meese 1990; Moi 1985; Showalter 1985), and antiracist studies (Bulkin, Pratt & Smith 1984; Simone 1989; Young 1987) have long since uncovered the ways that literature operates on behalf of dominant myths, but they have still not gained enough of a foothold in mainstream teaching to have any substantial impact. Teacher education is still tacitly and overly organized around the study of the specific subjects and details to be taught. Not enough work has been done on the general effects of these subjects within larger social systems. Thus, in much mainstream teaching, "good" narratives are still stories that have value because they are seen to be natural truths about the world. They attempt to create the myth of individual redemption as if we all stood on the same playing field with equal advantage and access to advantage when in fact we do not. Popular culture can help change the conditions of play.

The disenchantment with print among students has unmistakable effects. We all know that students have become adept at passing tests and essays about books they never finished; they are becoming skilled at reading encapsulated versions of the larger texts (so-called study guides) or getting the information from their fellow students without reading anything (buying or cribbing other student work). Some simply refuse to engage literacy at all, and the threat of failing has no impact on them. In part, this condition has to do with the dissonance between much of the curriculum and students' social realities. If we hope to have students engage critically with Shakespeare, we must first engage their ironic understanding of *The Simpsons*. The dissonance is not the effect of a particular individual alienation or "dishonesty" but rather of a social alienation. It is certainly not the result of teacher incompetence! Teachers who encourage and facilitate popular cultural forms, ones that students can actually work with, are not pandering to the personal and subjectively understood desires of individual students. Rather we are looking at how the dissonance of canonic reading and student social reality is created through our own closed-down social understanding. We are looking at all the possible and valid ways there are to have knowledge about the world.

How the Classroom Might Work

To begin with, a study of what and how much television narrative our students watch could help alert us to the students' competencies on many levels. The notion that students are competent because of their television viewing is a concept foreign to many teachers, but recognition of such student competence can begin to break down the hierarchical barriers in schools. Students who are regular viewers of narrative television have a vast store of information. On their own they know history and character. They are also adept at discussing the personalities and problems of their favorite characters and at trying to problem-solve for these characters. They can give a variety of reasons for their likes and dislikes of characters, even identify instances when they like a character who might be a "bad" person, thereby also possibly describing their relationship to power in another way.

In varying degrees, students have the verbal ability to present some sophisticated analyses of the programs they watch. When given a chance to express themselves differently, even those students for whom verbal skills are not strong can be very intricate in their analysis of their viewing. Students bring to the classroom a series of structural and analytic knowledges and competencies that are often not accounted for in schools. Making room for, and allowing for, these competencies and knowledges is an important first step in democratic schooling.

Although we are aware that interacting with our students is an important avenue into democratic pedagogy, correspondences between privilege and narrative choices within a race, class, or gender framework are not always as clear-cut as I have characterized them here, and they must be made visible. Although choices are constantly entangled with contradiction, struggle, and nonlinearity, we cannot avoid them. Even in a postmodern world, one that would deny linearity and stability, we must continue to identify dominance and oppression in people's lives. For me, finding out why I choose to read certain texts that are forms of the dominant/submissive structure stimulates fuller understanding of student choices and their relationship to power and hence to literacy. The more we recognize that we, as well as students, make narrative choices based on expressions of our relationships to power, the more we may be able to work with the ways that younger people also make these choices.

For example, young people often love television that features children with power (*Home Alone*), adults in the process of losing power (*Married . . . with Children, The Simpsons*), or young people and adults negotiating power equally (*Beverly Hills 90210*), conditions that speak to a young person's frustration with helplessness. These programs are not an expression of any misguided aesthetic understanding of culture or any failure of the school system to teach the "right" things, they are an expression of social meaning. Our interaction with popular culture is an expression of our social and historical understanding. It is key in any democratic educational relationship. Popular culture begins to unravel how the power of class, race, gender, ability, sexuality, and so on is experienced by our students. Teachers who come to popular culture knowing that they can expand their knowledge will be better teachers.

Furthermore, teachers of literacy will have an easier time identifying the social conditions of students' meaning making if we use texts the students choose outside the constraints of schooling. Television's

narratives often offer more opportunities for insight into the ongoing
social relations of our students than does print. A white middle-class
boy's choice of *LA Law* is likely to indicate that he will have an easier
time reading the canon (that is, his choice of TV narrative already
indicates the possibility of print literacy) than another middle- or
working-class boy who chooses exclusively to watch action/adventure
or sports narratives. He may be indicating print avoidance in such
choices. These latter choices often indicate some opposition to dominant social forms and literacies and are found more often, but not
exclusively, among working class "lads" (Willis 1981). Under the right
circumstances the choice of *LA Law* indicates the potential for social
actuality. Social and cultural theorists have indicated the many examples of how class, race, and gender interests operate in the lives of
people, either as connections or disconnections to power (Alvarado &
Thompson 1990; Hall 1990; Kaplan 1987; Kuhn 1982; Mulvey 1975).
So it is also important to note that the pull toward power and domination, when it is available to the young, is regularly the strongest of
all. Youth itself is powerless. These pulls toward and the access to
power are in themselves forms of literacy. Some will choose *LA Law*
because it mirrors future social possibility. Some will choose the power
of violence because that is often the only possibility available. These
narrative choices are important starting points for the teacher of literature.

Teachers might begin with an informal survey of students' viewing practices to illustrate whether the material conditions of their everyday environments are encouraging print or media or both as forms
of literacy. But there is a caveat here. Literature teachers who begin
their interaction with any student group based on a classification of its
members as print literate (or not) must guard against the possibility of
categorizing these students on a superior-inferior continuum. Such a
form of classification can actually become part of the process that encourages resistance to school among some students. Students who are
already advised of the ways that they fail within a system can spot all
the devices teachers have of identifying their inadequacies. As many of
us have asked ourselves before, why would any students want to continue to struggle in an environment that describes them as handi-
capped and inferior? Thus a survey of student literacies must be
constructed as one that looks at, respects, and acknowledges all the
levels of student competency. It can be the first step in a genuine vision
of all students as differently abled and competent in literacies.

Traditional teaching strategies can be remobilized to allow for the
presentation of students' already-in-place competencies. Students
who are not yet print literate can, for example, be asked to outline
their favorite television stories. The intricacies and complexities that

become apparent at just this level of retelling their favorite programs is a good entry point into the exploration of student skills. In one ninth-grade general-level class, a teacher versed in this type of exploration sidetracked her intended reading of the Helen Keller story when she realized that her mainly male class wanted to talk about a recent boxing match. She began the discussion with structuring questions about the setting (a large and resplendent Las Vegas hotel), the characters (the two fighters and their managers), the nature of the conflict (who was the underdog, who the favorite, and why), the history of the main characters (one Canadian, one American, one with a reputation for wife beating, and so on). The detail and eagerness with which this topic was taken up made the class dynamic and interesting. The result was that the teacher was also able to investigate the features of the way professional boxing is put together. She was able to talk to these competent students about the way violence is sanctioned in sport and elsewhere and to ask about other areas of sanctioned violence such as the Gulf war, which was going on at the time. In a subsequent class, a discussion about the differences between male and female responses to boxing was also possible. This second-hand form of oral storytelling is an age-old technique that affirms a student's literacies and abilities to analyze.

Technology can also be used to facilitate some of this type of storytelling. A tape recorder can be used to capture the story retellings. After listening to and critiquing their own tellings, the students can then edit their work. Under certain circumstances a video camera might be used to tape the student version of the story. If the students are amenable, this form of recording can be valuable in letting the students know where their storytelling falls short in producing excitement and suspense. It is often a motivator for the students to rethink and restructure their own skills. When it comes, the switch to print has to be accompanied by a student's sense of skill, not inadequacy. Students can be encouraged to transcribe their stories. Word processing can often be a motivator in this area. Literacy teachers, for instance, are becoming aware of the increased writing that takes place when students are allowed to use word processors. The link between video games and computers/word processors can be profitably used. One teacher reported that students who cannot be cajoled into handwriting more than a page of journal in a month are writing over a page every time they are at the computer.

The investigation of student televisual skills cannot, however, stop with establishing their competencies. A democratic pedagogy that allows student skills to enter the curriculum has not gone far enough unless it also makes visible the ways these skills fix (and often arrest) the students in a power hierarchy. The pedagogy must also push the students to critique the conditions of their own choices and, therefore, of aspects of their own knowledge. We must determine how we are also used by media—print included. As the investigation of students' interest in televisual narrative continues, it becomes apparent to teachers what it is that students actually like in popular culture, not what they might like. What they do like is, as I have said, a statement of the possible limits of their worldviews and their everyday choices. We can enable students to look beyond the limits of their biases and worldviews to engage social change if we begin with their knowledge and literacy. Questions about their preferences for, for example, *Married . . . with Children* and *The Simpsons* have revealed stories of abuse. How can any student in the grip of abuse be sanguine about sweet renditions of middle-class families? How can girls trapped in images of thin, beautiful models be ready for independence? Students know a lot; but like adults they have not asked all the questions and they have not been freed from some very debilitating notions of truth and normalcy. Students must at least be given a chance to investigate the parameters of their worlds and the ways they have (or do not have) access to social change. Girls (girls of color in particular) need to find the tools to ask the questions that expose their doubly, triply regulated lives.

Critical pedagogy has begun an in-depth analysis of the conditions and questions that teachers might ask in order to bring our understanding of schooling up to date (Aronowitz & Giroux 1985; 1991; Giroux & Simon 1989; Weiler 1988). Critical pedagogy brings us face-to-face with important issues, but it has also been the site of some considerable intellectualizing that can be alienating for teachers in the classroom (Ellsworth 1989). And yet, as I have argued, matching theory with what we know to be actual in schools brings us closer to democratic pedagogy. Teachers find themselves, as do their students, in many contradictory locations and must struggle to see the implications of all literature as a social as well as a literary practice. We are overworked and often feel discouraged by the additional requests made upon our time and effort by socially conscious pedagogies. It is especially difficult when the curriculum does not generally encourage seeking such an expertise. Unfortunately, without these interlacing perspectives, teachers are as much "used" by their discipline as students are. The inequities simply continue. Popular culture is a good place to begin to break down some of these disproportions.

References

Alvarado, M. & J. O. Thompson, eds. 1990. *The media reader.* London: British Film Institute.

Aronowitz, S. & H. Giroux. 1991. Textual authority, culture, and the politics of literacy. In *The politics of the textbook,* ed. M. W. Apple & L. K. Christian-Smith. New York: Routledge.

————. 1985. *Education under siege.* South Hadley, MA: Bergin & Garvey.

Barthes, R. 1973. *Mythologies.* London: Paladin.

Bulkin, E., M. B. Pratt & B. Smith, eds. 1984. *Yours in struggle: Three feminist perspectives on anti-semitism and racism.* New York: Long Haul Press.

de Lauretis, T. 1987. *Technologies of gender: Essays on theory, film and fiction.* Bloomington: Indiana University Press.

Ellsworth, E. 1989. Why doesn't this feel empowering? Working through the repressive myths of critical pedagogy. *Harvard Education Review* 59:297–324.

Fiske, J. 1982. *Introduction to communication studies.* 2d ed. New York: Routledge.

————. 1987. *Television culture.* New York: Methuen.

Giroux, H. & R. Simon, eds. 1989. *Popular culture: Schooling and everyday life.* Toronto: OISE Press.

Kaplan, E. A. 1987. *Rocking around the clock: Music television, postmodernism, and consumer culture.* New York: Methuen.

Kuhn, A. 1982. *Women's pictures: Feminism and cinema.* London: Routledge & Kegan Paul.

Lazere, D., ed. 1987. *American media and mass culture: Left perspectives.* Berkeley: University of California Press.

Lentricchia, F. 1980. *After the New Criticism.* Chicago: University of Chicago Press.

Meese, E. A. 1990. *(Ex)tensions: Re-figuring feminist criticism.* Chicago: University of Chicago Press.

Miller, M. C. 1988. *Boxed in: The culture of TV.* Evanston, IL: Northwestern University Press.

Moi, T. 1985. *Sexual/textual politics: Feminist literary theory.* London: Methuen.

Morgan, R. 1987. *English studies as cultural production in Ontario, 1860–1920.* Ph.D. diss., University of Toronto.

Mulvey, L. 1975. Visual pleasure and narrative cinema. *Screen* 16(3):6–18.

O'Sullivan, T., J. Hartley, D. Saunders & J. Fiske. 1983. *Key concepts in communications.* London: Methuen.

Rose, J. 1985. State and language: Peter Pan as written for the child. In *Language, gender and childhood,* ed. V. Walkerdine, C. Urwin & C. Steedman. London: Routledge & Kegan Paul.

Showalter, E., ed. 1985. *The new feminist criticism: Essays on women, literature and theory.* New York: Pantheon.

Simone, T. M. 1989. *About face: Race in post-modern America.* Brooklyn: Autonomedia.

Walkerdine, V. 1990. Video replay: Families, films and fantasy. In *The media reader*. See Alvarado & Thompson 1990.

Weiler, K. 1988. *Women teaching for change: Gender, class and power*. South Hadley, MA: Bergin & Garvey.

Willis, P. 1981. *Learning to labor: How working class kids get working class jobs*. New York: Columbia University Press.

————. 1981. Patriarchy, racialism and labour power. In *Politics, patriarchy and power*, ed. R. Dale, G. Eoland, R. Ferguson & M. MacDonald. Sussex: Falmer.

Wolf, N. 1990. *The beauty myth*. Toronto: Vintage.

Young, J., ed. 1987. *Breaking the mosaic: Ethnic studies in Canadian schooling*. Toronto: Garamond.

12

Teaching English:
Who's Subject to What?

Ursula Kelly

A fundamental assumption that governs the study of English and the study preparation of English teachers is that "the subject of English is always the site of subjectivity" (Humm 1989, 39). As used here, subjectivity refers to the process of the production or the making of the "thinking, speaking, acting, doing or writing agent" (Kristeva 1980, 19), that is, the human subject. Here, it is necessary to emphasize both "process" and "production," for it is these claims about human subjectivity that make the work of teaching English possible. Human subjectivity, who and what we are, is produced through, among other things, our life experiences and how we understand these experiences, an ongoing process in which change is both possible and real. It can be argued that the study and teaching of English accelerates and accentuates this process, actively encouraging the production of certain kinds of subjectivities while actively discouraging others.

The implications of these arguments are enormous. English teachers often see themselves as "moral arbiters," teaching sanctioned language and canonized texts to produce a literate, informed citizenry, that is to say, state subjects. Yet, the history of English has other sides to its story than the sounding of this "old myth" may allow to be heard. Through an examination of some of the predominant notions of what English is and what it does, through a rethinking of these notions and through an envisioning of a more critical approach to English, this chapter offers a reexamination of English and traditional ways of teaching English to certain ends. It provides perspectives that challenge teachers and students of English to engage more fully in "a process of becoming different by thinking critically and creatively" (Smyth 1989, 485) about our literary worlds and their interrelationships with our real worlds.

"Cultural Missionaries" and English

When providing reasons for wanting to teach English, many preservice teachers often refer, either directly or indirectly, to the often cited objectives of English teaching: to develop and enhance communication skills, to nurture the discriminating reader of "great literature" and, through both, to disseminate so-called high culture. Often, it is because English has enriched and transformed their own lives that preservice English teachers choose to shape their future work lives around it. In a very real sense, then, these preservice teachers are in training to become the "cultural missionaries" to which Margaret Mathieson (1975, 210) refers. Having been inculcated with a certain culture and being convinced of its righteousness, even if ambivalent of their chances of success, they wish to proceed with the conveyance of that culture to the more or less uninitiated.

Undoubtedly, these students do not underestimate the work of English teaching and the power of language and literature. Nor are they alone in their assertions about what English is for. Their explanations are reiterated daily in classrooms at all levels of formal schooling (Doyle 1982). But in many of these reiterations, what might be considered the insidious underbelly of the traditional study and teaching of English goes unexplored and unrecognized. Little is mentioned in English teaching, or in study preparation for the teaching of English, of the historical roots of English as a curriculum subject developed to establish and sustain the language, culture, and power of the middle class in England. Through schooling in the subject of English, certain forms of language and culture were established as superior, while others different from these were deemed inferior. This dominance was gained and is still sustained today through the continued suppression, subjection, and regulation of all forms of language and culture (Belsey 1982; Doyle 1982; Lovell 1987) in all social sites, for example, schools, business, and media.

Also largely ignored in the study of English is the imperialist nature of the subject as it was exported from England and, in many ways, continues to be taught in the now former colonies, Africa, India (Batsleer, Davies, O'Rourke & Weedon 1985), and Canada (Morgan 1990; Walker 1990). That is, what is chosen for study in English classrooms cannot be disassociated from the history of English colonial rule and the establishment of the "British Empire." English, in this form, still presents a major obstacle for peoples attempting to reclaim their historically subverted language and culture. In South Africa, for example, English in state schools works explicitly to "teach" black inferiority through a Eurocentric curriculum saturated with the beliefs and works of mostly white and mostly male English writers (Dlamini 1990). Similar arguments may be made about state and provincial curriculums, as they work against many disaffected social groups, in most school systems in the world, so widespread is this English imperialism.

Face-to-face with such aspects of the history of English, it seems important to consider the possibilities of a different moral imperative from the unquestioning acceptance of the legacy of domination and oppression that is a large part of what we know as English. At present, powerful "normalizing" (Greene 1988, 476) forces work to encourage a taken-for-granted attitude toward English, that is, such hierarchization and stratification of language and culture appear as normal, natural, and inevitable rather than socially produced, struggled over, and clearly changeable. However, alternative practices are possible and are illustrated in the two examples that follow, the establishment of the "standard" English speech and the "canon" of [L]iterature.

In the teaching of "standard" English, it is often not sufficiently acknowledged that the so-called standard is only one instance of English usage brought to dominant status through state- and provincially legislated formal and informal curriculums. As a result of such official sanctioning, this "standard" is now one against which all other forms of spoken English are measured. In imposing the "standard," little regard is given to either its arbitrariness or the need to preserve, respectfully, the language of community and culture that is a student's "first language." In this scenario, lost are the opportunities to study the richness of language difference, to explore the connections between language, culture, and identity, and to affirm social difference.

Instead, what often happens in English classes is that a homogenizing process begins, a process in which there are losers on all sides, whether or not the homogenization is ever fully effective. Many who have acquiesced to the so-called standard English know painfully and well the resulting isolation and alienation from their original communities and cultures whose practice of English differs from this "standard." Rarely, it seems, is such "academic terrorism" (Batsleer, Davies, O'Rourke & Weedon 1985, 28) acknowledged; too rarely is it questioned. That it is so rarely questioned speaks to the effectiveness of the imposition, through English teaching, of dominant value systems. On the one hand, this imposition can work to produce an acquiescent human subject accepting of the constructed yet very socially real superiority of the imposed forms of language. On the other, the imposition can reproduce a human subject who is already privileged in the larger social order and whose value system is reinforced through and by schooling.

While the study of literature is very much the focus of English teaching (Green 1990) and as such was and still is the main instrument of promoting and reinforcing "standard" English, literature is also effectively and overtly used in an "apprenticeship in discrimination" (Batsleer, Davies, O'Rourke & Weedon 1985, 29) where "beneath the [apparently] disinterested procedures of literary judgement and discrimination can be discerned the outlines of other, harsher words: exclusion, subordination, dispossession" (30). Research has, by now, well established that excluded, subordinated, and dispossessed within the history of English, particularly within the "classics," the so-called canon of [L]iterature, are many voices, those representative, for example, of women, many ethnic and racial groups, gay men and lesbians, and working classes (Lovell 1987; Russ 1983; Spender 1989).

The accuracy of this claim may be evidenced by the contents of and accompanying author biographies in most school literature anthologies. English curriculums have been slow to reflect a more accurate representation of our pluralistic and globally dependent world. In the face of such biased selection and study of texts, other measures can be enacted to encourage a "reading against" this elitism. Students of English can, for example, be directed to ask questions that probe the implications of the inclusion of some writers and communities and the exclusion of others. Students might well benefit from discussions of what constitutes quality in writing, how such decisions get made and transmitted, and who gains and suffers by such established biases of quality. Literature classes can become places in which students learn to question representation, voice, text, and context in the development of "readings" of the world and the relationship of literature to that world.

Each of the preceding examples points to the need for teachers and students of English to avoid begging the questions of English, [L]iterature, and curriculum by exploring the assumptions and histories that inform our present practices in this school subject. Without examining "the historical conditions which motivate our conceptualizations" (Foucault 1982, 778), teachers of English are in some ways disarmed, while unwittingly armed for allies unknown to them, going forth into classrooms bearing a creed the conditions and effects of which have not adequately been confronted. In recent revisions of particular imperialist moments in history, missionaries have been getting a "bad name." Is it now time that the "cultural missionaries" take stock—and begin to revise our own histories through rewriting and transforming our futures?

English, Cultural Politics and Critical Practice

As Phyllis Rose (1985) argues, "there is no neutrality. There is only greater or less awareness of one's bias" (77). It is quite possible and even likely that preservice teachers have had little opportunity in their studies to explore the connections between the historically entrenched biases of English and the unequal relations of power— among social classes, between men and women, among races and ethnic groups, to name a few—that form our larger social contexts. Providing the possibilities for such insights means, at the very least, providing spaces for alternative ways of understanding both English and society. Such spaces may arise through the formulation of certain reflective questions about one's teaching: In what ways do the happenings of my classroom represent and/or mirror the problems of society? In what ways do the happenings of my classroom challenge the injustices of the world? In what ways do I allow for the expression and affirmation of difference in my classroom? If, indeed, English does nurture the process of the production of human subjectivities— for example, the patronizing male, the white racist, and the self-deprecating woman, to name some of the more prevalent and oppressive forms—can challenges to these forms through literature nurture the production of alternative, less oppressive subjectivities?

Chris Weedon (1987) suggests that "forms of [human] subjectivity are produced historically and change with shifts in the wide range of discursive fields which constitute them" (33). Many contemporary literary and critical theories do pose alternatives to those theories most commonly posed to students of English. For example, feminist literary theorists have been instrumental in calling into question the lack of significant place of the voices of women, First Nations people, African Canadians/Americans, and lesbians, groups marginalized in the literary canon. Given the opportunity to trace the historical factors leading to a rationale for such exclusion, students can rethink the usual claims about the underrepresentation of women within the canon, for example, that few women wrote or that their work was in some ways outside the "objective" standards of good literature (Russ 1983; Spender 1989). English students can be challenged to move beyond the assumption that women did not write or did not write well, into more productive questions around what women did write, what their publishing experiences were, how these experiences differed from those of men of the same era, and why, with a few notable exceptions, the often superb writing of women went unnoticed.

This more "constructive reading" of English entails not only a shift in the subject, English; it provides, too, the basis for a potential shift in students' understanding. Through a wider range of perspectives and practices, students may realize a more compassionate and informed understanding of many unexamined and largely taken-for-granted attitudes about literature, reading practices, language, and culture. Students may learn to question the historical, social, and personal implications of one kind of writing being considered

"[L]iterature" and another "trash," of one reader being "discriminating" and another "low brow," of one type of culture being "high"
and another "pop." Further, students may well begin to talk about
what they perhaps already know, that is, that reading and reading
choices are much more intricately tied to people's lived realities and
to social relations of power than is ever usually acknowledged in
English classrooms.

The provision of alternative positions to those usually posed to
students of English and English education shores up the reality of
English as a site of struggle—for power, for position, and for
meaning—that is, English as a form of cultural politics (Green 1990).
To question the teaching of "English" in this way is to acknowledge
that English is the terrain on which are fought out answers to such
questions as, What culture? Whose culture? Under what circumstances? For what purposes? With what meanings?—questions that
are fundamentally about power, social relations, and human subjectivity. Included in any of the multiplicity of answers to these questions are moments in which some voices, some forms of human subjectivity, are affirmed, while others are devalued and silenced.

Yet, in very real ways, these struggles are already lived out in
English classes. The ambivalence with which many students and preservice teachers approach the study of English attests to the very real
suspicion by both that something is amiss. The perennial protests by
many students about the "relevance" of curricular materials speaks
to this disquiet as well. These feelings may well be a part of the resistance out of which a more exciting and informed study of English
might come.

Recognizing and accepting that human subjectivity is at the heart
of English teaching does not, in and of itself, necessitate any sort of
change in content and pedagogy. Concluding that the forms of human
subjectivity encouraged in and through the present circumstances of
the teaching of English are limiting and often oppressively sexist, racist, and elitist necessitates changes in both. Reformulating English,
then, and in so doing, hopefully enhancing the possibilities for remak-
ing the human subject of English, demands "a pedagogy of possibility" (Simon 1987, 370) in which the bias of all forms of literary knowing is acknowledged and critiqued and in which multiple realities are
celebrated and interrogated. It is a pedagogy in which students may
come to see more clearly the forces that work to make them who they
are, in which they imagine greater possibilities for what they may
become, and in which they can discern those qualities they no longer
desire. Such an informed citizenry might well strike a resounding
commitment to social justice once the conditions of injustice are more
fully realized.

What is suggested here is a pedagogy in which students and teachers of English can engage in the dynamic articulation of issues of power in language, culture, history, and experience—those fundamental aspects of the study of English—in more diversified, less monolithic, and more democratic ways. Central to such a pedagogy is the use of what Ira Shor and Paulo Freire (1987) call the "dialogical" method of teaching, attempts in classrooms to establish a more "democratic communication which disconfirms domination and illuminates while affirming the freedom of the participants to re-make their culture" (99). What such a method entails is the decentering of teacher authority and teacher claims to sole arbitration over the agenda and meaning of English. Instead, the forum is set for dialogue that can be as much contestation as affirmation and that is the explication of what it means to do English as cultural politics.

Through this venue, the proprietors of "standard" English, Great Literature, the discriminating reader, and the literary canon are challenged to reveal their politics—who benefits, who loses, what is gained, what is lost—not just at the level of the individual but at the level of the larger cultural community. Of course, the same challenge faces those proprietors of alternative, more critical approaches as well. In any case, the perspective of interrogation and critique (Kelly 1990) is one that enhances the possibilities of classroom democracy and encourages subject change as a necessary precursor to positive social change.

The basis for altering the politics of English teaching is already very much underway. As John Willinsky (1990) points out, "the New Literacy," that is, "those strategies in the teaching of reading and writing which attempt to shift the control of literacy from the teacher to the student" (8), for example, whole language and reader response, are fertile ground for enhancing the "social enterprise of literacy" (226). However, Willinsky, too, acknowledges that much more must be made of the social constitution of the individual self who, in the New Literacy, is put at the center of meaning production. Most important to realize is the extent to which that very self, that human subject, is constituted through the discourses available to it in the social context of the classroom, the community, and, in fact, the entire available signifying world. A pedagogy that has as one of its fundamental principles a critique of all perspectives—traditional, alternative, elitist, democratic, progressive—is that which might lead to the necessary evolution of the New Literacy into a more explicit form of cultural politics.

While teaching English as cultural politics is a healthily unsettling practice, it is certainly an important and necessary move "beyond communication." In many ways, to decide, explicitly, to put the construction of human subjectivity at the center of English is to put at the center of English studies the social order out of which communities of human subjects are formed. Further, it is to assert consistently that what we do in English classrooms matters in terms of such questions as, Who I am? How do I belong? What can I hope for? To what degree we provide the spaces for such questions to challenge all that is done in English classrooms may well be the most important criterion by which English teaching may be judged.

References

Batsleer, J., T. Davies, R. O'Rourke & C. Weedon. 1985. *Rewriting English: Cultural politics of gender and class.* London: Methuen.

Belsey, C. 1982. Re-reading the great tradition. In *Re-reading English,* ed. P. Widdowson, 121–35. London: Methuen.

Dlamini, S. N. 1990. *Critical teaching under the Bantu education system.* Master's thesis, Saint Mary's University, Halifax, NS.

Doyle, B. 1982. The hidden history of English studies. In *Re-reading English,* ed. P. Widdowson, 17–31. London: Methuen.

Foucault, M. 1982. The subject and power. *Critical Inquiry* 8(Summer):777–95.

Green, B. 1990. A dividing practice: Literature, English teaching and cultural politics. In *Bringing English to order,* ed. I. Goodson & P. Medway, 135–61. New York: Falmer.

Greene, M. 1988. What are the language arts for? *Language Arts* 65(5):474–80.

Humm, M. 1989. Subjects in English : Autobiography, women and education. In *Teaching women: Feminism and English studies,* ed. A. Thompson and H. Wilcox, 39–49. Manchester, UK: Manchester University Press.

Kelly, U. A. 1990. "On the edge of the eastern ocean": Teaching, marginality and voice. In *Critical pedagogy and cultural power,* ed. D. Henley & J. Young. Winnipeg: University of Manitoba Press.

Kristeva, J. [1977] 1980. *Desire in language.* Trans. L. S. Roudiez. New York: Columbia University Press.

Lovell, T. 1987. *Consuming fiction.* London: Verso.

Mathieson, M. 1975. *Preachers of culture.* London: Allen & Unwin.

Morgan, R. 1990. The "englishness" of English teaching. In *Bringing English to order,* ed, I. Goodson and P. Medway, 197–241. New York: Falmer.

Rose, P. 1985. *Writing on women: Essays in a renaissance.* Middleton, CT: Wesleyan University Press.

Russ, J. 1983. *How to suppress women's writing.* London: Women's Press.

Shor, I. & P. Freire. 1987. *A pedagogy for liberation: Dialogues on transforming education.* South Hadley, MA: Bergin & Garvey.

Simon, R. I. 1987. Empowerment as a pedagogy of possibility. *Language Arts* 64(4):370–82.

Smyth, J. 1989. A critical pedagogy of classroom practice. *Journal of Curriculum Studies* 21(6):483–502.

Spender, D. 1989. *The writing or the sex?: Or, why you don't have to read women's writing to know it's no good.* New York: Pergamon.

Walker, L. 1990. The ideology and politics of English grammar: An 1894 Newfoundland example. In *Bringing English to order,* ed. I. Goodson & P. Medway, 162–84. New York: Falmer.

Weedon, C. 1987. *Feminist practice and post-structuralist theory.* Oxford: Basil Blackwell.

Willinsky, J. 1990. *The new literacy: Redefining reading and writing in the schools.* New York: Routledge.

Contributors

Deborah Appleman is Assistant Professor of Educational Studies and Director of the Summer Writing Program at Carleton College, Northfield, Minnesota. Dr. Appleman taught high school English for nine years before receiving her doctorate at the University of Minnesota. At Carleton, Dr. Appleman teaches educational psychology, multicultural education, and English methods. Her primary research interests include adolescent response to literature, teaching literary theory to secondary students, and adolescent response to poetry. She has written numerous book chapters and articles on adolescent response to literature and has coedited *Braided Lives,* a multicultural literature anthology published by the Minnesota Humanities Commission. In addition to being active in the National Council of Teachers of English and the American Educational Research Association, Dr. Appleman works regularly with area school districts on the teaching of literature.

Deanne Bogdan is Associate Professor in the Department of History and Philosophy of Education, Ontario Institute for Studies in Education, University of Toronto, where she teaches courses in the philosophy of literature and literature education, literature and values in education, aesthetics, and feminist literary theory, aesthetics, and pedagogy. Her articles have appeared in the *Journal of Aesthetic Education, Journal of Philosophy of Education, Journal of Education, Educational Theory, English Quarterly, English Education, English Journal, English Studies in Canada, Journal of Educational Thought,* and the annual *Proceedings of the Philosophy of Education Society.* As well as being coeditor with Stanley B. Straw of *Beyond Communication: Reading Comprehension and Criticism,* she is the author of *Re-educating the Imagination: Toward a Poetics, Politics, and Pedagogy of Literary Engagement,* both published by Boynton/Cook. She has contributed chapters to *Young Readers, New Readings* (edited by Emrys Evans, Hull University Press/Garamond, 1992); *The World in a Grain of Sand: Twenty-two Interviews with Northrop Frye* (edited by Robert D. Denham, Peter Lang Publishers, 1991); *Reading and Response* (1991) and *Reassessing Language and Literacy* (1992) (Open University Press), both edited by Mike Hayhoe and Stephen Parker; *Literature in the Classroom: Readers, Text, Contexts* (edited by Ben F. Nelms, NCTE Forum Series, 1988); and *From Seed to Harvest: Looking at Literature* (edited by Kathleen B. Whale and Trevor Gambell, CCTE, 1985). Currently Chair of the Women in Literature and Life Assembly for the National Council of Teachers of English, and of the Status of Women in the Profession of the Philosophy of Education Society, she is former Coordinator of Publications for the Canadian Council of Teachers of English.

Trevor J. Gambell is Professor of Curriculum Studies at the University of Saskatchewan, where he teaches undergraduate and graduate courses in English/ language arts education, literacy, and writing. He has published articles on language research and education in the *English Journal, English Quarterly, Journal of Educational Thought, Canadian Journal of Education, Reflections on Canadian*

Literacy, Canadian Journal of English Language Arts, and *English in Australia.*
With Kathleen B. Whale, he edited the book *From Seed to Harvest: Looking at
Literature* (1985) for the Canadian Council of Teachers of English. Currently, he
is coediting a book with Mary Clare Courtland entitled *Curriculum Planning in the
Language Arts: A Holistic Perspective K to 12.* Published book chapters include
contributions on teacher education in *So Much for the Mind* (edited by D.
Cochrane, 1987, Kagan & Woo); on cognition, literacy, and curriculum in *Understanding Literacy and Cognition: Theory, Research and Application* (edited by C. K.
Leong & B. Randhawa, 1989, Plenum Press); and on the teaching of English/
language arts in Canada in *Teaching and Learning English Worldwide* (edited by
J. Britton, R. Shafer, and K. Watson, 1990, Multilingual Matters). His research
interests include academic writing requirements and processes of university students across the disciplines and the ways in which English/language arts interns
change their constructs of English teaching over the period of the fourth-month
internship. He is also very much interested in developing students' personal writing skills through writing workshops using computers. He and his wife and four
children make their home in Saskatoon, Saskatchewan.

Robert J. Graham is Associate Professor of Secondary English/Language Arts
Education in the Department of Curriculum: Humanities and Social Sciences at
the University of Manitoba, Winnipeg. His publications on various aspects of literacy instruction and the literary curriculum have appeared in the *Canadian Journal of Education, English Quarterly, Journal of Aesthetic Education, Journal of
Educational Thought,* and *Journal of Curriculum Studies.* He is also the author of
Reading and Writing the Self: Autobiography in Education and the Curriculum,
published by Teachers College Press. His current research interests lie in theorizing a rhetoric of inquiry into narrative approaches to teaching and in developing
the literary curriculum in secondary schools as a form of cultural studies.

Mary Beth Hines is Assistant Professor in the Department of Curriculum and
Instruction at the University of Houston. She has written articles, presented conference papers, and coauthored technical reports on the teaching and learning of
literature. She is particularly interested in the possibilities and problematics of
forging new frameworks for literature instruction from contemporary literary theories.

Russell A. Hunt teaches literature at St. Thomas University in Fredericton, New
Brunswick. Since the early eighties he has been attempting to teach in ways that
make students' writing and reading instrumental and meaningful and that invite
students to take responsibility for initiating and assessing their own learning in
social contexts. He studied eighteenth-century literature and critical theory at
Northwestern University, and has studied and taught in Chicago and Fredericton,
with extended periods of study and teaching at Indiana University; the Center for
the Study of Literary Education at Deakin University in Geelong, Australia; the
Institut für Empirische Literatur- und Medienforschung in Siegen, Germany; and
the Discourse and Rhetoric Group in Loughborough, England. He has attempted
to bring to bear on his teaching and writing interests ranging from early literacy
development, sociolinguistics, the psychology of reading, and critical theory. He
has presented his work at conferences, seminars, and workshops in Canada, the

United States, Australia, Germany, Denmark, the Netherlands, and England, and has published on these matters in journals such as *College English, Poetics, Language Arts, Reader, English Quarterly, TEXT,* and in a range of edited collections. He is currently the learning and teaching development officer at St. Thomas, and says he is working on a book on literacy learning through literacy use.

Ursula Kelly has a Ph.D. from the Ontario Institute for Studies in Education at the University of Toronto. Her teaching, research, and writing focus on feminist poststructuralist critiques of English studies in particular, and education, curriculum, schooling, and pedagogy in general. She is the author of *Marking 'Place': Cultural Studies, Regionalism and Reading,* an examination of the politics of reading as they relate to specific cultural forms and subjectivities of place and region in Canada. At present, she is Assistant Professor in the Faculty of Education at Saint Mary's University in Halifax, Nova Scotia.

David S. Miall moved to Canada in 1989 and is currently Associate Professor of English at the University of Alberta. He previously taught for ten years at the College of St. Paul and St. Mary in Cheltenham in England, and for three years at University College, Cardiff. He holds degrees from the University of Stirling and the University of Wales and a diploma in music from the Guildhall School in London. He has been developing alternative methods in the literature classroom and carrying out research in reader response since 1984 and has published a number of papers on these topics in such journals as *English Quarterly* and *Poetics.* He is now collaborating with Don Kuiken in an extended program of research on textual and personality factors in literary response. This has included the development of a literary response questionnaire now being used by a number of researchers in the United States and Europe. At Alberta, he teaches courses in British Romantic writing. He is particularly interested in Coleridge's thinking as a psychologist, as shown in both the poetry and prose writings, and has published several studies of particular poems as well as discussions of Coleridge's writing on dreams, love, memory, and emotion. He is director of the biannual Coleridge Summer Conference, held in Somerset, England. He is also interested in the use of computers in research and teaching in literature. He has edited *Humanities and the Computer: New Directions* (Oxford, 1990), and is now producing a series of electronic editions of Romantic texts for Oxford University Press.

Judith Millen taught language and literature in secondary schools in Ontario for eighteen years, half of which time was also spent as a department head. Her interest in media, a long-standing general interest, became focused in 1983 when she began her M.Ed. at the Ontario Institute for Studies in Education in Toronto. After nearly two decades of teaching English, she realized that there was a pressing need for contemporary education to address the changing face of literacy in North America. The decline of students' involvement with the medium of print was being seen as a crisis in education. With this in mind, she pursued the few courses available in media or media-related studies at OISE. Her qualifying research paper, entitled "The Empty Set: Television Reflections," was a study of the complex and contradictory offerings of contemporary television, especially entertainment television. She completed her M.Ed. in 1985 and continued with doctoral studies, which were completed in June 1991. Her Ph.D. thesis was an examination of traditional modes of sociology as cultural production. The thesis takes an interdisciplinary approach to suggest how the still-continuing practices of scientific, positivistic sociology might be transformed by other disciplines, especially those that come out of feminist, antiracist, and socialist literature and media studies. Dr. Millen is completing a postdoctoral fellowship at the Ontario Institute for Studies in Education. She is continuing her studies in media, this time looking at the correlation between adolescent narrative choices, their television viewing, and the possibility for strategies for classroom teachers with particular emphasis on gender, race, and class.

Lorri Neilsen is an educator, researcher, and writer whose work includes studies in literacy, gender and education, literacy and technology, and teacher growth. She is on the faculty of Mount Saint Vincent University in Halifax, Nova Scotia.

Michael W. Smith is affiliated with Rutgers University, Graduate School of Education. His research interests were developed during his eleven years of teaching high school English at Elk Grove High School in suburban Chicago, where he daily confronted the question of how he could help prepare students to have more meaningful transactions with texts. His work on autobiographical writing before reading is part of this line of inquiry, as are his investigations of the effects of direct instruction in interpretive strategies, the nature of adults' discourse in their book-club discussions, and the specificity of the knowledge readers employ when they read literature. His publications include two monographs in NCTE's Theory and Research into Practice series and a variety of articles in such journals as *English Journal, Journal of Educational Research,* and *Research in the Teaching of English.* He is currently chair of AERA's Literature Special Interest Group and the newsletter editor for NCTE's Assembly for Research.

Stanley B. Straw is Professor of Education and Associate Dean (Graduate Programs and Research) of the Faculty of Education, University of Manitoba, Winnipeg. He has coedited a number of books, including *Research in the Language Arts: Language and Schooling* (with Victor Froese, University Park Press), *Beyond Communication: Reading Comprehension and Criticism* (with Deanne Bogdan, Boynton/Cook), and *Social Reflections on Writing: To Reach and Realize* (with Sandy Baardman, Literacy Publications). He has also written chapters or entries for various books, including the upcoming *International Encyclopedia of Education* (Pergamon Press), *Perspectives on Talk and Learning* (edited by Susan Hynds and Don Rubin), *Foundation of Literacy Policy in Canada* (edited by Linda Phillips and Stephen Norris), and the *Encyclopedia of English Studies and Language Arts* (to be published by the National Council of Teachers of English and Scholastic). He is presently working on a coauthored chapter on the foundations of language learning for *Language Arts Across the Curriculum,* edited by Victor Froese to be published by HBJ/Holt. He has published articles and research reports in *Reading Research Quarterly, Reading-Canada-Lecture, English Quarterly, Reflections on Canadian Literacy,* as well as a number of other journals. For six years, he was coeditor of *English Quarterly,* the research and scholarly journal of the Canadian Council of Teachers of English. Dr. Straw has had a continuing interest in the relationships among different aspects of language and learning, which has led to work in the effect of writing on reading and listening comprehension (specifically, grammar and sentence-combining instruction), the relationship between talk and learning (specifically cooperative and collaborative learning models), the relationship between reading comprehension and response to literature models, and the relationship between theories of rhetoric and how we comprehend, respond to, and create meaning from text. He has also worked in theories of curriculum and has carried out a series of historical studies of the development of theories of reading and teaching.

Jack Thomson took voluntary early retirement in 1989 from Charles Sturt University, Mitchell, at Bathurst New South Wales, where he was Senior Lecturer in English in Education and Director of Postgraduate Courses in Language in Education. Previous to his twenty years there, he was head of English in a secondary school in New South Wales. He has worked in the faculty of education at Birmingham University (England) and in the school of education at the University of East Anglia at Norwich. He was visiting research fellow at Edith Cowan University in Perth, Western Australia. He has presented addresses and workshops at national and state conferences and conducted inservice courses in all states of Australia as well as in England, Canada, and the United States. He now works as an educational consultant and continues his interest and active involvement in research into all aspects of literacy education, with a particular emphasis on reading, writing, and thinking processes. His publications include many articles on English teaching and research published in Australian and English journals; and several books, including *Understanding Teenagers' Reading* and *Reconstructing Literature Teaching.*

Brian F. White is Assistant Professor of English at Grand Valley State University in Grand Rapids, Michigan, where he teaches courses in composition pedagogy, response to literature, and English education. His work with autobiographical writing before reading began in his own seventh- through twelfth-grade classrooms, and is part of a larger concern with how teachers can authorize students as interpreters of meaning in both their reading and their writing. This concern extends to his work with preservice teachers of English in their initial field experiences, where he has been exploring ways in which cooperating teachers and university supervisors can enhance the "reflections" and interpretations of student teachers. His work has been published in the *Journal of Reading,* the *Middle School Journal,* and elsewhere.

John Willinsky is Professor of Education and Director of the Centre for the Study of Curriculum and Instruction at the University of British Columbia. He has worked as a teacher both in the schools of northern Ontario and University of Western Canada, and is the author of *The Well-Tempered Tongue, The New Literacy,* and *The Triumph of Literature.* Among his current projects is an international venture in developing the basis for an explicitly postcolonial education with a focus on the context of the Pacific, and after recently completing a historical treatment of the construction of authority in the *Oxford English Dictionary,* he has begun work on a second, more general book on the dictionary that will deal with it as a primary instrument in the shaping of language and literacy that has yet to receive the critical treatment that it warrants.

Index

Also available from Boynton/Cook. . .

Beyond Communication
Reading Comprehension and Criticism
Edited by **Deanne Bogdan** and **Stanley B. Straw**

Beyond Communication is a collection of essays by well-known scholars and teachers in reading comprehension theory and literary criticism, particularly reader-response approaches. These two fields have traditionally been divided by their respective appeals to elementary and secondary education people. In creating this book the editors have sought to repair this unwarranted split.

The book presents a rationale for teaching reading comprehension with literary texts that integrate the two pedagogical approaches. It encourages teachers to include literature and reader-response approaches in daily sessions with students regardless of grade level. It provides teachers with alternatives for meeting new language arts curriculum requirements. And it gives an overview of this field from both Canadian and American perspectives. Contributors include Russell Hunt, James Moffett, Evelyn Hanssen, Jerome Harste, Kathy Short, and Pat Sadowy.

Boynton/Cook   1990   384pp

Re-Educating the Imagination
Toward a Poetics, Politics and Pedagogy of Literary Engagement
Deanne Bogdan
Foreword by **Margaret Meek**

Thirty years after his landmark radio talks aired in 1962, Northrop Frye's conception of the educated imagination has become a major theoretical and practical touchstone for many of today's English teachers at the senior secondary and college levels. Within the educated imagination, the three crucial issues in literature education address why literature is taught, what is taught, and how it is taught—what Deanne Bogdan terms respectively the justification, censorship, and response problems, all of which form a complex of assumptions about the place and function of literature within the curriculum.

Both a critique and defense of literature education, *Re-Educating the Imagination* examines the implications of Frye's theory. Using as a dialectic the idea that the educational value of literary reading stems from its effects as a form of real experience, Bogdan analyzes the educational context of literary engagement, offering a revision of the educated imagination in terms of real readers reading in the classroom. Questioning the humanist underpinnings of the traditional claims of literature to instruct through delight, the text incorporates and reconfigures those claims within their social and educational context.

This book will appeal to classroom teachers of literature committed to a reflective approach to their profession, pre-service and in-service practitioners, school administrators seeking a philosophical base for language arts policy, and graduate students and professors in literature and language arts education. At a time when so many scholarly books seek to divide and create chasms rather than discussions, *Re-Educating the Imagination* makes connections and builds bridges: between canon and curriculum, between the disciplines, between the schools and the universities. It is a book which prods the reader to consider the most basic assumptions underlying the profession of teaching literature.

Boynton/Cook   1992   408pp

Heinemann-Boynton/Cook
361 Hanover Street
Portsmouth, NH 03801-3912
(800) 541-2086